KEY NEXT DOOR

LESLIE D. WEATHERHEAD

KEY
NEXT DOOR

ABINGDON PRESS

NEW YORK   NASHVILLE

KEY NEXT DOOR

Library of Congress Catalog Card Number: 61-6395

PRINTED IN THE U.S.A.

Dedicated

to

The Rev. Professor

JAMES S. STEWART

M.A., D.D.

Professor of New Testament Language,
Literature and Theology in the
University of Edinburgh.

A great Christian, a great Professor,
a great Preacher,
and
My Friend

Preface

In this volume of sermons I have picked out twenty-five of those which I preached at the City Temple, London, towards the close of my twenty-four-year ministry there. They are printed more or less as preached and inevitably ideas are repeated. Nearly all of them appeared in "The City Temple Tidings," our church magazine which month by month often reaches a circulation of five thousand copies.

Since a sermon tries to state the "truth through personality," a printed sermon loses much of its value. Further, in church I had the immense asset of preaching at a point in the service when the minds and hearts of the congregation—a congregation I knew and loved—had been prepared for my message by three-quarters of an hour of worship. That worship owed an immense debt to my Choir and Organist at the City Temple. Working in co-operation with my friend, Eric H. Thiman, Mus.D., Hon. R.A.M., F.R.C.O., and the Choir I loved and admired, was an immense privilege and one of the factors that made it so hard to leave. Their music made an "atmosphere" in which preaching came easy. Between us we had worked hard to make each service an ideal example of Free Church worship.

However, without these aids I hope the messages may be of help to some. I have tried to be mentally honest and realistic. More and more I have come to feel that in some quarters glib phrases, hoary clichés and, to the congregation, unfamiliar theological terms are used which, when put to the test by the listener, are simply not true. Four years ago when I had two spells in hospital and a good deal of pain, I felt what a lot of nonsense there is in some of the hymns, and indeed in some of those teachings of the Bible which are out of harmony with the mind of Christ. I felt challenged by what I myself had said from time to time and determined to test every utterance more severely. Poetic imagery, beautiful language, traditional theology, religious words made familiar by centuries of repetition, all, I felt, must be tested anew by the tests of sincerity and truth and realistic usefulness to the hearer. For a long time in my preparation, I, first of all—having chosen the subject—made myself write down at the head of my blank paper an answer to the question, "What do I expect this sermon to accomplish?" It is a good discipline if one is honest with the answer.

Once more I must thank my secretary, Miss W. E. Haddon, who has given me nearly twenty years of splendidly efficient and devoted service, and I must thank my wife also for she does an invaluable job in proof-reading and giving me advice and counsel.

My old friend, Leonard Cutts, Director and Managing Editor of Hodder and Stoughton's Religious Books, has given me that same warm encouragement which he has shown me for thirty years.

Most of all, perhaps, I want to thank the listeners to these sermons for their patience and tolerance. It has been a great privilege to preach to them, especially in the new City Temple to which we have now safely returned after more than seventeen years in borrowed premises. I shall miss my listeners very much. After twenty-four years I know many of them better than their relatives do, and have been the confidant of many of them from childhood upwards. I admire their courage so much and have been so enriched by their affection and their prayers. It has been a great privilege to have been in such a church for so long.

My wish for the City Temple I can partly express in a prayer which I saw framed in a church in a lovely country village (Much Hadham, Herts) and which I copied down:

> O Father, fill this House with Thy spirit. Here may the strong renew their strength and seek for their working lives a noble consecration. Here may the poor find succour and the friendless friendship.

Here may the tempted find power, the sorrowing comfort, and the bereaved find the truth that death hath no dominion over their beloved.

Here let the fearing find a new courage and the doubting have their faith and hope confirmed.

Here may the careless be awakened, and all that are oppressed be freed.

Hither may many be drawn by Thy love and go hence, their doubts resolved, and their faith renewed, their fears at rest, their courage high, their purpose firm, their sins forgiven, and their hearts aflame with love. Through Jesus Christ our Lord. Amen.

LESLIE D. WEATHERHEAD

The City Temple,
London.

THE SERMONS

Key Next Door

John 13⁷: Jesus said, "Thou shalt understand hereafter."
1 Cor. 13¹²: Now I know in part; but then I shall know
fully. (R.V. margin).

I REMEMBER once wanting very much to see over a house. It
was an empty house standing in its own grounds and that
made the next house a good deal farther on. I went up the
drive of the house I wanted to look over. The doors were shut
and barred and the windows tightly fastened. I took the liberty
of looking in through the ground-floor windows, and I could
see a little. By walking round the house I could get some idea
of its general plan. But, of course, from the outside one could
really only have the vaguest idea of what the house might
contain and what in detail had been the plan of the architect.
One could only "know in part".

Then I noticed that there was a card in the window of a
downstair room facing the front gate, and on the card were the
words: "Key Next Door." So I had to go farther on, obtain
the key and come back and enter the house. Then a good many
things that had been obscured from me were made plain. The
beauty and design of the house were revealed. The plan of
the architect could be appreciated.

It seems to me that this is a parable. The house of life's
meaning is like that. So many doors are shut, so many windows
fastened. We peep in and we get glimpses of meaning. By
walking round we may get a general idea of the lie of the house
but there are bound to be many things that puzzle us and upon
which no clear light shines. Yet, if I may press the parable,
there is a notice that says, "Key Next Door." We may have
to go farther on, perhaps even into the next phase of being,

and indeed, perhaps the next phase after that—for there must be many stages of spiritual progress—before we can understand all, but we are promised that at last we shall understand. "Thou shalt understand hereafter."

* * *

You can imagine the setting of our text. The words were probably spoken on the very night before our Lord's death. Let us look at the situation. The disciples are very puzzled. They have tried to follow Him and they have left a good deal to do so, but He has talked about going away and even said that that was expedient. He has told them that He has many things to say to them, but they cannot bear them now. He has said, "What I do thou knowest not now," and then He has offered them the golden promise of our text: "Thou shalt understand hereafter." They had peeped through the windows. They had seen glimmerings of light. They had begun to understand, but they so badly wanted to see more. "Show us the Father," clamoured one of them, "and it sufficeth us." But He could only show them Himself. Often they must have been bewildered to the point of being dismayed, just as we are, but there was given to them, and we may say given to us also, the gracious promise, "You shall understand afterwards."

* * *

It is a message we need, for life to most thoughtful people is incomprehensible. It contains so many puzzles. There are such terrible inequalities in it; experiences that look like injustice at the heart of things, or even carelessness. Cruel things happen to people, frustrating things that do not make sense, and sheer accidents that alarm us. Things of enormous importance seem to depend on things that look like luck or chance. Big doors swing on such tiny hinges. What are we to do in the face of the problems that we cannot solve?

I want to say first that it is an act of faith to believe that there is a key anywhere. It is an act of faith based on the nature of God. If there is a God at all, He cannot be a cruel fiend, for if He were, we should be His superior, for we *know*, if we know anything at all, that kindness is better than cruelty, love is better than hate, goodness is better than badness, humility is better than pride, and unselfishness is better than egotism. If we know anything at all, we are sure of our fundamental moral values. We hardly need the poet to tell us that

> A loving worm within its clod
> Were diviner than a loveless God.

If there is a God at all, in whose being are included the moral values man treasures, He could not create a creature capable of asking such questions and yet incapable of ever finding out the answers. I believe that though evil is very powerful, it cannot keep the key out of our hands for ever, even though now we have to say that the key is next door. "Then I shall know fully."

* * *

I wonder if you feel that it is a feeble thing to say the key is next door. I wonder if you are put off by the very phrase. Are you in your mind thinking, "He is giving us the old religious dope, talking to us as parents sometimes talk to children, and saying, 'Of course, you cannot understand now, but you will one day'"? Few things, I think, are so aggravating to the eager, questioning minds of children than to be given that sort of dusty answer. Is it a kind of variation of 'pi in the sky when you die' to say to people, "Well, one day you will understand and all will be made clear"?

I used to think it was, but, after all, if you go to the theatre to see a play, you do not rise up at the end of the first act and say, "What a rotten play! What a feeble affair! What a stupid plot! What a meaningless business!" If I took you to the theatre and you said things like that at the end of the first act, I should say, "Sit down and see it through! You cannot judge a play at the end of the first act."

I must have quoted to you before the famous words of Gheyserlink:[1] "If a cinema film of the history of the earth

[1] *The Restless Earth* p. 101 (Scientific Book Club).

were to be produced, and if that film were to last twenty-four hours from midnight to midnight, then the first twelve hours of the film would show a history not yet discovered, and *man would not appear until the last five seconds of the film*." Well, if that is true, we have not got to the end of the first act yet, have we?

Though man is made in the image of God and every individual is infinitely precious to God, this does not deny the truth that at the present stage in the world-drama we call history, man is only a very little child. I am holding in my hand a little bar of steel with a knob at one end. It is three and a half inches long and is shiny because I have had it in my pocket for thirty years. You would never guess what it is. It is the axle of a little boy's engine, and when my second son was scarcely four years of age he was playing with it, holding it between his finger and thumb and putting the end of it in his mouth. He was nudged by his older brother and he swallowed it, and it lay jammed in the intestine. That experience with him taught me many things which I must not talk about now, but we had to take him to the Infirmary in Leeds and leave him there to be X-rayed every few hours. I shall never forget my feelings as I parted from him. How on earth could I explain to a little boy of that age the necessity of being X-rayed every few hours? How on earth could I combat his own thoughts which might reasonably have been thus—"Here am I in pain. I thought Daddy was my friend. He takes me away from home to a strange building and into a terrifying thing called a ward, full of other children. He hands me over to a complete stranger called a nurse, and when I need him most he deserts me utterly and goes home to have tea with Mummy." What an illustration of the words, "I have many things to say unto you, but you cannot bear them now. . . . What I do thou knowest not now, but thou shalt understand afterwards." The key to the house of meaning for that little dearly loved son was farther on. Now he understands. He knows that love was my motive.

We must try to realise that man is apt to forget what a baby thing he is and what a tiny power he has to comprehend what God is doing. I admit that I often see unintended humour, but the other day I heard a woman praising her husband. She said he was marvellous. She said things about him that could not possibly be true of anybody! You would think that the business of the City of London would come to a standstill if anything happened to him! But as she talked, I saw the angels behind her giggle, and one nudged the other and said, "Just listen to her!" I suppose to the angels it was the sort of situation that we might be in if we overheard a female slug boasting to another that her husband left the finest streak behind him on the garden path of any slug in the garden. As the slug is to man, so is man to those higher beings who inhabit the unseen. Our bravest deeds, our noblest efforts must get quite a different perspective when viewed from the heights of heaven, and here is little man standing up and throwing out his chest with an egotism that must make all heaven laugh, and being hurt that he does not understand what God is doing. I am imagining a tiny ant creeping along the front of this pulpit and coming to this break in the cushions, and finding it a real problem to know how to cross the gulf here, where my finger is, and get home in time for supper, and I am realising that he does not even know that he is in the pulpit of the City Temple! He has never heard of the City Temple! Poor little insect! What does he know of London, or England, or Europe, or the world, or its place in space? Even the name Krushchev means nothing to him!

Honestly, without diminishing man's importance to God because he is a loved object, our *mental* grasp of things is probably as fractional as an ant's grasp of the world. If the majesty and wisdom and power of God are infinite, as we glibly say, is it any wonder that I cannot understand what He is doing? Indeed, it is amazing that the One who had the greatest insight and saw farther than any of us, could tell us with His divine authority, "You *will* understand afterwards," and that Paul by faith could say, "I shall know fully."

* * *

After all, even with our limited vision there are glimmerings of meaning. I talked about peeping through the windows of the house of meaning and seeing a little. But, you see, if there is the faintest glimmer of meaning about anything, it must mean that there is mind behind everything. If there is anything in the universe that makes sense—such as the eternal value of human values—then there must be mind behind all phenomena. If your little boy threw out on the carpet a whole boxful of wooden bricks each bearing a letter of the alphabet, it is incredible that as they fell they would make a word, and if after a brief absence you came back and even found a word of three letters, you would say, "A mind has been at work." I must admit that the universe often seems to me quite incomprehensible, events seem unrelated, accidents happen, and sometimes you would think there is no more meaning in the world than there is in blocks thrown out by a child's hand on a nursery floor. Then suddenly, with insight rather than intellect, you become aware of meaning. Beauty, for instance, seems to me meaningful, or we get a glimpse of truth, or see an act of goodness, or regard a mother's love for a child. They make sense. I feel that I "know in part". So I say to myself that although I cannot understand much, there is Mind behind some things and therefore Mind behind everything. And I feel that that Mind, more than personal in any human sense of that word, is saying to us tiny children with the minds of insects, "I know you cannot understand, but hold on! You shall understand afterwards. The key is next door."

* * *

In my own philosophy of life I have a place for accidents. I do not mean that they cause surprise to God, but His knowing about them, even beforehand, no more causes them to happen than my knowing that you will go out of the doors of this church after the service, is the factor which causes you to do so. By accident I mean a thing that God did not intend and man could not foresee. Surely there must be such happenings in the criss-cross of human freewill.

A week yesterday at the Cup Tie Final at Wembley, Dwight got his leg broken. You read about it and perhaps saw it on television. I never read that Dwight sat down on the field and said, "Why should this happen to me?" or "What have I done to deserve this?" or "Why did God allow this to happen?" He probably said, "Well, it's bad luck, but it's just one of those things." Just as the rush of bodies together broke his leg, the rush of wills together has broken many a heart, and the criss-cross of freewills, acting sometimes through ignorance, or folly or sin, has brought seeming disaster to many lives.

But let us in our illustration leave the football field and come to the home. Let us imagine that you are bringing up little children. You do not pad the walls with eiderdowns and put foam rubber on the floor. Your little boy can meet with quite a nasty accident on the edge of the fender, perhaps, or the table leg. But you do not leave razor blades about, or saucers of sulphuric acid. In other words, as far as you are able, no situation arises so disastrous that you cannot deal with it. In this way you guard your home. In this way God guards His universe. Many troublous things can happen to us, but nothing with which He cannot deal. To change the figure, nothing can go so wrong that He cannot weave it into an overall plan, though when you rise up, as a child rises up, crying out in anger and even in despair, He cannot explain because you are too little. He comforts you and says, "You shall understand afterwards."

* * *

Frequently I find myself amazed at the degree to which, by peering through the windows, we *can* know in part and make sense out of life, and, in my reading, illustrations occur repeatedly that light up my theme this evening.

I remember so clearly going out "birding" in Yorkshire with a dear friend of mine. We watched some jackdaws apparently building a nest in the crevices of an old ruined tower. They gathered their material and they pushed it into the crevices. Apparently they could not realise that it was dropping right through the crevices on to the floor inside the hollow tower. If they can feel frustrated, they must have felt terribly frustrated about that. Believe me or not, when we walked into the tower, there was a heap of nesting material almost up to my shoulders. But when we went to a farmhouse adjoining the ruins, an old lady, crippled with arthritis, came out and talked to us, and she said this, "You know the jackdaws are doing me a wonderful service. They gather my kindling for me. I use what they push through the holes at the top of that ruined tower to start my fire."

I do not often attempt to write poetry, but I did make up this verse:—

> In my frustration make me sure
> That Thou, my God, art He,
> Who buildest something to endure
> From what seems loss to me.

Do you remember how blotting-paper was first made? In a large paper-mill an employee omitted one of the ingredients of writing paper and he came and confessed his fault to his employer. The employer tried to write on the paper and found that it was useless, but the way in which the ink ran suggested a new use for this type of paper. Up to then, fine sand had been used to dry the written page. The carelessness of an employee was not willed by the employer. You might call it an accident. You might call it ignorance, or folly, or sin. But it was the origin of something very useful. Out of what looked like meaningless accident, something useful was born.

Perhaps a more impressive illustration is offered in the conquests of Alexander the Great (356-323 B.C.). Land after land, people after people, fell to his conquering might, but wherever Alexander went the Greek language was spoken and good roads were put down. Over three hundred years later the Gospel spread as it never could have done unless there had been roads called the Greek language in men's minds, and roads across the country called Greek roads. Many a slave, lashed by tyranny into servile labour, was all unknowingly spreading the Gospel of Christ, but he couldn't know it then. The key was next door.

The Psalmist guessed that God might even use "the wrath of man to praise Him", and as Principal Oman once said, "Without a trust that God has a purpose He can make it serve, human cruelty dethrones for us either God's goodness or His omnipotence; and one is a mockery without the other."

We have not to go far in this church to see the perfect illustration of my theme. Look at that Cross. It is illuminated from behind until late every night, so that any one passing by and looking through the glass doors from the street can get a glimpse of its meaning and significance, and feel that there is light behind his cross too.

But when it happened, it looked like defeat, it felt like defeat, it was called defeat. Did you say you were frustrated and that you were hurt? What do you think He felt, and what did they feel who had committed their lives to Him and risked everything for Him? There was no key to get into that house of darkness on Good Friday. The key was next door, or next door but one. They found it on Easter Day and entered the house of meaning.

Do look through the windows. Do gather any light there may be now for your problem. But lest you become bitter or cynical, take home with you this golden word of our Lord—Thou shalt understand hereafter.

Some years ago I had a strange dream. I am not making this up for the purpose of the sermon. I was passing through a time of great difficulty and unhappiness, and in my dream I was to be offered a personal interview with Christ, and I thought, "Ah, I will ask Him this. I will ask Him that. Now I shall get an answer to all my questions and the key to all my problems." Believe it or not, in the glory of His presence it was not that I forgot to ask Him anything. It seemed utterly unnecessary and meaningless. Somehow I had an overwhelming feeling that even He would not be able to explain to me because my mental grasp was so tiny, but there came an overwhelming feeling of supreme joy that questions no longer needed to be answered. It was sufficient to know there *was* an answer. I *knew* that all was well and somehow I knew that all was well for everybody. Another text came to my memory: "In that day ye shall ask me nothing" (John 16²³).

*　　*　　*

As we close, have in your mind again, if you will, the picture with which we started, of the house shuttered and fastened and standing in its own grounds. Imagine that you and I are together at the gate. Then recall the words that our late King George VI loved so much. "I said to the man who stood at the gate . . . 'Give me a LIGHT that I may tread safely into the unknown.' But he replied, 'Go out *into the darkness* and put thy hand into the hand of God. That shall be to thee better than light and safer than a known way.'"

"What I do thou knowest not now, but thou shalt understand hereafter." The key is next door.

> I do not ask thy way to understand,
>   My way to see;
> Better in darkness just to grasp Thy hand
>   And follow Thee.

The Robe of Christ

My text, taken from the story of the Prodigal Son, is "Bring forth the best robe and put it on him". (Luke 15^{22}).

Together with that sentence I want you to meditate on some sentences used by St. Paul. Here they are:

Romans 13^{14}: "Put ye on the Lord Jesus Christ."

Galatians 3^{27}: "As many of you as were baptised into Christ, did put on Christ."

Ephesians 4^{24}: "Put on the new man."

Colossians 3$^{9-10}$: "Ye have put off the old man with his doings and have put on the new man."

We might remember also that passage from the Old Testament when Elijah cast his robe over his successor, Elisha (I Kings 19^{19}).

* * *

Those who know their theology will recognise, I hope, that what I am trying to restate in modern language tonight is that great doctrine which played such a large part in the thought of St. Paul, and afterwards in that of Luther and Wesley, which we call Justification by Faith. Wesley's conversion, which led to the changing of the face of England, was precipitated by hearing an anthem in St. Paul's Cathedral, and then hearing someone read Luther's exposition of the doctrine of Justification by Faith. In parenthesis, let no one belittle the evangelical value of a lovely anthem well sung. I must confess that for me it is devotionally very often the high-spot of a Church service and never more so than at present.

A problem of real magnitude puzzled the early Christian thinkers. How could a perfectly holy God have anything to do with sinful men? God is holy beyond our power to imagine.

Our own sin prevents any real appreciation of Infinite Purity. We may think how terrible it would be to sleep with a leper, to be in intimate contact with someone who had a loathsome disease, but even such contrasts cannot picture for us the horror and loathsomeness of sin to God. Our fathers met the problem by saying that God imputed to men a righteousness that was not their own, but was Christ's. God treated them *as if* they were righteous, because Christ had become their Brother and identified Himself with them. He Who knew no sin was "made sin", as Paul put it, "on their behalf."

Now before you dismiss all this as theological wangling—and I admit that theologians do sometimes wangle—let us go back to the story of the Prodigal Son. Here he is, back home at last, with the dirt of the far country on his clothes and the dirt of the far country on his soul. But *at once* he is forgiven and clothed in the robe which is the symbol of a son. He was far from perfect. He still smelt of the pigs, but *he was treated as though he had never been away*, and that is the essential point and at the same time the miracle of forgiveness. *Relationships* are restored as though they had never been broken. The Prodigal may have taken weeks to recover from the far country experience, but *at once* the robe was on him. It was the symbol that the old relationship was restored.

So, you see, Paul's message to those who are far from God is not primarily, "Try harder, undergo a long discipline and one day you may graduate and be worthy of sonship." That is not much of a Gospel. Gospel means good news, and everybody has heard the advice, "Try harder," and many have found it barren. Religion, thus taught, is an added burden where it ought to be "the kind of burden that sails are to a ship and that wings are to a bird". It is no good going to India as a missionary if all you have to say is, "Try harder!" The Indian knows already the value of trying and carries it out better than we do.

Paul says, "Accept forgiveness! Come home! Accept a changed relationship! Allow yourself to be called a son! Change your picture of yourself! Wear the robe of Christ's loving acceptance and forgiveness! And do it now!" In any case a relationship is not something you can enter by making an effort. There are only two ways into a family. You can be born into it, or adopted into it, but you cannot do either by trying. Effort does not alter relationship. Christ was born into God's family, but God is willing to adopt us so that we too can call Him Father. We are "heirs of God and joint heirs with Christ."[1]

*   *   *

Now is this all unreal and silly? You may think so at first. You may say, "What's the good of my calling myself a son if I'm a swineherd? What's the good of my wearing the robe which is the mark of a son if Im a swineherd underneath? Your imagery," you might say to me, "is misleading. You can't make a man a Mayor by buying for him a Mayor's robes. You can't make a man a graduate by buying for him a gown and a hood. This is pretence! You make a hypocrite of him!"

But wait a moment! Let me speak for a moment about the psychology of clothes—and I think I shall have the ladies of the congregation with me here.

I used to wonder why women change their clothes so often. They look perfectly nice to me in the kitchen in the morning. What's the matter with that pretty jumper and pleated skirt anyway? But in the afternoon they say they must go and change. If you ask them why, they give a revealing answer that lights up my theme. They say, "Oh! Changing makes me *feel* so different."

Paul says, "Put on Christ. You will feel different! You may not *be* very different underneath, but you'll feel different and that's a great start." "Bring forth the best robe!" Let him begin to feel like the son he really is. You have heard of a man feeling that he could not disgrace his uniform. Clothes make you *feel* different. To be well dressed gives you confidence, helps you to hold up your head.

We know the spiritual equivalent of all this. All of us here probably believe in the transforming power of Jesus Christ to change men's lives. Except for that, Christianity would have

[1] Romans 8[17].

23

faded out long ago. If you believe that Christ changes men's lives, answer me this question: When does that change begin? My answer is that *it begins when a man changes his mental picture of himself, when he begins to feel that he might be other than he is.*

As long as a man believes himself to be a dirty dog, a morally defeated person, an unchangeable bad-egg, so long will he remain unchanged. When he sees himself as different, as a son, then he has started the process by which he will be changed. Let that soldier who in his heart funks the battle, look in a full length mirror and see himself as one of Her Majesty's Life Guards, and he feels braver at once. He believes in himself. I have an old friend who has that horror of horrors, a nagging wife. One day, when he had been scolded by her, he was slinking out of the room, and she shouted, "And where are you off to now?" To which he replied, "I'm going upstairs to polish my medals." And sometimes, when he felt a bit down and defeated, he would slip away and put on his old uniform with his modest medals. It made him *feel* better.

"Blessed are they who heal us of our self-despisings," some-one has said. Yes, blessed are they who, even while we confess to them our sense of defeat and failure, say in all sincerity, "Well *I* never think of you like that. I don't believe that about you. You don't look like that to me." Blessed are they who see past the labels other men stick on us and beyond the labels we stick on ourselves. Blessed are they who believe in what we might become, who see us already as the men we want to be. Do you see what they do? In a sense they put the robe of Christ upon us for they see us already not as pig-men, but as sons. And *by doing so they help to change us.* They make us *feel* better, and they help incredibly because feeling is to effort what petrol is to the machinery of your car! Who wants to push his car home if someone can tell him how to make it go?

*　　*　　*

Centuries ago Formosa was governed by a Chinese Governor named Goho. He was a man of humane and liberal outlook, and one of the things which he did when he became Governor was to induce the savage tribes under his rule to abandon the established custom of offering each year a human sacrifice. He persuaded them to be content instead with an ox or a pig as their victim: For forty years this continued. But at last, after an unusually bad harvest, the leaders of the people came to him and said that this would not do; their gods were angry, and now they must have a human victim once more. Goho expostulated and pleaded with them, but in vain. Finally, seeing that it was no good, he yielded. "Go," he said, "tomorrow morning to such and such a place in the forest, and you will find the victim ready—a man tied to a tree, wearing the red robe of sacrifice and a red cloth over his face and head! Strike! for he is your victim."

Next morning the men gathered at the appointed place, and there they saw the victim dressed in red, his face covered with a red cloth. In a frenzy they rushed upon him, and struck off his head. But as the cloth rolled away from it, they saw the face of the victim they had killed. It was Goho himself. From that day to this no human sacrifice has ever been offered on the island of Formosa. So Goho reconciled those crude savages to himself. By the sacrifice of his death he did what by his rule and teaching he had so far failed to do—he changed their whole minds, and changed them permanently.

And what happened? A red robe became the symbol of a changed life. A man discarded his former dingy robe and wore a red one, as if to say, "I am one of Goho's men. I am different." They became known as the men of the robe.

*　　　*　　　*

My friends will you now do something in your own mind? You need not move a muscle. If you are in earnest about Christianity, please do this. Imagine that you are at this moment looking at yourself in a full-length mirror. You are clothed in black, the black of self-despising and failure and defeat. Then, as you continue to look in the mirror, Christ, wearing a red robe (and it would be red, wouldn't it?) comes alongside you, and He puts His red robe right round you. Now, when you look in the mirror, you are a person clothed in red, and you are a person very close to Christ, and that blessed union will make you like Him. It may take time admittedly, but already, *already*, you are a changed person, allied with Him in a new closeness of relationship. Something has begun—and I don't mind how much you emphasise the time it will take to complete the process—but something has begun which has already made you a person clothed in red instead of a person clothed in black. His radiant personality has done something already. In faith that the old self is dead, its mourning has been covered with resplendent crimson. You have "put on the new man". You have "reckoned yourself dead to sin". You dwell in Christ. You are one with Him. Your life is hid with Christ. You abide in Him. You have put on Christ. You are His man now. You belong to Him. You are a man of the robe.

*   *   *

Let me emphasise that in another way, deserting for the moment the metaphor of the robe.

One glorious summer I stayed a few days in the country with some dear friends of mine. I remember sitting one day on the lawn in their lovely garden under a cedar tree. You can see the picture. The air is sweet with the scent of the cedar and of a lilac tree in full bloom. A chaffinch is singing a rhapsody above my head. At my feet is a dog, Pete, aged and feeble. He is a dog without much to commend him as far as appearances go. For some time his back was red-raw with disease and his destruction was contemplated. Indeed, one veterinary surgeon recommended that he should be "put away". He is the property of Mike, the only son of my host and hostess. Mike had to interrupt a university course to serve with the Forces. He is in the Navy. Knowing my host and hostess well, I could, without rudeness, make a comment, not too complimentary, about Pete, though I did not know that Pete was Mike's dog. Although Pete has now fully recovered, he totters about the garden. He cannot run. He is not in any pain and appears to be happy, but no one would claim that he is either useful or ornamental. My hostess explained that Pete certainly was a great care and something of an anxiety. "But," she added, her eyes softening, "we love him *for Mike's sake.*" They saw the dog as something Mike loved. They couldn't have done away with the dog because the dog was bound up with Mike and Mike with the dog. They would hardly like to meet Mike's eyes after the war if he said, "Where's Pete?" and they could only answer that he had been "put away" because he was a nuisance and no use and not worth saving.

Not worth saving? Why they saw past the label which I, in ignorance, had affixed to him as a wretched, useless, old dog! He had meaning, dignity and worth because *he was Mike's dog.*

Supposing some angelic cynic could look on this world of men. Can't you imagine his saying to another angel, "I can't understand why God doesn't wipe them off the earth as their Bible says He did at the Flood. Look how they've wrecked His plans. Look what dirty swine they are. . ."?

But we belong to Christ. "Ye are Christ's!" cries St. Paul, and Christ is God's, and God, holy though He is, cannot turn away one who wears the robe that establishes that man, even while yet a sinner, is one of the family. "They shall never perish," said Christ, "and no one shall snatch them out of my hand."[1]

So we say, "For Jesus Christ's sake." So we plead, "Through Jesus Christ our Lord." So we pray that God will "only look on us as found in Him".

* * *

I see, in imagination, two boys. I am going to imagine that they are twins. Twins, especially uni-ovular, often have a strange psychical link between them and are frequently devoted to one another. The prison-walls of the flesh, the barriers of temperament and outlook which separate most people, seem to have less power to separate twins. They almost seem to pass in and out of each other's personalities, and sometimes appear to know what is happening to one another even though separated in space. Let me call them John and Jim and suppose them to be in their early twenties. Let us imagine John the

[1] John 10²⁸

ideal Christian man, and Jim a man who has done some great wrong; a wrong which reacts cruelly on others, spoiling their lives and frustrating their plans, dragging the family name in the mud, bringing pain and sorrow to many. I think I know what John would do. As soon as possible, he would be at his brother's side. He could not bear his brother's *guilt*, but he would bear a greater sense of shame and sorrow, even than his brother. He would do his uttermost in putting right what was wrong. He would be willing, so closely to identify himself with his brother, that, what with the inward shame and sorrow and the outward hostility shown by others, he would in a real sense bear his brother's sins. He would be "made sin" on his brother's behalf. He would "become a curse" for his brother. And he would give himself to the task of winning his brother to the ways of righteousness and know no respite until the task was done.

Then I imagine them returning to their father who, we will suppose, is ideal in character. John has his arm round Jim's shoulder, —and remember that an embrace frequently symbolises the desire to draw another within one's own personality, to identify oneself with him, and to suffer for him in one's own being. There is no weak excusing of the wrong done by Jim. There is no pretence, no sham. But the father, whose nature, let us imagine, for the illustration's sake, is perfectly shared by John, knows that John will stand by Jim and never leave him, that the twins are one in an identification for which we have not the right word, and that, while nothing can ever lessen the father's hostility to evil which has wrought such harm in Jim and through him to others, he not only loves Jim, but can receive him and *treat him as innocent* (= justification) for he and John are one. We often use the phrase of two close friends, "They are wrapped up in each other," as if one had thrown his robe around them both.

Charles Wesley has said it, hasn't he?

> No condemnation now I dread;
> Jesus and all in Him is mine!
> Alive in Him, my living Head,

And *clothed in righteousness divine,*
Bold I approach the eternal throne,
And claim the crown, through Christ my own.

*   *   *

I am going to make another suggestion. Do you know what a loofah is? Our chemist, following the Americans, spells it LUFA. It is a kind of sponge people use in a bath. I want you to go and have a bath! Let it be—what I myself often try to make a bath—a sacramental ceremony. Pray that as the water cleanses your body, His grace may cleanse your soul. Say out loud "L. U. F. A. I am *L*oved, *U*nderstood, *F*orgiven, *A*ccepted." Then get out of the bath and imaginatively put on the robe of Christ's friendship, the robe of a restored relationship, the symbol of a son. Tomorrow shall begin a new chapter in your life. You are home now; back in God's family.

My friend, you may have come into God's house tonight feeling entirely satisfied with yourself. If so, I have no message for you just now. But if you have come in wearing the dark robe of self-despising, of guilt, or any kind of shame, of depression and frustration and defeat listen to a Voice which says, "Bring forth the best robe and put it on him!" You are a *son*. He will treat you as a son. You are loved, understood, forgiven and "accepted in the Beloved". Friendship is offered, and the restoration of a relationship, *as if you had never been away.*

Why not accept tonight the robe of Christ? Now, as we bow in silence, just listen to that Voice speaking about you: "Bring forth the best robe and put it on him. *He belongs to me.*"

Loneliness: Man's Need and God's Answer

Two sermons preached at the first Festival of the "Friends of the City Temple."[1]

Morning Sermon

I want today to be an especially happy day of fellowship. It is exactly a year today since we had our first service in this new building and we thank God for all the blessings of the past.

I was asked to speak today on the subject of Friendship. The Chapel at the end of the church is called "The Chapel of the Divine Friendship" and it is the particular responsibility of the members of this movement.

I have often preached on the Divine Friendship. I find that in over twenty years I have never begun—as it were—at the other end and preached on Loneliness, and I should like to think with you on that subject today.

*   *   *

What is loneliness? Let us differentiate it from solitude. Solitude is a state of being geographically alone. Loneliness is a state of being spiritually alone. Solitude is a good thing and one that, if not enforced, can be enjoyed at frequent intervals. Indeed, the religious man knows that he *must* arrange it, for as Professor H. H. Farmer once said, "In the solitary places of the human hearts is to be found the meeting place of God and man."[2] There are things God cannot possibly say to us if we are everlastingly protected by our friends, or even by one friend, if that friend is one who never criticises us adversely.

[1] There are over 1200 members of this organization. Thirty-three countries are represented in the membership, including all the commonwealth countries and fifteen of the States of America.

[2] H. H. Farmer, *The Healing Cross* p. 193 (Nisbet)

Loneliness is a disease, in its original meaning, dis-ease, something that ought not to be there. It is an evil thing. "It is not good that man should be alone, saith the Lord God."[1] It is a craving for human relationships. And it is very much to do with religion, for one definition at least of religion, based on its very name, is that it is the conscious bond (ligare, to bind) between the soul and God—or, of course, in the case of some religions, the gods.

Dr. T. M. Ling, a psychiatrist, called loneliness "one of the major social evils of our day." It is a disease which is on the increase in that twice as many people are living alone today compared with twenty-five years ago, though many people who live alone are never lonely. They have solitude but no loneliness. Here, indeed, is one of the few psychological diseases which could be called a killing disease, for it has often led to fatal alcoholism and it can lead to suicide. In four hundred and nine suicides recently studied by one psychiatrist, Dr. Peter Sainsbury of the Maudsley Hospital, London, one hundred and twelve—more than a quarter—were of people who lived alone.[2]

Most of us do not see such severe cases as these, and yet probably all of us know of some cases which are severe enough to cause great unhappiness. We shall not waste our time if we study the matter today, though I must leave until this evening a discussion of practical remedies.

* * *

Let us see the picture as completely as we can. The moment I speak of loneliness, many minds will think of the awful, one-room flat with four walls often covered with hideous wallpaper and with nothing provided but a gas-ring. We think, with a shudder, of elderly—often unmarried—women who live in flats, hardly ever visited by anyone. Day after day, one of them who kept a diary wrote on page after page, "No one called," and a weekly visit of a minister or deaconess for

[1] Genesis 2[18]

[2] Dr. Cyril H. Powell, *The Lonely Heart* (Arthur James)

perhaps half an hour is no real remedy for this condition. If the lonely one can get out, it is something, but even then, the walk, the bit of shopping, the bus ride, how futile and pathetic they must seem to a hungry soul who wants companionship and love.

But loneliness is not circumscribed by such cases. William Canton's book, "The Invisible Playmate," reveals a ghastly loneliness in the heart of the only child, and no one should ever laugh if such a child invents a playmate. When a second child arrives, the attention he receives frequently drives the first into serious loneliness.

Who is lonelier than the child at boarding-school, particularly the child who goes to a new school at the age when his or her contemporaries have already made and fixed their circle of friends?

To see the picture completely we must include the young man who goes to the university, who was so bright when he only had the other boys of his school to compete with, and who, when the standard of ability jumps to university level, finds himself very ordinary and very lonely and very insecure. The bright, school prize-winner is almost a duffer and cannot now maintain the superiority which gave him the feeling of security. The number of suicides amongst new undergraduates at Oxford and Cambridge has recently been a great worry to the authorities.

Turn to the business world and remember how lonely a youngster feels during the first weeks in a bank, or an office, or a factory. How shy he can be of his own ideals if he finds no one who shares them! How easy it is to get into a thoroughly bad set if one of its members at any rate ends a youngster's loneliness! Christian ideals can be lost in a month if loneliness throws a youngster into situations where such ideals are scorned.

You would think that marriage would end loneliness, but many a young wife is suddenly cut off from the associates in her business or profession and has many lonely hours. And who has not seen a young bride, full of Christian idealism, lose it because it is too lonely to maintain it? Her husband scorns it.

32

The "set" in which they move despises religion. Church-going soon disappears. Saying their prayers follows. Secret prayer does not last much longer. The children are brought up without any reference at all to the Divine Friend of little children, when, if once the fellowship of a good church had been entered, the loneliness—in this matter—of husband or wife would have been ended, and the spiritual values, the maintenance of which are the only hope of the nation, would have been maintained.

The loneliness of old people I will not dwell upon. Again and again one meets them. On average people are living twenty years longer than they did when I was a child. By 1975, says one writer, one person in seven of the entire population will be sixty-five or over. In 1900 the proportion was one in twenty-one. If not chronically ill, many old folk never feel really well. Growingly they feel unwanted and unloved. Frequently they feel in the way. Their ideas are regarded as old-fashioned. Their advice is never sought. Their companionship is not regarded as worth seeking. They are a drag on everybody. The only power they now possess with which to please others, is the money they will leave. Many old people wish they could die, and the wish is sometimes secretly shared by those who look after them, so unhappily wide is the gulf between the generations.

*　　*　　*

I suppose there may be a few people present who have never known loneliness. But most people have known it at some time or another, even the young, the companionable and the popular. Take a look at a few examples.

Few could have been more popular than young Rupert Brooke, the handsome poet. Yet how pathetic is the true story of his setting off for America in May 1913, with no one to see him off at the Liverpool Docks. Everyone else seemed to have friends. He had none. Looking down from the liner he saw a dirty little ragamuffin on the quay, and, running down the gangway. Rupert Brooke found that the boy's name was William. "Will you wave to me if I give you sixpence, William?"

"Why yes," said William. Back to the ship went the poet. And when the great liner slipped away from her moorings and friends waved to friends, a dirty rag was waved by a dirty hand. "So," wrote the poet later, "I got my sixpennorth and my farewell—Dear William!"[1]

* * *

Florence Nightingale lived as busy a life as anyone and was ceaselessly surrounded by others, but Sir Edward Cook wrote of her, "She was very lonely. She felt that everything she said or did was a subject of vexation to her sister, a disappointment to her mother and a worry to her father." She wrote to her mother, "I should be as happy here as the day is long if I only had your smile, your blessing, your sympathy, without which I cannot be quite happy." Her ideas and her ideals made her lonely.

* * *

Few preachers have been so popular as F. W. Roberston of Brighton. Yet his ideas made him lonely. He wrote: "I shall be left alone as my Master was. I am hated by some who loved me once, not for what I do, but for what I think. Yet a sublime feeling of a Presence comes about me at times which makes inward solitariness a trifle to talk about."[2]

So we could go on. The Old and the Young, the Great and the Obscure, the Rich and the Poor, the Wise and the not so Wise know this grim battle with loneliness.

And, of course, the poets know it. Writes Matthew Arnold:

> "Yes, in the sea of life enisled,
>   With echoing straits between us thrown,
>   Dotting the shoreless watery wild,
>   We mortal millions live *alone*."[3]

And Longfellow calls us

"Ships that pass in the night and speak each other in passing,

[1] *Collected Poems of Rupert Brooke* p. lxxxi (Sidgwick & Jackson)
[2] *Life and letters of F. W. Robertson* Vol. 2, p. 99 (Dent)
[3] "To Marguerite"

Only a signal shown and a distant voice in the darkness,
So, on the ocean of life, we pass and speak one another,
Only a look and a voice, then darkness again, and a silence."[1]

* * *

Well, there is the problem. What solution have we? I believe that God has the answer, though the detail of that solution I must leave until this evening. It seems futile and almost wicked to say to a really lonely person, "God is your friend," for God to most of us is so unreal. The word "God" lights up only a misty Abstract Idea. The idea needs translating into warm human love before it can remedy loneliness.

But let us take hold on two considerations before we close. The first is that Jesus Christ was very lonely and He illustrates poignantly my contention that solitude is geographical and occasionally good. But loneliness is spiritual and of the nature of disease, or as conparable with disease as is starvation.

Jesus loved solitude. He disliked loneliness. Jesus often went away that He might find solitude. Yet He took steps to try to ease His loneliness. He called His disciples, in Mark's beautiful phrase, "that they might be with Him." He needed human companionship. He took Peter and James and John as far into His transfiguration experience as they could go. But they went to sleep. He took them as far into the Gethsemane experience as He could, but though He rebuked them—"Could ye not watch with Me one hour"—He could not keep them awake.

His Mother let it be known that she thought Him mad and His own brothers repudiated Him. His was a sensitive soul, yet He knew what has been called "the solitude of human hate". He was no hard man of steel and stoicism. He laughed. He wept. He loved little children. He loved birds and flowers. He was compassionate to the sick. But His ideas and purposes made men hate Him, reject Him, crucify Him, and even His own men "all forsook Him and fled", just when He was most lonely and needed them most.

[1] "Tales of a Wayside Inn," The Theologian's Tale.

35

My friend, here is one thing to remember. You will never be as lonely as Christ was on Good Friday morning.

* * *

Then take with you this thought which I confess I never realised so fully until I started collecting passages that spoke of God's friendship. All through the Bible you will find words about God and His relation to man which express the idea that God is trying to end man's loneliness.

We cannot read five chapters of Genesis before we read that Enoch walked with God. Abraham was the Friend of God. Moses met with God on Sinai. The promise came to Joshua, "As I was with Moses so I will be with thee." David says he can face the valley of the shadows because "Thou art with me." Micah says, "What doth the Lord require of thee, but to do justly, to love mercy and to walk humbly with thy God?" Then God comes Himself in Jesus, Who is no ascetic in a cave to be sought by pilgrimage, but who loves to be with men— the Friend of publicans and sinners; "the most precious slander," said T. R. Glover, "that ever oozed from slimy lips." Christ's last recorded word in one Gospel is, "Lo, I am with you every day until the consummation of the age," and when His physical presence was removed, He promised His Spirit "that He shall be *with you* for ever". "With you," "with you," "with you." The words take us very near the heart of the whole message of religion.

One could not but be moved by the story of the soldier who asked his officer if he might go out into the "No man's land" between the trenches in World War I to bring in one of his comrades who lay grievously wounded. "You can go," said the officer, "but it's not worth it. Your friend is probably killed, and you will throw your own life away." But the man went. Somehow he managed to get to his friend, hoist him on to his shoulder, and bring him back to the trenches. The two of them tumbled together and lay in the trench-bottom. The officer looked very tenderly on the would-be rescuer, and then he said, "I told you it wouldn't be worth it. Your friend is dead and you are mortally wounded." "It was worth it though, sir." "How do you mean, 'worth it'? I tell you, your friend is dead." "Yes, sir," the boy answered, "but it was worth it, because when I got to him he was still alive and he said to me, 'Jim, *I knew you'd come.*'"

If true of a human friend, how true it must be of the Divine Friend. He must not make religion an insurance by saving us from the waters of trouble. But He does promise that when we pass through them, He will be there too. "With you, with you. . . ."

Still the word of the Gospel is Immanuel, for God is *with us.*

Evening Sermon

This morning we diagnosed loneliness, noted its nature and its widespread incidence; tried to understand Christ's loneliness and saw how God seeks to end it. But we did not specify the practical things which the lonely person could do.

I think they are all included in the realm of religion. For loneliness is an insufficiency of relationships and to me the very heart of religion—as the word implies—is relationship. If I were asked to say in one sentence what Christianity is, I think I should say that it was *the acceptance of Christ's friendship.* It was that friendship which transformed the disciples and still transforms those who take it seriously. To me, the unanswerable argument for Christianity is that it changes men's lives. What they believe intellectually is very much a secondary affair in my view. The services and ceremonies they attend are of less importance still. But to enter into Christ's fellowship and *to follow the implications of that entry,* will bring a soul into fellowship with Christ's other followers and end his loneliness, and as the young Christian meditates and listens and thinks, the Christian sense of values and the great Christian verities will be established in his mind. In a *live* Church a new life will begin for him in company with Christ's other friends.

Christ never imposed beliefs on the minds of His followers. Said T. R. Glover, "Christianity began in friendship." To be a Christian is more like falling in love than accepting beliefs.

37

A man meets a girl and thinks how wonderful it would be if he could share her life. Peter saw in Jesus One with whom he felt it would be wonderful to live. So Christianity *began* in experience, and as the experience deepened, certain great truths grew up in his mind. They formed his creed. But he did not *begin* by swallowing a parcel of statements. Peter had probably never heard of the Virgin Birth, but he became more loving and easier to live with and that is far more important than believing what the authorities have labelled orthodoxy.

* * *

But let us turn to the practical things a man or woman can do to cure the disease of loneliness. I have grouped them as follows:

(1) Something to question
(2) Something to remember
(3) Something to feel
(4) Something to try out in action.

(1) *Something to question.* It is a question we must ask ourselves. Is my loneliness my own fault? I once read about a woman called Edith, of whom this was—perhaps cruelly—said, "Edith is a very small island, bounded on the north, on the south, on the east and on the west by Edith."

I once knew a wealthy woman who lived in her own house, had her own servants, her own car and even someone to drive her about, but she was for ever moaning how lonely she was. She wanted people to visit her, and she wanted notice to be taken of her, and, like everybody in the world, she wanted to be loved. Then one day she made a great discovery which I expect you made long ago, that the way to be loved is to love. Instead of waiting to be visited, she *invited* people to tea who could not afford to ask her back. She went to see people so as to ease *their* loneliness. She joined in fellowship groups, really *joined in* instead of sitting like a wall-flower waiting to be admired, pitied and fussed. Within one year she was so busy that she wondered how on earth she had once looked out of the window after breakfast and said, "How on earth am I going to get through today?" When asked if she was lonely, she said—amusingly to those who had known her earlier—"Lonely? I haven't time to be lonely."

Let us first ask whether the fault is not our own that we are lonely. Are we so proud that we cannot be anything else but lonely? Have we ever offered to others hospitality and loving service, or are we imprisoned in self, a self full of a self-pity and bitterness that drives people from us and makes our loneliness worse?

*   *   *

(2) *Something to remember*. I want you to remember that you *belong*. You *belong* to God. You *belong* to the Christian family. You can *belong* to a church. You can make a beginning today by belonging to "The Friends of the City Temple".

I remember so well being told by an old friend of mine, then a professor of theology in one of our colleges, how that when he was a little boy and his father was away from home, he did something naughty and was sent to bed by his mother just before his father, whom he adored, came home after several days' absence. When the boy heard his father's key in the front door, he could bear the loneliness no longer. He put his dressing-gown on over his pyjamas and came down-stairs. He feared a rebuke, but his father opened his arms and said, in loving tones, "My own, wee son!" My friend said he would never forget the delicious sense of *belonging* to the family. Christ has not called us servants, but friends.

There is power in belonging. I knew a man who, one Sunday evening in Berlin, was very lonely and very tempted to enter an evil house. Photographs outside allured him. Bodily needs tortured him. He was far from home. . . . No one would know. . . . Suddenly he moved away. (I have often wondered if prayer at that moment was being offered for him at home.)

When asked what sudden thought had moved him out of temptation's power, he said, "I *belong* to a church at home. I couldn't have gone back and faced them if I had let them down. I belong to them."

*   *   *

(3) *Something to feel.* I want you to feel that you are sent.

When you poke the fire, it may be that only the tip of the poker touches the coal, but every molecule in that steel rod, every atom, every electron is involved, and so is the strong thrust of the arm behind the hand that grasps the poker.

The poker is the fellowship of the Church. The hand is the hand of Christ. The strong arm is the arm of God, and again and again you may be the part of the poker that touches life. But you are empowered. Others are involved. You are not alone. To change the figure, you are sent.

Can you take this message from Christ's own lips. Listen! "I am not alone *because* the Father is with Me . . . the Father *sent* me." Let me read to you more of this message. As it helped Christ to face His loneliness, so it will help you.

"My meat is to do the will of Him that *sent* me."

"He that receiveth you receiveth not Me, but Him that *sent* Me."

"The Spirit of the Lord is upon Me. for He has *sent* Me to bind up the broken-hearted."

"I came down from heaven not to do My own will, but the will of Him that *sent* Me."

"He that hath *sent* Me is with Me. He hath not left me alone."

"I must work the works of Him that *sent* Me while it is day."

"The word is not Mine, but the Father's Who *sent* Me."

And best of all, "As the Father hath sent Me, *even so I send you.*"

What a glorious thought! He *sent* you into that bank, that office, that hospital, that school, that hostel, that college, that home—and for His glory!

I often wonder how men can stick the monotony of life. To rise, to shave, to dress, to come downstairs, to eat bacon, to put on a coat, to catch a bus, or worse, a tube train, to arrive at an office, hang a hat on a peg, sit at a desk for four hours, to eat a chop and a little rice pudding, to return, sit for four more hours on a stool, to leave the office, walk along the same street, go in with the latch-key, hang up the hat, wash the hands, eat a meal, light a pipe, read the evening paper, yawn at the wireless and go to bed. And tomorrow the same, and tomorrow and tomorrow and tomorrow. . . .! Sunday is a change, of course, and Saturday afternoon and evening. Oh, yes, and there is a wife and perhaps kiddies and summer holidays and hobbies and pictures and music and fun.

But take the great majority of the hours. What do they all lead to? To what purpose are they spent? To saving a little money, to retiring, to passing away, let us hope into a world where the meaning of existence is made a little more clear.

But supposing He *sent* you into that office, to show forth in terms of your personality, His glory. Suppose that it *is* man's chief end, after all, to glorify God. *Sent* by the most high God to that little business, Smith and Co., off Tottenham Court Road, to reveal the glory of God.

Look at that humble, middle-aged little woman getting off the bus and going into that drab place of business—monotony? Oh, yes, but she isn't only doing her best for Smith Ltd. She believes she is *sent*. The glory of God is round about her. Every day as she steps off the bus at the corner of Tottenham Court Road, the angels sound their trumpets for her in heaven and the hosts of the shining ones watch her with pride and joy. Would it be absurd to press our analogy and say, "She is the contact point of their poker? They are in it with her. She is *sent*!

*　　*　　*

(4) *Something to do.* Now here *you* must decide. I think it makes people angry who complain of loneliness and are told, "Well, why don't you take up golf or gardening?" I remember seeing a lonely man "take up golf". When I saw him, he was taking up the course! I've never seen a more miserable object! Many of my friends have for years told me that I ought to have a hobby. "Take up gardening," they say. I *hate* gardening! Nothing ever grows if I put it in, even if I put it in the right way up!

No, here we have to think things out for ourselves. But I think that to cure loneliness what we do about it *must include some kind of service to others.*

Let me only hint at some things you may have overlooked. If you cannot get out much, could you pray regularly for certain people? There are six Prayer Circles here, and you could join one of them without leaving your home. You could write loving and enheartening letters to those who are passing through a bad time. You will get some lovely letters back, to read in lonely hours. Sometimes a whole day is brightened for me by one sentence in one letter in my morning mail. Could you sometimes ring a person on the phone with a cheery message?

Some of you who can get out, perhaps possess a car. Could you give a lift to people sometimes, when they want to come to church, or do their shopping, or see a relative? Could you go and baby-sit, or relieve that tired soul who can never get away from her invalid charge? Could you who can cook, sometimes make something tasty for the gas-ring slaves? Listen in on the wireless to the "Week's Good Cause" until the one turns up that you could help.

I feel that those who will come into the fellowship of a live church would soon, by giving and receiving, be able to cure their loneliness. We help one another. And as far as my experience goes, I can say one thing without fear of contradiction; nothing in the world is so enheartening; nothing so quickly banishes that dark mood we call loneliness, than the response of those whom we succeed, however simply, in helping along the way. Here the words of Christ are once more so amazingly true: "He that loveth his life, loseth it. He that loseth it for My sake, shall find it unto life eternal." Shall find LIFE! The thing we are all looking for! Fulness of LIFE. Let me translate the wonderful words differently: "He who hugs life to himself, loses all joy in living, is lonely and self-excluded from joy. He who *gives himself away to others* shall find a fullness of life that will develop into the wholly satisfying life that is everlasting."

Can We Cast Our Burden Upon The Lord?

A T my request the Choir opened the service this morning with the lovely introit, "Cast thy burden upon the Lord," but I want to ask whether in truth we can really do this.

I have been asking myself for some time now whether religion does not fail to grip people because often it uses language which is beautiful, but which just is not true. Are we too glib in the claims we make for religion? Do we paint it too rosily? Do we claim for it more than it can sustain? Do we resort to aphorisms and clichés and old-fashioned language which we do not even expect to be realised?

We have often said, "You cannot think better than the truth about God." But a child might *think* a diet of jam *better* than meat, and an adult might think something given *better* than something earned.

On one of my holiday Sundays I attended a service at which the Psalms were chanted, and in one of them the most impossible things were promised by the congregation. A dear old lady, a few seats in front of me, chanted quite lustily:

"Whoso privily slandereth his neighbour, him will I destroy. . . .
Morning by morning will I destroy all the wicked of the land,
To cut off all the workers of iniquity from the city of the Lord."
(Psalm 101).

Well, we may look forward to better times and Khrushchev had better look out, but as far as I could see, she only had her umbrella with her, and whether she will destroy the next person who slanders his neighbour, we must leave in serious doubt!

* * *

Seriously, the matter is of high importance. It can only lead to an unreality most unattractive to all men and women of honest mind to stand up in church and chant nonsense or say things one cannot mean in any sensible use of words. And many of the Psalms chanted in modern worship are far worse than that. They breathe a spirit of fierce cruelty that is the opposite of the teaching and example of Christ.

This sin of unreality is not confined to any one branch of the Church. Some of the hymns must have struck you as utterly unreal.

> "Take my silver and my gold;
> Not a mite would I withhold."

How few can sing those two lines with sincerity!

> "With Thee conversing, we forget
> All time and toil and care.
> Labour is rest and pain is sweet,
> If Thou, my God art there."

Pain sweet? I do not think even the greatest saints would call pain sweet, and to sing words like these is wrong. Either it makes people hypocrites or it makes sincere people suppose that the words are true for others. Thus they suppose their own experience is of poor quality, and they feel depressed. They suppose that if they were all they ought to be, then pain would be "sweet".

* * *

But all this is negative. I want to bring three texts to your notice this morning.

Psalm 55[2]: "Cast thy burden upon the Lord and He shall sustain thee."
Galatians 6[2]: "Bear ye one another's burdens."
Galatians 6[5]: "Every man shall bear his own burden."

Are they all true? *Can* they all be true? The last most certainly contains truth, though, in my view, not the whole of the truth. Can we look at that one first?

Every man shall bear his own burden! In this text we catch a haunting glimpse of life's essential loneliness.

44

Let us imagine a situation which is not very fanciful. A man —a husband and a father of little children—in the prime of his life is suddenly stricken down by some killing disease. Never before perhaps has he known a day's illness. Like so many people, he had read and heard of sudden illness, but in a queer way he has always thought that though it came to others, it would never come to him. His friends prayed for him, sympathised, sent messages and flowers. But there comes the moment when, perhaps, he goes up early to bed, he who usually went to bed after midnight, and he looks at himself in the glass and the loneliness of suffering falls upon him. Or he wakens in the morning before the day breaks and has to accept once more a day of pain and weakness. Inwardly he knows his days are numbered. Some burdens you cannot accept once and for all. You have to accept them again every day. And there falls upon the spirit an awareness—"This is my burden, mine alone." As Jeremiah said, "This is a grief, and I must bear it" (10¹⁹).

Says Siegfried Sassoon:

"I thought how strange we grow when we're alone,
 And how unlike the selves that meet and talk,
 And blow the candle out, and say goodnight.
 Alone—The word is life endured and known.
 It is the stillness where our spirits walk
 And all but inmost faith is overthrown."

"Every man shall bear his own burden."

*   *   *

But thank God that is not all the truth. "It is not good that man shall be alone," saith the Lord God. Many of us—I for one—can speak from experiences for which we thank God, that our dear ones share our burdens.

This is true even about the small burdens of every day. What a rich thing it is to have a friend to whom you can pour out the story of your burdens! My mind goes often to the definition of a friend which I first heard amongst the Arabs. It is the loveliest definition of a friend I think I know. "A true friend is one to whom you can tip out all the contents of your heart, chaff and grain together, knowing that the gentlest hands will take and sift it, keep what is worth keeping, and with the breath of kindness, blow the rest away."

At the end of the day to be able to share with a dear one the burdens one is carrying, this is a blessing indeed, and perhaps one of the richest things in a happy marriage. To be able to pour out one's heart without receiving a sympathy so cloying as to drive one into rancid self-pity, and yet without receiving the cold shoulder and the bored indifference, is to be built up and renewed and strengthened to bear bravely the burden of the next day. Real love, of course, *desires* to share the burden of the beloved. The late Dr. W. R. Maltby once told a revealing and true story.

A man in a position of trust was found guilty of shameful conduct, dismissed his post and his disgrace made public. As so often happens, the burden of it all fell most heavily on his relatives. One of them was his daughter who had made a place for herself in society and was much looked up to and admired. But when one of her companions said, "It is terrible that you should be involved in his disgrace and your name dragged down into the mud," she, who had the right Christian attitude, was almost indignant, and replied, "When I heard of it, I said, 'Well, thank God I can share it.'"[1]

Side by side with that story I would place one told by Professor W. M. Clow. It is of a young man who deserted a widowed mother and, like the prodigal, departed to another town to embark on a life of profligacy. His minister wrote to him repeatedly, but he would never reply. Finally, the minister wired the boy that his mother was dying and the prodigal returned. But as the boy entered the room, his mother gave one fleeting smile of welcome and died. When the boy looked at that still form and noted in the lined face and the silver hair the signs of anguished suffering, he knelt down by the bed and shook the room with his sobs.

"Every man shall bear his own burden"—true in a sense,

[1] W. R. Maltby, *The Meaning of the Cross*, p. 10 (Epworth Press).

but he could never bear all the burden. She had carried the heavier part for his sake.

*   *   *

Now we are ready to draw near to the words of the Introit again. Says the Psalmist: "Cast thy burden upon the Lord."

We hardly need to "cast" it, for love always desires to share the burden of the beloved.

But let us be very honest: I used the word "share," not "bear". There is a hymn that contains this verse:

> "To Thee I bring my care,
> The care I cannot flee.
> Thou wilt not only share.
> But bear it all for me."

The last line is not true. The burdens of life are part of our discipline. You do not help your schoolboy son by doing his sums for him. You help him by sharing, teaching, encouraging, explaining, standing in with him in all that puzzles and troubles him.

This seems to me the true teaching of Christ about His yoke. He never said it was easy in the usual sense of the word. He had made yokes Himself; heavy ones too, but He had planed them smooth.

> "The yokes He made were true,
> Because the man who dreamed
> Was too
> An artisan.
> The burdens that the oxen drew
> Were light.
> At night
> He lay upon His bed and knew
> No beast of His stood chafing in a stall
> Made restless by a needless gall."[1]

The Greek word "easy" means "well adjusted", and I have read that a carpenter's shop in ancient Palestine frequently

[1] Gladys Latchaw, *Masterpieces of Religious Verse.*

bore a notice saying, "My yokes are well-adjusted." Jesus may have been quoting from a notice outside his own father's shop.

If I had a lantern and a screen, I could show you from my own slides what is called a "training yoke". The Mosaic law forbade an ox and an ass being yoked together with an ordinary yoke because, to use a modern idiom, the ass "couldn't take it." When a young ox was being trained for ploughing, a "training yoke" was devised. The younger animal was yoked to the older, stronger, and more experienced animal. The heavy end of the yoke was the burden of the stronger. The stronger was placed at the end of the furrow. The stronger kept straight in the furrow, under the guidance of the ploughman. All the weaker had to do was to keep steadily "pulling his weight", as we say, and keeping parallel to the stronger. If, in youthful, bovine pride, the smaller animal pulled away to some fancied path of his own, of course trouble followed. The furrow would have to be ploughed again unless the younger accepted the discipline of both the yoke and the goad. Any such action would make the yoke chafe the shoulders of *both animals* and could rub them red-raw. The younger animal during his training must drop his pride, be meek and lowly in heart, give up his will to the stronger, who took the responsibility as well as the burden. Then, for the younger, the yoke would be smooth and free from galling (easy, as the Gospel says), and the burden light.

Many of us are carrying heavy burdens and at times the loneliness of it all will fall upon us with a stab of terror. But in fellowship with others, we shall find the load lifted a little, particularly if we do not become self-pitying but seek to ease the burden of another. And here is a closing parable. The wings of a bird are a burden. In some birds its wings weigh more than the rest of the body. But when it carries its burden and at the same time *trusts the air to support and sustain it*, it finds that *its very burden becomes the means by which it learns to fly.*

God is like the supporting air around a bird. We learn to fly when we trust this upholding power.

"Cast thy burden upon the Lord; He shall sustain thee."

The Christian Reaction to Grief

Jeremiah 10¹⁹: "Woe is me for my hurt! my wound is grievous: but I said, Truly this is my grief and I must bear it."

THIS sounds a dark subject for a bright summer evening, but perhaps for that very reason this is a good time to face a dark problem.

I must have repeated before the story told by the late Dr. Boreham of an awful night in Scotland, when the snow lay deep and the wind shrieked around a little house in which a good Presbyterian Elder of the Kirk lay dying. His daughter brought the family Bible to his bedside. "Father," she said, "shall I read a chapter to you?" But the Elder was in sore pain and only moaned. She opened the Book and began to turn the pages, and then she heard him say this, "Na, na, lassie, the storm's up noo; I theekit (thatched) ma hoose in the calm weather."

When grief is heavy upon a man, it is not the moment to hand out explanations. When grief falls upon us, we cannot immediately receive carefully thought out advice. It is wise to thatch the house before the storm arises, and even though it is a dark thing to say, the storm will arise. I should not think there is one middle-aged person in the world who at some point has not had to come to terms with grief, and sometimes with devastating grief.

Grief is as old as humanity. Four thousand years ago, Alistair Maclean tells us, on a sunny afternoon in Egypt, heart-broken parents laid to rest in a carved sarcophagus the body of their beloved little daughter. A few years ago two English explorers discovered the tomb. They entered a cave that had been shut all that time and they found the sarcophagus. On it were inscribed these words: "O my life, my love, my little one! Would God I had died for thee!" The two English explorers uncovered their heads and from the darkness of the cave went back with dim eyes into the blazing sunshine of the Egyptian desert. Then they sealed the entrance, leaving love and death to their eternal vigil. Yes, how old a thing is grief! How wise we should be to come to terms with it!

*　　*　　*

The sermon falls into three parts and each of the three falls again into three sub-headings. I want to speak of three faulty ways of meeting grief, three mistaken ways of meeting it, and three true ways of meeting it.

(1) *FAULTY WAYS*

(i) Resentment is only too common a reaction to grief. "Why should this happen to me?" we ask. "What have I done that God should treat me thus?" We look upon the apparent escapes of others, and we feel envious and jealous and in our hearts we manufacture one of the deadliest poisons of the soul, a bitter resentment of spirit.

The terrible thing about resentment is that it poisons ourselves, and does more harm to the man who harbours it than to anyone else. There is not time here and now to take up all the psychological aspects of this matter, but it can be broadly said that many physical ailments develop through the long continuance of emotional poison in the deep mind. I must speak very carefully here, but it is known that arthritis is *sometimes* touched off by resentment. Now do let me make this clear. It would be false, as well as cruel, to suppose that every case of rheumatoid arthritis has been set up because the patient is resentful about something. At the same time, it would be foolish to overlook the fact that some illnesses are what we now delight to call psychosomatic. That is to say, they show in the body, but they are caused or touched off in the mind, and arthritis is one of them. Asthma is another; the gastric ulcer is another. Skin diseases are *sometimes* in this category. There can be no doubt that resentment, long harboured in the mind, is a faulty reaction to grief and *capable* of setting up actual physical illness. Let us then try to get rid of our resentment.

(ii) Self-pity. This was called by the late William Brown, one of our greatest psychiatrists, "the most disintegrating of all emotions." It is admitted that the human mind needs love and appreciation, and if at any time of grief the mind does not receive this support in positive and healthy sympathy, then it can lapse into self-pity, and a person can really wallow in it without even attempting any positive solution of his difficulties. He can thus make himself far less able to cope with life. So this is a second faulty way of reacting to grief.

(iii) The third is fatalism. I do hope that by now at the City Temple there is not one person left who believes that a grief that befalls him is the will of God in any intelligent use of that word. That which is willed is intended, and the idea that God intends a mother to lose her baby child, or a wife her husband, or that God hands out cancer to this man and polio to this child, is, I think, one of the most terrible heresies of our time. Even Christians used to sing a hymn that contained the verse:

> "Though dark my path and sad my lot,
>   Let me be still and murmur not,
>   But breathe the prayer divinely taught,
>   Thy will be done."

Do not let us in an hour of grief try to find solace in a false thought that makes God into a devil. If you brought such grief to a human being, you would be shut up in prison or a lunatic asylum. So it is hardly likely that God is that kind of person. If you want to say, "Thy will be done," say it on the morning when cancer can be prevented or cured; say it when your baby is safely born and "both are doing well"; say it on a bright sunny morning when you are throbbing with life; say it at five minutes to one on Christmas Day; say it when your heart is pulsating with that joy, the source of which is the heart of God.

*　　*　　*

(2) *MISTAKEN WAYS*

Now let us look at some of the mistaken ways. I differentiate here from faulty ways because faulty ways are our own fault. There are some ways of reacting to grief for which people should not be blamed, but from which they should be delivered.

(i) The first is belittlement. I feel strongly that we should not encourage this reaction, even where a little child is concerned. I remember so well a little child I knew picking up the pieces of a dearly loved doll which had been broken by the carelessness of someone who was cleaning out her bedroom. The little girl was broken-hearted, but, irritated by the child's sorrow, the cleaner said, "Don't cry. It doesn't matter. You will get over it. They will give you another." It did matter, and everybody who understands a child's heart knows that it did matter. It was a vulgar, an almost obscene thing to say, "You will get another." A brand new, painted doll of high price thrust into the child's arms would be a vulgar insult when a much loved doll, with all the paint kissed off its cheeks, lay in unmendable fragments on the nursery floor, and the reaction just made a gulf between the two of them. Of course, the sorrow will pass. But it will take time, and the reaction to grief is not helped by belittlement. It is better to go right into the sorrow with the child, and perhaps the best thing you can do *then* is to show the child that you do understand and that you share her sorrow.

Now when grief falls on a person, in many ways he does become a child again. Every psychologist would agree that during a time of sorrow, there is in many ways a regression to childhood's level and to help to overcome one's grieving one needs comfort and sympathy and love, not, I beseech you, the belittlement of the cause of one's grief from the superior heights of another's immunity.

(ii) The second mistaken way is that of comparison. This has often been applied to me. "Yes, you may be in this or that trouble, but think of so-and-so, and how much worse he is." "Never mind," people tell us, "you have lost a child, but Mrs. Jones opposite has lost both hers. You are unhappy, but Mr. Smith has been unhappy for years. Think of so-and-so, he has never had what you have had . . ." and so on and so on.

I think Tennyson must have had this mistaken reaction to grief thrust upon him when his friend, Hallam, died. Listen to this!:

> One writes that "Other friends remain,"
> That "Loss is common to the race"—
> And common is the commonplace,
> And vacant chaff well meant for grain.
>
> That loss is common would not make
> My own less bitter, rather more:
> Too common! Never morning wore
> To evening, but some heart did break.[1]

Frankly, is it any comfort to find that somebody else has had occasion for grief? For myself, I find it depresses me even more to think how widespread grief is. And ought one to try to feel happy that somebody else is worse? Is not that a subtle form of selfishness and pride, as though a punishing hand had at any rate dealt with one more lightly than was the case with one's fellows? The mere recital of other people's woes does not assuage my grief, though to recall their courage helps.

(iii) A third mistaken way of reacting to grief is contained in the advice, "Put it out of your mind." I am sure those who give this advice mean well. They take us to the pictures, or they suggest a holiday, or they say, "Take up your work again," and they try to distract us, and for a little while it may work. But always the mind knows its own grief and swings back

[1] In Memoriam, vi.

to its sorrow. We have only postponed a true reaction. We have not made it by mere distraction. "Time will heal you," we are told, and there is a measure of truth in that, but we cannot apply the anodyne of long years to our present grief. We can only hope that in the end we shall get over it, and I am always suspicious of the glib sentence that time will heal. Time only makes a young sinner into an old sinner, a young fool into an old fool. A dislocated elbow *not skilfully treated at the time*, will not be cured by the passing of time. Rather will the whole arm become helpless. A repressed fear will not be cured by time. It will be buried in the deep mind only, perhaps, to break out in nervous breakdown at some time of special strain. And sorrow, as we have seen, can become bitter resentment which can poison both mind and body. These are mistaken ways. The pagan knows them and tries them. Surely Christianity has some deeper word to speak.

(3) *TRUE WAYS*

(i) The first I want to mention is acceptance. I do not mean the grim, bitter acceptance of those who are fatalistic behind their acceptance. In the common sayings of our ordinary life there is frequently concealed a great deal of wisdom, and in my heart I honour those who look their grief straight in the face and say in the modern phrase, "Well, it is just one of those things." This seems to me very near to the words used in our text by Jeremiah. "This is my grief and I must bear it."

I think the Christian has a lot to learn from that attitude. In the rough and tumble of life, with the jarring of personalities, the action of one freewilled person on that of another, the general ignorance of things like the cause of disease and the essential slow learning of the rules that govern the universe, we are all of us, at some time or another, likely to get hurt. But it is not God's intention. He does not single us out. There is no place for fatalism, no place for resentment, no place for self-pity. I think we are to try to accept our grief as our share of the sorrow of the world, a sorrow which God Himself eternally shares.

(ii) The second true way of reaction is to share our grief with the right person. The important words there are *with the right person*. We are not to tip out our symptoms into every willing ear, for that *deepens* the sense of grief. It is likely to make us feel defeated. He who continually claims sympathy turns himself into a person who needs sympathy, viz. a defeated person. At the same time, a sorrow shared is a sorrow halved. The listener need not be a priest or a minister. Someone with a robust outlook on life and a faith in the over-all purposes of God can help us enormously merely by listening to our sorrow. There is a very wise psychology behind the practice of confession, as long as the practice is properly safeguarded, and I do not mean the confession of sin only, but the confession of grief. Said Shakespeare:

> "Give sorrow words; the grief that does not speak,
> Whispers the o'er-fraught heart, and bids it break"[1]

Spenser, in "The Faerie Queene", reminds us that

> "He oft finds present help who does his griefs impart,"[2]

and I have tried to show in another place that many poets would agree.[3]

(iii) The third, and perhaps the most important, way of reacting to grief is to sit down and confront it. Don't try "to put it out of your mind." Put it into the centre of your mind and steadily stare at it. "This is my grief and I must bear it." But then go on to say, "How can I turn this into an asset? How can I make this grief of mine serve God's purpose in my life?"

Believe me, it can be made to serve Him. Maybe it will make you more sympathetic with others. Maybe in some hour when another calls upon you, it will strengthen your advice. Maybe it will break your own pride. . . . Whatever happens to us, I believe, can be woven into the purposes of God. This is one

[1] *Macbeth* Act iv, Scene 3.
[2] Book 2, Canto 1, verse 46.
[3] *The Afterworld of the Poets.* (Epworth).

of the fundamentals of my own faith. Even the Cross, you see, was willed by wicked men, but God wove it into the redemption of the world, and your thorns too can become a crown.

*   *   *

Look briefly at illustrations which show the difference between a faulty reaction to grief and a true one.

"Your wife has not been to church lately," I said to a man some time ago. "No," he said sadly, "when our boy was killed she stopped saying her prayers and stopped going to church. She put her Bible away and she has become sour and bitter and very difficult to live with. Her very face has altered. Her mouth turns down at the corners. She seems unable to relax and is resentful, bitter and cynical about everything."

Compare that reaction with a true story told by Dr. Stanley Jones. A widow in Australia had two splendid daughters both serving as missionaries in Fuchow, China. During a terrible time of rioting both the girls were murdered. When the news reached the widow she was sixty-two years of age. She did not press her lips together in bitter resentment. She set off for China, learnt the language, went to the very place where her two daughters were murdered, and for twenty years served on the staff of the same mission. She died at eighty-two and was buried by the side of her daughters. What a difference!

Those who have read the life of Mrs. Josephine Butler will remember her reaction to grief. She and her husband went for a holiday in Europe and left their one child, a little girl, at home. Eagerly the child awaited the return of her parents, and at last, after she had gone to bed at night, the great moment came. There was the sound of wheels outside the house and a great commotion in the hall downstairs. The excited little lassie jumped out of bed and rushed on to the landing and jumped on the banister rail to get the first glimpse of Mummy and Daddy. And then the lost balance and the terrible fall! "Never," says Mrs. Butler, "can I lose that memory, the fall, the sudden cry and then the silence. It was pitiful to see her

56

helpless in her father's arms, her little drooping head resting on his shoulder and her beautiful golden hair, all stained with blood, falling over his arm. Would God I had died that death for her! If only we had been permitted one look, one moment of recognition!" But the world knows that Mrs. Josephine Butler rose up from her grief and devoted herself to wayward and motherless daughters in the outside world. A tragedy which God certainly did not will was not met with resentment, self-pity or fatalism. There was no comparison with others, or belittlement of grief, or distractions to take it out of the mind's focus. There was the perfect reaction of acceptance and turning the grief into an asset, so that the world in one sense can even be glad at the grief of that brave heart.

Do not think that such illustrations are confined to famous people. Here is part of a letter I received since last Sunday from a brave woman who lost her husband:

"I woke one night to find the dearest thing I loved in life dead beside me. . . . Many of my friends were filled with deep love and they longed to help me and they prayed that God would guide me and allow me to sleep. And then during a little sleep I saw my husband. He had a most wonderful look on his face and I awakened full of the strangest happiness I have ever felt. I knew how Mary felt at the tomb. I wanted to live because Jim (the husband) was alive and I knew that all that God had promised was true. I lay and cried, but they were tears of happiness, and ever since I have slept every night without a drug.

Then I began to feel a strange longing to do something, but I could not make up my mind. I tried several things which led nowhere, so I asked God again to guide me, and in a few weeks He had directed me to nurse in a great hospital. When you realise that I had only been in the Red Cross and had never heard of an Assistant Nurse, you will see how wonderfully I was led. I served in a ward kept for women with Parkinson's Disease and disseminated sclerosis, and when I confessed that my nursing experience was small, the sister said that the patients did not need so much skilled nursing as love and kindness. . . .

I feel that this is what God wanted me to do and what my husband is pleased to know I am doing. God has put healing balm on to my broken heart. There are still days when I feel I am kneeling in the Garden of Gethsemane, but I find God there and there is always help to put me on my feet again, and we walk back to life together. . . . When I enter a ward a great compassion comes over me. I suppose you could say that love goes out from me.

I would like to tell you one more thing. One day when I came home and opened the door I thought, 'If only I could go in and find him there, or go into the garden and see him,' and it was as though God replied, 'One day, my child, you shall come home and find the door open to life eternal. You won't need to look for your husband or go into the garden. He will be just inside the door waiting.'"

What a wonderful reaction to grief and what a privilege to receive such a letter!

*   *   *

There is a haunting and terrible picture in the second book of Kings (2 Kings 6 [24]). Samaria was being besieged by the Syrians. The city was famine-stricken. Everyone was wearing sackcloth, the sign of distress, save only the King. He still wore the royal purple. One day as he passed along he heard two women quarrelling. They had made a pact that on one day the son of one of them should be boiled and eaten, and on another day the child of the other. The first child had been devoured. Then the mother of the second child would not give the baby up. The king was horror-stricken. He expressed that horror in the customary way. He rent his robe. The women started back. *The king was wearing sackcloth underneath his royal robes.*

What a royal thing to do? Sackcloth underneath. The splendour of the purple without. Can we be great enough to follow? Our disappointment, our frustration, our sorrow there underneath, known to ourselves and perhaps our closest friends and advisers, but outside, the robe of cheerfulness, the royal ministries of love, the garment of praise. Not a sorrow resentfully buried, but put out of sight and revealed only when the revealing would help another. Thus self-pity is banished. Irritability and resentment are cured. The toxins of bitterness and cynicism are neutralised.

Let us wear in sight of men a royal robe flashing with jewels of courage and hope and kindness. For when we look at Jesus, the Man of Sorrows Who was acquainted with grief, we know that man is too royal to let all men see the sackcloth and too divine to believe that grief can be the final word.

It Doesn't Matter as Much as You Think

(A New Year Sermon)

I WONDER how your New Year resolutions are getting on! On the first day of a new month, the second month of the year, it seems a good time to recall our New Year resolutions and check up as to whether we are still maintaining them.

I would like you, if you will, to think with me this morning about one that I myself made, and perhaps you made it also. I made the resolution that I would try to keep my perspective right; that I would try to develop such a spiritual sensitiveness that I could quickly recognise when a thing was a trifle that did not matter and when a thing was important. I crave to have enough grace, common-sense and courage to react to trifles as trifles and to important matters as important.

If we fail to do this, we find our inner serenity disturbed by things as trifling as a wet day, a burnt pudding, a dismal dinner-party, a torn dress, a missed train, a letter lost in the post, and so on.

If we are honest with ourselves, we must admit that there are occasions when we have been slighted, or irritated, or hurt, and we have said the quick, angry word or maintained the slow, sulky silence, so that for ourselves a whole day has been spoilt and the shadow of our depression has darkened the pathway which others have to tread. Indeed, one sulker at a meal can pull down such a darkness upon the happy fellowship of the table that even little children are robbed of their merriment, and everybody's life is made gloomier than it need be.

I expect you know what it is to do something and to have your motive for doing it doubted or even impugned, or to have done something for which another gets the credit, and so on.

There are people here who would love to have been married, to have had their own home and family and the security of another's love, and for no clear reason they have been deprived. There are others who have married happily, and then somehow the marriage has gone wrong and they are faced with its break-up or by the permanence of a bored distaste with one another's company, with ill-concealed hostility and scarcely suppressed resentment. There are some who have watched others get wealthy and live in comfort, when they themselves have put out just as much energy, and have had just as much ability and have tried as hard, and yet they have failed and now struggle on in something near to poverty, with the future so lacking in security as to frighten them in the dismal hours of sleepless nights. There are some who, though it is no credit to themselves, have had robust health, or unbroken luck in business, while others have always had to struggle against threatened illness and the feeling of being unable to cope. Some face this New Year, only a month old, with feelings of immense confidence. For them the future is rosy with promise. Others, no less deserving, face the future listlessly and drearily, and wonder indeed what the New Year will bring.

Most people at some time or another have said, "If only I had had this or that advantage. If only this had happened. If only that had come my way. If I had married Jane instead of Joan. If I had been to a university. If I had passed that examination. If I had been offered that directorship. . . ." There are moments like these in all our lives, when that terribly insidious enemy of inward peace which we call self-pity, undermines our morale, and, if unhampered, will multiply and produce its morbid progeny—resentment, bitterness, dislike of others, hatred, envy, and even despair.

I wonder if this morning we can get our perspective right and say about something that has loomed too large, "It doesn't matter as much as I thought."

*　　*　　*

Look with me, if you will, at some of the pictures in Scripture that light up our theme.

I want you to look first of all at John the Baptist. There are a number of preachers worshipping with us this morning. I think all preachers must have a great affection and a great regard for John the Baptist. I am so glad that our Lord Himself paid John such a wonderful tribute. Here is a man who schooled his body, disciplined his mind, forswore marriage and practised asceticism that he might give himself entirely to the great cause, the cause of the spiritual welfare of his fellows. Here is a man who went out into the inhospitable desert and lived on locust beans and wild honey and the meagre fare which the barren desert offered. Here is a man who eschewed the wealthy, the influential and the great, and was content to cry to his fellows, "Repent! Believe!" We are told that "all Jerusalem came out to meet him and to be baptised in Jordan, confessing their sins". All Jerusalem! That must have warmed a preacher's heart! Here is a man at the peak and triumph of his career. He commands enormous crowds. His name is on everybody's lips. And then look what happens! His cousin, a joiner from Nazareth, became his competitor for the crowds, and to John's eternal credit, when he might have been forgiven if he had wanted to be first, he said of Jesus, "He must increase, I must decrease." He saw himself as one who prepared the way for someone greater. He saw in a flash that his own popularity did not matter, but in that recognition he showed his greatness.

If there is anybody present who has risen to the top of his own particular tree, and in the hour of his triumph has had to make way for somebody else, he will know how John felt. Yet John had the insight that all sincere preachers must cultivate, the insight by which a man says, "It does not matter through whose lips the message comes. It only matters that the people respond to God." So from that moment, John fades in importance. This lonely man becomes lonelier still. What follows is the obscurity of a prison cell in the grim fortress of Machaerus by the silent shores of the Dead Sea, followed by a terrible death at the whim of a dancing girl. Yet I think at the end, John, reviewing his misfortunes, would have said, "They do not matter as much as I thought."

*　　*　　*

Turn to another story which seems to me to light up the same theme—the story of the Good Samaritan. I must not stay on it, or even try to deal with it adequately, but let me sketch in its outline. Here is a poor Jew lying in the ditch by the roadside. As we should say now, he has been beaten up on a road that is still called the Bloody Way. The way from Jerusalem to Jericho is notoriously a dangerous path. I went down it myself in a motor car in 1934. On this very road, we were told, the police had been searching for a brigand who had built a wall of stones right across the road, had stopped all the cars and robbed all the passengers. The brigand, it was reported had chopped a finger off a woman's hand to get her rings more quickly. One could say that this road is still the Bloody Way, and Jesus must have been in far greater peril than the modern traveller as he walked along it, for indeed it does seem as if this story is based on facts.

You will remember that along the road came a priest on his way to an appointment. I have a great sympathy for this priest. In my job it is almost unpardonable to be late for an appointment and keep a congregation waiting. Besides, who was this poor nobody in the ditch and what was his misfortune to do with a priest? If the hand of God had smitten the traveller—and the Jew of that time would thus interpret misfortune—why should he, the priest, interfere? But more than this, if the priest touched the man, he would become ceremonially unclean. If, by any chance, the man were dead, the priest would be unable to fulfil any priestly duties for twenty-four hours and he would have to spend them in cleansing ceremonies. Do not let us sneer at him too quickly. Besides, perhaps the priest looked over his shoulder and saw the Levite coming along, and said, "Oh, he will see to this man." But unfortunately the Levite also passed by on the other side.

Both of them, you see, had their perspective wrong. It would have been better to keep a congregation waiting than to pass the wounded man, unhelped, by the wayside. It would have been better to spend a week in cleansing ceremonies than to befoul one's spirit by callous indifference to desperate need. The things they thought mattered, did not matter nearly so much as they thought.

*　　*　　*

Look briefly at just one more picture from the Scriptures. Can you sense the situation that confronted the apostles after the Ascension? Judas had gone. He had committed suicide. He was out of it and the remainder felt it of enormous importance to make up the number to twelve. They were in such a hurry that although they prayed, they finally adopted a heathen practice and cast lots. And the lot fell on Matthias. His unimportance seems to be established by the fact that he is never mentioned again in the Scriptures. Filling the vacant place in a hurry was not nearly as important as they thought. It really does look as though St. Paul was the man they would have appointed to the apostleship if only they had waited, and St. Paul does seem to have had his perspective right. Do you remember how he wrote to the Corinthians and said, "What are you all making such a fuss about? One of you says, 'I am of Paul.' Another says, 'I am of Apollos.' Another says, 'I am of Cephas.'" And, says St. Paul, in effect, "It doesn't matter nearly so much as you think."

*　　*　　*

Now can we relate our theme this morning to modern situations? Before we do so, I would make one caveat. My message does not mean that we can be complacent about things. My message does not mean concerning *anything* that it does not matter as much as we think. We must make our stand on some things like nuclear weapons, like apartheid, like prostitution.

64

There are some outstanding questions of the day concerning which the true Christian cannot dilly dally. He must say the brave word, take the definite step, make up his mind, speak out bravely, stick to his guns.

*   *   *

But that having been said, there are some things which, in my opinion, do need pushing into a different perspective.

Let us begin with the Church. It is good to see our own sins before we dwell on the sins of other people. Do you feel that the Church gets far more excited about its doctrines than about its duties; far more excited about its orthodoxy than about its relevance to human need? I have been criticised lately for preaching a sermon on sex, but I was confronted by some young people who presented an inescapable challenge. "The Church teaches its doctrines," they said, "and some of them are doctrines concerning which no one ever trips up. No one has ever gone to the devil because he has not understood the Trinity. But thousands of people trip up on sex and the Church is nearly silent about it." I tried to answer that challenge and I think I was right in doing so, especially when a Harley Street doctor writes that one woman in three admits to pre-marital intercourse, that one in twenty of all births is illegitimate, that one in six of all babies is conceived ahead of marriage or right out of wedlock, and that one in eight of all brides is pregnant on her wedding day.

The matter of church unity is important to me. I do not feel at home amongst the Roman Catholics or even Anglo-Catholics. I admire the Salvation Army, but I do not speak the same language. If I go to a Quaker Meeting, I go to sleep in the silence. (I mean that I mentally go to sleep, just as some of you are doing now!) I am not trained to meditate in a silence of half an hour with no words to guide me. But I do not think these differences matter nearly so much as we think. If one man is in the Air Force, another in the Army and another in the Navy, they are all serving the Queen, and I do not feel that I have the right to say that my way of serving my King—and, of course, I mean Jesus—is right and another man's way is wrong. Some people say that you should not sprinkle a baby, but you should immerse an adult. That alone, they claim, is true Christian baptism. Other people say that you should not take the Holy Supper in the evening, but you should have it before breakfast in the morning. Some people say that Anglican Clerical Orders are superior to Free Church Orders, and they ask me to believe what to me is the impossible theory of apostolic succession. But about all these concerns I want to say to the disputants, "I don't think they matter nearly as much as you think." Serving our Lord, loving His little ones and interpreting His spirit in the life of the world today—surely these are the things which should be large in our perspective.

* * *

I would appeal to you in the life of our church here to try to keep your perspective right. Miss Jones has stopped coming to church because she does not like the size of the Cross in the apse. Mr. Smith is not coming any more because he was not re-elected on to that committee. Mr. Ponsonby says he "doesn't believe in Foreign Missions", and he won't come any more because a recent sermon on India made him uncomfortable and he called it "disgusting". Mrs. Thompson, her husband tells me, sobbed herself to sleep because she was not asked to pour out the tea.... Oh dear! Oh dear! Whenever I get my holidays I feel that religion is in the same category as great mountains and glorious sunsets, the calm beauty of the dawn, the majesty of the night sky, a great art, great poetry and great music. And then, when I come back to the day-to-day detail of a modern church, I find hours of time and immense energy absorbed by silly children of adult age and childish emotions who quarrel about trifles and have never emotionally grown up. How hard it is to keep our perspective right!

* * *

So in the life of the home! If that row you had with your wife had been incorporated in a play on the stage, you would

66

both have laughed heartily about it, and yet because it happened in your lounge, you did not speak to each other for hours. Years ago I actually interviewed a girl in her twenties who told me, when I was trying to find out the cause of her nervous unrest and lack of integration, that her father and mother had not spoken to one another for five years. I said, "Do they live together?" She said, "Oh yes! They live in the same house, but they leave little notes for one another on the mantelpiece." When I asked how it began, the girl said, "Well, mother wanted some people to come to supper and father did not like them and they had a terrible quarrel, and neither of them has made the first move to bring it to an end." Can you believe it? Think of the tension, the hostility, the built-up pride and the misery in a home for years. Apparently no guardian angel could make his voice heard, whispering in the ear of either of them, "It doesn't matter nearly as much as you think."

I should like to think that the value of this sermon would be that we look into our own hearts at the things that hurt and dismay and irritate us, and listen to that angel-voice which would tell us when a thing is important and when it is not.

* * *

Can we pass on one or two tips to one another in this matter? I think in a long life I have discovered one or two rules that help me when I am tempted to get my perspective wrong.

(1) Never make an important decision when you are angry or depressed.

(2) Never make a decision between midnight and five o'clock in the morning. One can lie awake through those hours at which body, mind and spirit are at their lowest ebb, and one's problems loom up with terrifying immensity so that one can be driven into a decision which one may regret all one's life.

(3) Never leave a quarrel unsettled. Never retreat into a resentful silence. Wait a few days and then write to the person concerned and arrange to talk things over together. Buried resentment can play havoc with physical health and mental serenity.

67

Here is a verse which is a great favourite of mine.

"In the castle of my soul there is a little postern gate
  Where, when I enter, I am in the presence of God.
  In a moment, in a turning of a thought,
  I am where God is.
  When I meet God there, all life gains a new meaning,
  Small things become great, and great things small.
  Lowly and despised things are shot through with glory.

My troubles seem but the pebbles on the road,
  My joys seem like the everlasting hills,
  All my fever is gone in the great peace of God,
  And I pass through the door from Time into Eternity."[1]

When we go into that peace, we get our perspective right. We discover there the things which are as big as the hills and the things which are as little as the pebbles.

* * *

Let us remember finally that we shall never feel so defeated, so depressed, so beaten, so cheated, as eleven men felt on Good Friday night. Why, Jesus had promised them the world! They were going to rule in a kingdom. Some of them were going to sit on His right and on His left. Life was going to be marvellous. They had become important. They were going to do big things. . . . And then He was arrested, tortured, crucified. We shall never feel as they felt then. No, not even crippling disease, financial failure, the broken-heartedness which comes from the deprivation of love, the desertion of friends, the death of dear ones, the injustice and disappointments of life—these cannot bring us so low as the Cross brought those eleven men. And then—a dawn, a voice, a testimony, a race, and a certainty, and they knew that even His death did not matter as much as they thought. Indeed, in a sense it mattered gloriously and became a new beginning instead of a dismal end.

Do you remember that night when you were only a little child

[1] Walter Rauschenbusch.

and somehow your doll got smashed, or your favourite teddy bear got burnt in the kitchen fire, or someone trod on your clockwork engine? I doubt if we can really recover now the anguish of spirit we felt then. And those adults who looked on said that we should get over it, or they would buy us another doll or another teddy or another train. But we did not believe we should ever get over it, and in the darkness of our despair we sobbed ourselves to sleep. And yet, now, we know it did not matter as much as we thought.

Men and women, I wonder if the day will come when we shall look back on disease and war, on disaster and misery, on pain and sorrow, on deprivation and frustration, and say, "Well, it was awful at the time, but it didn't matter as much as we thought." I think that moment will come. We shall adjust our perspective. I think we shall see those things—even death—as the little things, and the big things will be the hands of God that sustained you, the purposes of God that never let you go and that bring us all at last to the place where we understand and are utterly content; the place where in unbroken joy we "bless the Hand that guided" and adore "the Heart that planned".

May God help us to get our perspective right, to see the things that matter most; not just to want the things that peace of mind can bring, but the things which ultimately bring peace of mind. May God save us from ever hearing that Voice, in heartbroken rebuke, saying to us, "If thou hadst known in this day, even thou, the things which belong unto peace! but now they are hid from thine eyes."

The Harsh Words of Jesus

I was reading recently the *Autobiography of Charles Darwin*[1] and came across that sad passage in which he says that he was "very unwilling to give up" his belief in Christianity, but at last, he wrote, "disbelief crept over me at a very slow rate, but was at last complete." He adds this sentence, "I can hardly see how anyone ought to wish Christianity to be true; for, if so, the plain language of the text seems to show that the men who do not believe—and this would include my father, brother, and almost all my best friends—will be everlastingly punished. And this is a damnable doctrine."

Darwin continued to believe in God, but the harsh words of Jesus killed his belief in Christianity.

Some months ago I had an interesting conversation with an agnostic, and he put a most challenging situation which I summarise as follows:—"You Christians," he said "start with the assumption that Christ was divine and, therefore, perfect, and then try to fit everything in or explain it away. Now, I begin," he continued, "with the thought that He was like other men, though infinitely better than most. I then feel that He lost His temper, was sometimes intolerant and even childish."

I hate to hear anyone talk like that about the Master and I asked for illustrations. "Well," he said, "a man who chases people out of the Temple with a whip, and who overturns their tables, isn't turning the other cheek, is he? A man who says, 'If you don't believe in Me, you will go to hell,' (John 3[18]) is intolerant, and a man who curses a fig-tree for not bearing figs is childish, especially when we are specifically told that it was

[1] *The Autobiography of Charles Darwin*, Ed. by Nora Barlow, pp. 86-7 (Collins 1958).

not the season for figs anyway (Matt. 21¹⁸, Mark 11¹²). A man who says, 'No one comes to the Father except through Me,' (John 14⁶) is arrogant and exclusive. What about the Psalmists who called God 'Father', not to mention the Buddhists who surely find their way to God?''

Now we rather pride ourselves here at the City Temple on being honest-minded. Let us try to meet this challenge and face these issues, for not only men of the calibre of Charles Darwin, but many thoughtful people do find the Christian way not only hard to tread because of its moral demands, but hard to follow intellectually because of the difficulties involved in what I have called the "harsh words of Jesus".

*   *   *

1. Let us assume, for the sake of argument, that Jesus had no more of God about Him than anyone else; that He was on the whole a good man, but not sinless and not divine. Let us assume, for a moment, that He was no more than human, that He was self-centred and egotistic—as, for instance, when He said, "*I* am the Light of the World"—that He was intolerant and sometimes bad-tempered.

If you do this, you appear to answer some questions, but you raise others which are harder still to solve. Some problems are met, but bigger problems arise. For instance, He seems to have had no sense of sin. Now the agnostic agrees that He was a good man. But a good man has a keener sense of sin than a bad man. Sin blinds us to our own sinfulness. Goodness makes us sensitive to sin. Paul calls himself "the chief of sinners", and John Wesley used on his death-bed the same words of himself. But *Jesus* is alleged to have said, "Which of you convicteth Me of sin?" Jesus said, "When *YE* pray say, 'Forgive us our trespasses.'" "On every page of the Gospel," says Professor H. R. Mackintosh, "we encounter such imperial demands for obedience, as well as gracious promises of help and pardon, as it would have been an enormity for a sinful man to utter."[1]

For myself, as I study the records, I cannot feel that the

[1] *The Doctrine of the Person of Christ*, p. 36 (T. and T. Clark).

71

words "human" and "good" are big enough ships to carry the cargo of the evidence about Him. They are so loaded with the weight of meaning which the New Testament evidence piles into them, that they founder and sink. When someone says, "I am the Light of the world"; when someone says that the world is well lost if He be gained; when someone says that the final judgment of all men will have reference to Him, that His message is to be preached through the whole world, and that if He is lifted up He will draw all men unto Himself; when He accepts the worship of men and claims to be one with God; when He speaks of the glory He had with God before the world was; when He allows a sceptical disciple to call Him, "My Lord and my God," and does not rebuke him for blasphemy, then such a man is not good or bad, but *MAD*—or else a Divine Being, call Him, Son of God, or Avatar, or Incarnate God, or what you will.

If this is madness, it is more attractive than our sanity. If this madness spread, it would bring sanity to a mad world. If every man regarded his neighbour as Jesus regarded His, what problems would remain in this hectic, fear-haunted, selfish, materialistic scramble we call living?

*   *   *

2. Even so, more needs to be said. It would be absurd to try to explain away all that sounds like harsh language. Harsh words do not deny love. They are sometimes evidence of love. They frequently affirm concern. The measure of the violence may be the measure of the need to sound alarm. The measure of Christ's harshness to the Pharisees was the measure of the thickness of their protective armour of hypocrisy against the shafts of His truth, and the measure of His concern that they should learn that truth before it was too late. If, when children are playing at bedtime in a nursery, you see a little child in a flimsy nightdress walking backwards towards an unguarded electric or gas fire, you don't say, "Excuse me, I hate to interrupt your game, but there is a fire behind you." You shout, "Look out! Mind the fire!" It is love and concern which prompt the urgency and what may sound like rough speech.

How grateful I felt once, when I was riding with a friend in the desert, to a Bedouin Arab who rose up from the ground in the very path of our horses and shrieked out some cry of warning! I did not know then that there were sinking sands thirty yards ahead.

How unrealistic it would be to pretend that life has no hazards, no moral dangers, no lurking pitfalls; that you can sin and get away with it, that to all men at last a loving Santa-Claus-like Father in heaven will hand out a reward and say, "There, there, it's all right. You didn't mean any harm; nothing has been lost; all that awaits you is an eternal Christmas Party."

No! The gentlest lips in the world, lips that said the kindest, most loving things to sinners, said the most terrifying things about sin that the world has ever heard. In the most tender of all the parables—that of the Prodigal Son, in which the boy, after years of sin, is freely forgiven and his relationship with his father is completely restored—you read these words: "For this, my son, was *dead* and is alive again; he was *lost* and is found." "Dead!" "Lost!" So those are the words that describe what sin can do to us, unless in His mercy we are found and restored (Luke 15¹¹ff).

And we must accept *some* apparently harsh words as the measure of loving concern. If I am walking towards a cliff-edge and a man shouts violently, harshly, vehemently, I thank God he was violent enough to stop me. And we must realistically accept that life is built up on the foundation of goodness, and the penalty and consequence of self-chosen evil are terrible because goodness matters so much. We think that all talk of the results of evil points to a cruel God, but if a man who can see, walks in daylight over a cliff-edge, we don't say, "Wasn't life cruel to him?" We say, "Why didn't he look where he was going? Surely he had heard of the law of gravity." In the same way, surely we have heard of the law of morality, and some of the harsh words warn us with a terrible vehemence to look where we are going. Ask yourself, at the end of this road called today, or this week, or this year, whether tomorrow or

73

next week or next year—if you keep straight on the present path—will bring you peace of mind. Are you on the road that leads to what God desires for you?

* * *

3. When all this is understood, we can legitimately soften *some* harsh sayings by realising the language difficulties. Consider some of them:

(a) Words alter in meaning. Jesus spoke in Aramaic. The Gospels are in colloquial Greek. The Greek has been translated for us into English, some of it into 1611 English, since when many words have changed their meaning even in English. Imagine the gulf between the words we read now and the impact the original had on the minds of those who first heard them.

For instance, the words translated "thieves and robbers" did not have the same meaning as we give to them. Jesus did not mean Isaiah and John the Baptist when He said, "All that came before me were thieves and robbers." (John 10[8]). The reference must have been to those political revolutionaries who had led the nation astray. The man on the cross next to Jesus, whom we call the "dying thief", was a political revolutionary, not a brigand or a burglar.

(b) A second difficulty about our Lord's language must be noted. We are not meant to take words which He spoke to a certain individual in a certain circumstance, as if they applied to all individuals in all circumstances.

Because He saw that wealth was getting in the way of the rich young ruler's spiritual progress, he told him to sell all and give to the poor. He did not mean those words to be a universal rule applicable to all, for He Himself depended on the wealth of others. He stayed in the homes of rich men, used their accommodation and accepted their hospitality. He and His disciples depended on the gifts, probably, of rich women in Jerusalem who kept full the "bag" from which Judas pilfered.

Again, if every Christian took to himself the words that Jesus spoke to Peter, "Follow Me," and interpreted them to mean

74

leaving business, then the latter would be denuded of Christian influences, and, as Christianity extended, the work of the world would come to a standstill.

Again, if He did say that no one came to the Father save by Him, he was talking to Jews who had never heard of Buddha, and who would never find a way other than His own that led them to the Father. If He had been talking to a multi-racial community it is incredible to me that He would have excluded the devout seekers in other religions from finding their way to the Father of all. (See Acts 10^{35}.) [1]

(c) A third point should be remembered about the language ascribed to Jesus. The fourth Gospel was not written until 100 A.D. Jesus died in 29 A.D. What a time-lag! And though memories were more accurate before notebooks partially atrophied them, scholars tell us that the fourth Gospel is rather the meditation of a devout mind on what Jesus taught, than a verbal report of His exact words. Even the earliest Gospel, Mark, had a time-lag of perhaps twenty-five or thirty years, and we know how hard it is to recall the exact words of a person even one year afterwards. Indeed one week, or, in some cases, one day is enough for some people to get a conversation distorted.

(d) Again, no one denies that the Gospel writers were inspired. But inspiration does not preclude prejudice. It does not alter the colour of the glasses through which the writer is looking. It does not erase bias, or change viewpoint, or guarantee accuracy. Matthew may write of an angel at the empty tomb, and Mark may report a man. Luke speaks of two men and John of two angels. *But they all agree about the empty tomb.* Fancy never obscures *fundamental facts*, though the four variations present the fundamentalist who believes that every word of the Bible is verbally inspired, with an interesting question as to which Gospel he should accept as the true report, and as to what he thinks of the verbal inspiration of the others!

Matthew is keen on tracing all the happenings of Christ's life

---

[1] Of course the passage may mean that the eternal Christ is the interpreting and reconciling factor in non-Christian religions but this view does not seem to be relevant here.

to the fulfilment of prophecy. That is his bias or fad. He even thinks that Joseph and Mary, returning with the infant Christ from Egypt, are fulfilling an old prophecy of Hosea about the Israelites escaping from the Pharaoh. (Matthew 2[15]). "Out of Egypt have I called my son." This is nonsense to us.

Matthew speaks of a woman who had tried many doctors and spent much money, "but was nothing bettered, but rather grew worse." Luke was a doctor and he tells the same story, but he leaves out this slur on the profession!

(e) Nor have we made any allowance for our Lord's tone of voice, nor the smiling of His eyes. It sounds as though He talks harshly to a woman in Syria, who came and asked Him to cure her little girl. According to the Revised Version, He said to the mother: "It is not meet to take the children's bread and cast it to the dogs." (Matthew 15[26]). Three things are obscured from us by our English version. One is that He did not say "dogs" at all. He said "puppies." A second is that He was quoting, *for all we know with a twinkle in His eye*, a proverb which ran, "Children first, then puppies." A third is that "puppies", so far from being unkind, was a term of endearment in Syria, very like our English "kiddies", a word we use without even thinking of its literal meaning of little goats.[1]

* * *

4. What then are we to do? "Life is Commitment," says Dr. J. H. Oldham in a splendid book with that title. We must decide whether to accept the view of the agnostic whose words I quoted at the beginning, and think of Christ as only a man, and moreover a man with many faults, or whether He was and is a Divine Being whom we may worship and strive to follow, and with whom we may still have fellowship.

[1] It was, of course, impossible to deal in one sermon with all the difficult sayings of Jesus. I have dealt with a number, including the fig-tree story and the problem of Hell, in my book *When the Lamp Flickers*. In regard to the money changers in the Temple I feel we have done more harm with that whip than He did! I have heard the incident used to defend modern war! He may have used the whips only on the beasts and they, in their wild rush, may have upset the tables. Besides, is not bad temper one thing and righteous indignation another?

If He is the former, of course the Christian religion falls to the ground. If He is the latter, then it is agreed that there are still problems which we cannot solve and passages of Scripture which, as yet, we cannot understand. They have to be held *sub judice*, awaiting fuller light. From a general reading of all four Gospels I make my overall picture and await further light on those sentences which do not yet fall into a harmonious relationship with the whole. It is sounder to judge the Bible by Jesus than to judge Jesus by the Bible.

But when I think of what He has meant to the world, of the difference He has made where—in every country in the world—He has been taken seriously; when I think of some of the people whose lives He has changed, even some known to me, and when I try to imagine what my own life would be without Him, unworthy though I am to call myself a Christian, I am content to await further light on many things that He said and did. For that of which I am *sure* in my heart, compels my worship, claims my service and holds my heart in willing bondage.

I invite you to come with me in a quest. Let us by all means try to understand more. Let us try to see further. But let us in the meantime commit our lives to Him and try to follow Him. It seems unlikely to me that His Church, stretching, as it does, across the world, containing, as it does, its scholars and its saints, is wholly mistaken about Him and has been so for two thousand years; that what Schweitzer called "the mighty spiritual force which streams from Him and flows through our time also"[1] had its origin in the minds of a dozen Galileans of the first century who were completely deceived about Him. It seems to me very unlikely that His way is one of self-deception and leads at last only to final disappointment, darkness and despair.

Well, whatever our present thoughts and doubts, let's *do* something! Let us commit ourselves to His way of life and see what happens. After all, Peter, the fisherman, did not understand very much. He probably saw all the events that my agnostic friend holds against Jesus. He heard the harsh sayings.

[1] Albert Schweitzer, *The Quest of the Historical Jesus*, p. 397.

One of them was directed to him. But from a swearing fisherman, he became a saint.

Thousands, nay millions, have followed the Way of Jesus and found their lives changed. They have found Peace of Mind, and Joy, and Meaning in life. Maybe He is the clue for which you are seeking. Maybe He is the Way, after all.

The Nature of Christ's Temptations

IF you have been worshipping with us over Easter you will remember that we thought of Palm Sunday and of the Passion, Death and Resurrection of Christ from the point of view of the outsider, the man who is not uninterested in religion, but who fails to see its relevance to his own life. So in the last four services we have held we voiced the question of such a man and imagined him saying, "What is this to do with me?" If a Man *does* ride on a donkey into Jerusalem; if a Man *is* put to a terrible death by Jewish hatred and Roman tyranny; if it *is* true that a Man did rise from the dead on Easter Day, says the man-in-the-street, "What is that to do with me?"

This morning I should like us to think together about our Lord's temptations from the same point of view. What are they to do with us?

*   *   *

In the lesson we had read to us the vivid narrative in St. Matthew's Gospel which recounts our Lord's temptations, and one thing may have dawned on you already, that inasmuch as Christ was humanly alone, the account of His temptations must have come from Himself. We are told that He was with the wild beasts. We are told that the Devil tempted Him. We are told that angels ministered to Him. But, humanly speaking, He was alone, and I think He must have told the story in this pictorial and symbolic way because He wanted His men to realise that He was tempted too. Not one of us can say, "Oh it was all very well for Him. He did not have to put up with the things I have to put up with. He could not have been tempted as I am. He does not understand people like me." If ever we have felt like that, I think this story puts the matter right

79

and brings Him, as it were, within our reach. And if, as we believe, God dwelt in Him more fully than in any human being before or since, so that we may call Him indeed the Son of God and an incarnation of God, then the story of Christ's temptations leaves God not as an outsider, but as One Who, *from within*, understands what human temptation is like.

* * *

I am sure you would pick up also the significance of the second lesson that was read to us, where the author of the Epistle to the Hebrews tells us that Jesus was "tempted in all points like as we are".

It seems important to realise that that sentence does not mean that He had to face the same temptations that we face. Surely it is true to say that the higher you go in the scale of spiritual progress, there must be some temptations that fall away from you and which lose their power to attract you, but there will be new ones, far more subtle, far more fierce, and demanding more and more insight and more and more courage.

Let us look at this matter a little more fully. It would not seem to me true to suppose that the passage from "Hebrews" means that Jesus had the same temptations that some of us have. Even we have made *some* spiritual progress, and I can assure you, for example that if you invite me to tea I shall not even be tempted to steal the teaspoons! I do not feel tempted to run away with somebody else's wife—at least not at the moment! Seriously, some of the grosser sins have not the faintest attraction for most of us. We should not cosh an old lady on the head, break into a bank, forge a cheque or rape a child, and to me it would be incredible to suppose that Jesus was tempted to immorality, or to theft, or to drunkeness.

What does seem important to realise is that He was tempted *at all points*—at the point of His power, at the point of His weakness, at the point of His relationships and at the point of His longings. I surmise that where we should not have enough sensitive spiritual insight even to imagine temptation was present, He saw it in all its subtlety and fierceness, and at the point where we say "Yes" to evil, He said "No". It can be very, very difficult to say "No" if part of the temptation is to fail to see that there is a situation which demands a "No".

*   *   *

One of the ways, I think, in which we can understand the temptations of another is by asking ourselves the question as to where his deepest longing really lies. Help me to estimate a man's dominating desire and you will help me to estimate the fierceness of his temptations. Probably we all know someone who desired above all things to be wealthy and to have the kind of spurious security which it is supposed wealth can purchase. The temptation of such a man will be to become unscrupulous, if by shutting his eyes to moral niceties he can make more money, or if by doing a thing which cannot be found out, he can increase his financial reserves. His temptation is the reflection of his desire. Probably we have all watched a girl who very much wanted the kind of security which marriage to a wealthy person would provide, and her temptation will probably be to deceive herself about her own motives and blind herself to the size of the obstacles between herself and happiness. What is called "a good match" will overcome all her scruples.

The man in the first illustration will probably spend his old age regretting the things he did to achieve his ambition, because in old age what one hoped would be the dead past has a horrible way of becoming the living present, and remorse can make old age much more miserable than poverty *and a clear conscience* would have made it. Frankly, such a man's worst enemies would never inflict on him the pain which comes from the terrifying fact that memory never dies, and even when we slough off this physical body, it is probable that the past will be as present as the present is now.

Bishop Charles W. Stubbs wrote these rather grim lines:

> "The ghosts of forgotten actions
>   Came floating before my sight,
> And the sins that I thought were dead sins
>   Were alive with a terrible might.

And I know of the future judgment,
How dreadful so'er it be,
That to sit alone with my conscience
Would be judgment enough for me."

And as for the poor girl who wanted the security of a wealthy marriage and whose dominating desire was a good time, with plenty of clothes and cars, cocktail parties and continental holidays, one knows that her old age will be spent in bitter and futile regrets realising that no one ever succeeds in buying happiness, and that she might have had real love even though comparative poverty had been coupled with it. It is an old platitude that money does not make one happy, and I think it is a poor compensation to console oneself with the reflection that with money one can be miserable in comfort!

Surely all our dominating demands are to be subjected to the dominating demands of God. We often say, "He has made us for Himself and our hearts cannot find rest apart from Him," but many of us travel a long way before we realise that the platitude is true. It is true because God made life in that way. A motor car is made for the roads. That is why it has got wheels. If you drive it into a swamp, it stops and will not take you any further. Man was made with apparatus within him so constructed that life will only "work out" one way, and that is His way. If man's personality is driven another way, it stops, and blessed is he who, before the evening of his life falls upon him, realises in very truth that only in God's will is his peace.

*   *   *

Now if we seek to understand the temptations of Jesus, we must ask what His dominating desire was, and I think the answer in a sentence is that He wanted to get His message across to men for that is what He had come to do; that, for Him, was the will of God. When I read the Gospels it always sounds to me as though Jesus was chafing to be set free from the tasks of the carpenter's shop. Probably His father died when He was little more than a boy, so that caring for Mary and the other children—probably four brothers and two sisters—devolved upon Him. I imagine that at the first possible moment He must have handed over the carpenter's business to James, His eldest brother, and in spite of the criticisms and lashings of James's tongue (see the Epistle of James 3⁶), He began to declare the great message which He had come into the world to bring. There was not a moment to lose, and quickly He knew Himself to be the anointed of God. Quickly His personality flowered into something that we cannot call anything but divinity. Quickly He knew that there was power in His fingers not given to other men and wings to His words which would carry them through the world.

First of all, however, though the time was pressing, he must have a month to think things through, to plan His programme, to determine the way in which God would have Him act. So He goes out into that gaunt, bare and terrifying desert and there He fasts.

Imagine Him, therefore, in that stony, barren place, blazing hot in the daytime, unpleasantly cold at night. The wild beasts are around Him, and at His feet are the flat stones of the desert, irresistibly reminiscent of the cakes of unleavened bread His mother made at home. His hunger was poignant: His mind plays with the idea of testing His powers on the stones at His feet. But I am sure that is not the sharp point of the temptation. All around Him His people were starving. How can He ask a peasant people to listen to a new message of God when their stomachs are empty? He had a great concern about men's hunger. However we interpret the feeding of the five thousand it means that, and those who tell us we ought not to pray for material things must think again, since in the centre of the perfect prayer, we find the petition, "Give us daily our bread for the coming day."

The fierce centre of the temptation flashed upon Him in a moment. Why not lead a social revolution? Why not become first a social reformer? Why not give them bread? His sympathetic insight sees, in imagination, multitudes of men, their gaunt ribs nearly bursting through their chests, their womenfolk clutching starving babies to their flat breasts. How can He talk to them about spiritual things when they are beset with hunger?

Then the power of God breaks through and He sees the suggestion to be one from the Devil. The words break from Him involuntarily: "Man doth not live by bread alone." In other words, you must not try to buy men's allegiance, not even with bread. It is a word that has strengthened those who on the mission field have felt the same temptation, and if they have fallen to it have been taunted with the phrase, "Rice Christians." Jesus put the temptation behind Him. That was not God's way.

*   *   *

The second temptation was very similar because there was a legend that when the great Redeemer and Messiah came, He would float down from the heavens and land upon a pinnacle of the Temple and from that eminent height would call the faithful to Him. Supposing from the pinnacle of the Temple He throws Himself down and relies on His Father's power, would that not be a way of winning the ear of the multitude? Men love magic more than they love most things. To the conjurer they will always listen. Men are fascinated by the one who works that kind of marvel. Besides was it not written, "He shall give His angels charge concerning Thee, and in their hands they shall bear Thee up, lest at any time Thou dash Thy foot against a stone"?

What a terrible temptation? One catches one's breath to realise that *He might have thrown His divinity away*. If once He had betrayed the power God had lent to Him, He could no longer have claimed to be the perfect servant of God, or the perfect instrument of His will, or the Son completely obedient to the Father. In a sentence, Jesus realised that as He must not buy men's support with bread, He must not compel their allegience with magic.

I pause to point out how slow we all are to repudiate magic ourselves. Miracles still happen and we have often discussed them in the City Temple. But magic never happens. Magic is a break with law. God never does that. Miracles are different. They illustrate the extent of law and its ramifications into the physical, psychical, psychological and spiritual parts of the universe. But still men crave for magic. Much of the appeal of certain spiritual healers lies in man's lust for magic, his longing to take a short cut and get what he wants by unworthy ways without the labour of research and effort.

If only people could understand that, they would realise that to learn *how* God works makes an ounce of discovery worth a ton of futile prayer. Our question must not be, "*Can* God do this and that?" For that is a question no one can answer. But we are encouraged to ask the question, "*Does* God do this and that?"

I have seen cholera in an Indian village. In that village were some Christians who drew apart into the church to pray. But other Christians moved the patients so as to prevent the discharges from their bodies during washing operations getting into the village tank from which the whole community took its drinking water. Some were praying for God to intervene by magic. Others were praying that God would show them how to work His will.

When we read the sentence, "Thou shalt not tempt the Lord thy God," I know it may be translated, "Thou shalt not put the Lord thy God to the test," but surely that translation helps us little, for what else is faith but putting God to the test? I am convinced that the sentence means, "Thou shalt not try *to force the hand* of the Lord thy God and make Him work in the way you think He ought to work." If Christ *had* cast Himself down, He would have been destroyed, for God's hand must not be forced like that.

*　　*　　*

From one of the hillocks in the desert where Jesus was tempted, you can see, on a clear day, the blue waters of the Mediterranean, and round the shores of the Mediterranean was the whole of the known world. A terrible experience comes down to us in these picturesque words. "The Devil taketh Him up into an exceeding high mountain and showeth Him all the kingdoms of the world and their glory; and the Devil saith unto Him, 'All these things will I give Thee, if Thou wilt fall down and worship me.'"

Jesus was a patriot. All Jews were, and the Jew believed that he should dominate the world; indeed, that that was God's purpose for him. Jesus knew that if He raised a sword, ten thousand others would flash from their scabbards at a word from Him. That was just the kind of Messiah they wanted: someone who would rouse the youth of the nation and drive Rome into the sea. It must have been most tempting, especially when a Jewish-dominated world was thought to be God's will, and when the Messiah knew that He had unusual powers. The temptation was fought back. "Get thee behind Me, Satan!" This way too cannot be God's way.

We are not surprised to learn that the Devil left Him and that then the angels came, and whether we think of the Devil as a personality of terrifying evil potency, or whether we think of the Devil as a symbolic word for the human tendency to succumb to the lower trends of our nature, does not matter at all. Jesus said "No" to evil, and anyone who has done that knows that even on his lesser level of achievement, there is a wonderful sense of calm and peace. I see no reason to deny the reality of angels. Most of us have had some experience of their comforting ministry, especially when on our lower levels we have said "No" to evil.

We notice at once that all three temptations have something in common. They are temptations to take a short cut so as to satisfy a dominating desire. A social revolution, or a display of magic, or an armed revolt against Rome—any or all of them would have caught the ear of the people. All of them Christ resolutely set aside.

* * *

How relevant it all is to our own day! Do you notice that Khrushchev has succumbed to the temptations which Christ resisted? Is not Khrushchev working to bring all the kingdoms of this world and their glory under the domination of Russian power? Is he not eager to get the ear of mankind and bend all humanity to his will? The very thing that Jesus regarded as of the Devil, Khrushchev has enthroned.

The temptations of Jesus happened two thousand years ago, but this very morning on the wireless a voice reported the Chairman of the Foreign Relations Committee of the United State of America saying, "Now we have got enough nuclear power to smash Russia." You see the same dominating desire, the same quest for power over other people, the same short-cut to achieve good as we understand or misunderstand it.

Nor can we pretend that these temptations are far from us. I hope that we shall not watch with callous indifference or bored unconcern what is going on in South Africa. Let me read you four paragraphs not written by some hysteric revolutionary. The law is said to be unemotional and dispassionate. What I am going to read to you is the plain law about apartheid in South Africa.

(1) It is unlawful for an African worker to take part in a strike. If he does so he is liable, on conviction, to a fine not exceeding five hundred pounds, imprisonment for a period not exceeding three years, or both such fine and imprisonment.

(2) If there is only one waiting-room on a railway station, it is lawful for the station master to reserve that waiting-room for the exclusive use of White persons, and any non-White person wilfully entering it commits a criminal offence and is liable to a fine not exceeding fifty pounds or to imprisonment for a period not exceeding three months or to both such fine and such imprisonment.

(3) The Minister of Native Affairs may, provided that the urban local authority concurs, by notice in the Gazette, prohibit the attendance of Africans at a Church service in a town, if it is, in his opinion, undesirable that Africans should be present in the numbers in which they ordinarily attend that service.

(4) If an Indian (or a coloured or an African) sits on a bench in a public park, the bench being set apart for the exclusive use of White persons (by way of protest against the apartheid

87

laws), he commits a criminal offence and is liable to a fine not exceeding three hundred pounds, or to imprisonment for a period not exceeding three years, or to a whipping not exceeding ten strokes, or to both such fine and such imprisonment, or to both such fine and such whipping, or to both such imprisonment and such whipping.[1]

No one supposes that the temptations of Jesus recorded in our first lesson were the only temptations He had to face. He once praised those who had "continued with Him in His temptations."[2] They must have been constant and often so subtle that we in such a situation should not have recognised their existence. But do let us note that those He faced are still with us. In one place we hear the words, "Let's smash Russia before she smashes us." In another place we hear the words, "Let's dominate the Blacks even though Africa is their own country. The White man must be the master." In another place we hear a voice saying, "Let's shut the school rather than let Black children mix with White." And so the dreary voices go round the world.

*   *   *

I am to be asked shortly on a radio programme to answer the question, "What have you learned from life?" Well, I have learned a lot of things from life, but from my own failures, from the confidences of innumerable men and women, from the rough and tumble of forty-five years in the Christian ministry, and from my observations as a student of personal, national and international affairs, I will tell you the outstanding thing I have learned. It is this: Life will only work out one way, and that is God's way. He made it like that. Every other way has across it a barricade bearing a notice which says, "No thoroughfare this way." If you surmount the barrier, there is a precipice.

[1] Quoted from *This is Apartheid* (Gollancz 1959), by Leslie Rubin, who represents the Africans of the Cape Province in the Senate. Foreword by Alan Paton, author of *Cry the Beloved Country*.

[2] Luke 22[28]

Men will not learn the truth of half a dozen words:

"OUTSIDE GOD THERE IS ONLY DEATH."

*   *   *

After all, Jesus *did* say, "I am the Way." Perhaps He meant it. Perhaps He was right after all.

Thy Word is Truth

(A Sermon for Bible Sunday)
John 17[17]: "Thy word is truth."

TODAY is Bible Sunday. The whole Church of Christ cele-
brates the Second Sunday in Advent as one on which
special attention is given to the Bible.

Let us begin by being completely honest. We know that the
Bible is widely circulated and translated into almost every
language. We are told that it is a best seller and no one can
over-estimate the value of the truth it contains. But very few
people regularly read the Bible, and many who do, read it
perfunctorily without much benefit or enlightenment.

Let us be honest enough to say that this is not surprising.
Many of us in youth had to "mug it up" as a subject for
examinations, and so it is associated in our mind with tiresome
tasks. We can never quite recall all the Kings of Israel, and
we wish St. Paul had not been quite so enthusiastic and visited
quite so many cities in his missionary labours! Further, the
Bible is frequently printed in an unattractive book set out quite
differently from our more interesting reading. The Bible is
very dull in very many places, and it is often incomprehensible.
Where it can be understood, it is often completely irrelevant
to the kind of life we have to live today.

Further, I think the layman must get particularly exasper-
ated. He reads his Bible and thinks he has got hold of some
rich fragment of truth, and then some preacher, well versed in
research and higher criticism and the original languages, stands
up in the pulpit to tell him that the verse he had thought means
this, means that, or that a sentence which had become precious
to him is really no part of the original document, or that we

have no right to believe that even Jesus actually said words attributed to Him.

I remember how shattered a friend of mine was when I told him that his favourite text meant exactly the opposite of what he supposed! The text was, "I will lift up mine eyes unto the hills, from whence cometh my help." He thought that was a grand sentence to hold in the mind, and indeed it helped him to justify to his conscience spending a Sunday on holiday in the Lake District; taking his car to the foot of one of the great mountains and then climbing it and thoroughly enjoying the mountain air and the vigorous exercise! Was he not following the Biblical injunction and lifting his eyes to the hills? This is not the place to diverge on to a discussion of how we should keep Sunday. We have considered that before.[1] But the text to which I have referred is really a question, and behind the question lies the fact that the temples of the heathen god, Baal, were built on the tops of hills. The Psalmist is really saying, "Shall I lift up mine eyes unto the hills? Is it from thence my help will come?" And he answers it with a resounding negative, asserting that his help cometh from the Lord who made not only the hills, but the heavens and the earth. My friend finished his reading at Psalm 121. Psalm 122 begins, "I was glad when they said unto me, Let us go into the house of the Lord," and I am afraid I can offer him no alternative reading which would get him out of the obligation of going to church on Sunday!

So, with one thing and another, I think we should begin our meditation about the Bible by realising that the Bible is very little read, and if a book is as difficult as the Bible, one must not be obstinate and pompous, but admit readily that there are very good reasons why it should not be read in its present form.

Yet, of course, we must go on at once to realise that the truth by which men live is to be found in the Bible. Even the Old Testament was the Bible of Jesus. It was loved and treasured by Him and studied continually.

During the week that has gone I asked a dear friend of mine

[1] See *When the Lamp Flickers*, p. 125 ff. (Hodder and Stoughton)

who reads the Bible regularly and faithfully, "Why do you read it every morning?" Her answer, I think, was perfect. "To find out more about God and to get help for my everyday life." That is a great answer and that is the answer I want to offer you this morning. That is really what the Bible is essentially about. From it we may find out more about God and get help for our daily lives.

The second lesson this morning contained the text (John 17[17]). The first lesson contained that glorious opening verse, "As the hart panteth after (or literally, "over") the waterbrooks, so panteth my soul after Thee, O God."[1] The word for "waterbrooks" should be translated "aqueducts." It is a reference to those covered channels by which the Hebrew people brought the spring water from a hillside down into a town or village. The aqueduct was covered so that animals would not foul the water. The stag does not pant after or over the waterbrooks if it can get at the water and drink it, but the whole text lights up with meaning for me when I realise that the animal could hear the water and even smell it, as it were, through the air-vents in the casing. The animal knew the water was there, but he could not get it. So man's soul longs after God. Man knows that the Bible contains the truth he needs. Man is certain that religion would not have gone on so long, and nobody would buy the Bible at all, or bother to translate it, unless it contained the truth by which his soul is fed. Yet, in spite of this feeling, it is so hard to get hold of it. We feel like hungry men who arrive in a village full of grocers' and confectioners' shops. In the windows we see the food, but we find it is early-closing day, and we cannot get at it. Can we this morning help one another to *receive* those life-giving truths and drink of those streams that flow through the Bible from the heart and mind of God?

*　　*　　*

Two things I think we should remember as guiding principles. First of all, the Bible records a *progressive* revelation of

[1] Psalm 42[1]

God. Frankly, it opens with very crude thoughts about God. It closes with the God and Father of our Lord Jesus Christ. In earlier parts of the Bible, God is simply a local storm-God who lives at the top of Mount Sinai. At the end of this precious volume, He is the everywhere available One who loves all and longs to be in a close personal relationship with all men. In the earlier books of the Bible there are bloody massacres supported from God's word. Listen to this! "Joshua never withdrew the hand that held his javelin until he had massacred all the people of Ai, both men and women, even as the Lord God had commanded him." You could justify Russia going into Hungary on that basis, though, of course, the Russians never stopped to ask if they had a divine sanction. You think of Lot's lingering lady turned into salt, or of Agag, a helpless old man, hacked in pieces by Samuel. You read of Jepthah vowing that if the Lord would deliver the children of Ammon into his hands, he would sacrifice the first living thing that came to meet him on his return. He came back victorious and his only daughter came to meet him. Yet he carried out his vow and she was loyal to it also, both of them believing that God was the kind of person who would be pleased by that senseless sacrifice.

Men and women, do not hesitate to give up much that is in the Bible. The Bible *contains* the word of God. It *contains* the truth about God. But, as we have said so often, nothing is true about God—even if it is written in this holy book—nothing is the real word of God unless it is in harmony with the spirit of Jesus. He is the Word of God; the Word who became flesh and dwelt among us. You may, if you like, take your blue pencil and cross out huge chunks of Leviticus, crude stories of bloody massacres, and many sentences in Psalms that breathe the spirit of revenge and hate. Indeed, even in the New Testament you may put a bracket round some of Paul's worries about circumcision and some of St. John's imagery in the Revelation.

Indeed, I would go further. Let us pay every respect to those who wrote what they sincerely felt to be true, but the truth has been granted to us in greater measure and so has the power to

93

perceive the truth, and the first commandment is that we should love the Lord our God with all our mind. The important question is not, "Is every word in the Bible true?" but rather, "What sublime truths can I glean from the Bible which the witness of the Spirit in my own heart claims as truth relevant to my life and sustaining to my soul?" The rest can be rejected, or, at least, held *sub judice* awaiting further light, remembering that "the Lord hath yet more light and truth to break forth from His word."

The second guiding principle is that we must recognise a growing ethical standard, and some of the illustrations already given illustrate that fact. The invasion of another country, as the Hebrew people invaded Palestine, without any provocation or any reason, except that they wanted it for themselves, so far from being regarded as wrong, was regarded as the purpose of God. The success of the invasion was held as a sign of His goodwill, but in truth the Israelites had no better reason for invading and putting to the sword the Hittites, the Ammonites, the Perizzites, and the other inhabitants of Palestine, than Russia had reason for invading Hungary and putting her people to the sword. The only excuse we can make is that ethical standards were so much lower in those far-off days that the measure of guilt was proportionately less, and the Israelites at any rate *thought* they were pleasing God.

*   *   *

So now comes the question: With the Bible in my hands how can I extract from it the truth my soul needs? How can the hart drink at the waterbrook instead of just longing for the water? How can I get help for my everyday life by reading my Bible?

Many people, of course, already know it well enough to love certain great and sublime passages in it. There are others who say that every part of the Bible is equally inspired. What utter nonsense! The book of Esther does not mention the name of God once, and Leviticus is largely a list of rules for the priests carrying out the Temple sacrifices. Sir James Barrie would have had an answer to this question all ready. He said that his mother's Bible, held in the hand opened of itself at the fourteenth chapter of St. John. How ridiculous it is to take refuge in the theory of verbal inspiration, namely that every word in this great library, written over a period of one thousand years by hundreds of people differently inspired, is equal at every point of its inspiration! Some passages in the Bible, in the light we have now, are quite untrue, others are very misleading, others have been mistranslated, while some passages are sublime and one feels that their value will never deteriorate.

In these days we have many scholars to help us. If you decide to read the Bible regularly, you may care to join the Bible Reading Fellowship, or the International Bible Reading Association. Both will offer you short passages for daily reading with simple comments.

In case you do not know it, I would like to introduce you to the work of the Rev. Dr. William Barclay. He has written a number of commentaries on the books of the New Testament. They are divided into passages suitable for daily reading, and I would put his work an easy first over all such books on the Bible. Further, you can get them very cheaply.

But I would like to use an illustration of a personal kind which may be of some help to those who tend to put the Bible away from them, saying, "Well, it may contain the truth, but it is so difficult that I cannot receive it." My illustration is taken from the way in which I myself slowly came to love music. I am not a very musical person, though there are some classical compositions which mean a great deal to me. Yet much classical music I have not yet learnt to appreciate, and some modern music I just do not understand at all. Strange though it may sound, my two boys have helped me most. They were both educated at Kingswood School where Saturday night attendance at a concert was compulsory. I have a great regard for the headmaster whom I regard as one of the great headmasters of our time.[1] He would arrange for very distinguished artists to sing and play to the boys. At first I remember that

[1] Mr. A. B. Sackett, M.A., now retired.

my elder son resented having to be present, but when he left school, he had a real love for great music, and when he lived at home for a time, he would buy gramophone records and play them to us. Sometimes I would say, "For goodness sake, turn that off," but he would often persuade me to sit down and relax and listen. Gradually the music began to speak to me and I began to enter into that world which to musical people is so wonderful.

Is not this parallel with our approach to the Bible? Almost everybody loves some tunes and almost everybody loves some passages in the Bible, but just as great music eludes a lot of us in its significance and beauty, some of the great passages of the Bible seem so difficult that we turn away from them. But if we will attend to modern translators, it is rather like having someone sit down and help us to appreciate Beethoven. Gradually a new world of truth and beauty is entered and the starved soul is fed.

I want to take the analogy a little further. It is no good pretending that a sonata is beautiful because somebody else tells you it is by Beethoven. Either you appreciate it and love it, or you do not. You must be sincere. If you do not love it, you are probably missing something great because it is admitted that Beethoven is a great composer. Yet even these admissions cannot compel the admiration of the sincere listener. He would be wise, however, to listen and to go on listening and to have whatever exposition his musical friends can give him, until Beethoven's world opens to him.

It is the same with great art, painting or sculpture. There is a great deal of insincerity about and people will rave over pictures they do not understand. But let us have sincerity above all things. I either like a picture or I do not like it. If I do not like it, it is no good my being told it is by a great artist, though this information might well make me sit longer in front of it and let it speak to me. I remember once sitting for an hour in front of one of Epstein's sculptures until it gradually dawned of me what the sculptor was trying to say. Then I was deeply impressed by his artistry.

So it is with the truth in the Bible. It is no good having a superstitious and insincere regard for words because they are "in the Bible". Either they speak to you or they do not. Remember that truth has no value for personal living until you see it to be true; until, as we say, "the penny drops." But since these words in the Bible have been written for our guidance, and since so many great souls have been satisfied by the Bible, it is good for us to read and ponder and "sit down before truth like a little child," in order that the great world of truth about God and ourselves, with which the Bible is concerned, may open to us. Like beauty, truth will gradually authenticate itself *and that is its authority.* Men crave for what they call an infallible Book, just as some crave for an infallible Pope, or an infallible Church, or an infallible conscience, but these are lazy ways of evading the discipline of sitting down before truth until it authenticates itself in the mind. It is an attempt to escape from the discipline of having to think. The only real authority is perceived truth. Until it is perceived to be true, it has no authority for us. For this reason when Jesus taught He did not thrust on men a heavy exterior "authority" as though to say, "Believe this because I say so." He took infinite pains with parable and simile, so that truth would authenticate itself in simple minds. Men *saw* that what He said was true.

There is really no such thing as an external authority where spiritual truth is concerned, if you mean by authority the power to convince. The power to convince is that of man's inner perception guided ever towards the truth by the Holy Spirit, remembering that he who refuses to move cannot be guided anywhere—a fact which fundamentalists overlook.

*   *   *

I hope all this does not put you off attempting to read the Bible, for remember that there is no experience through which the human heart can pass—at least, I ought to say I cannot think of one—but you will find that somebody whose story is recorded in the Bible has gone through that experience and

G   97

gone through it victoriously because of the power and help, the comfort and sympathy of God. If you are lonely, if you are depressed, if you are worried by private cares or by the state of the world, if you are ill, if you are bereaved, if you have been let down by your friends, or if you carry a dread burden of guilt about the past, if you are unhappy, or if you are glad and young and full of the joys of life, you will find every experience enriched in its significance by the record of men who in these pages found the relevance of God to human need. Indeed, you will find one of the most wonderful things that can be found, namely, the way in which every experience which befalls us— whether God intended it or merely allowed it, whether it is born of His good, or man's evil—contains an inner significance. It is trying to flash a message from Him. Remember that to signal His messages to us, God uses lamps which He did not light. He can use even what evil does to us. The word of Jesus make one feel that nothing can befall us which does not contain a message which God wants us to heed.

I do not suggest that you start with Genesis in a great burst of enthusiasm. If you do, you will flag a bit in Exodus and die in Leviticus! I do not suggest that you start reading backwards, for Revelation talks about beasts with numerous eyes and horns and the imagery is often meaningless. St. John in one place says he saw a woman sitting on a scarlet-coloured beast, "having seven heads and ten horns,"[1] but I don't think she has any message for us in London this morning! The author is writing in code and we have lost the clue. I would suggest that you begin with one of the Gospels. Mark or Luke would have my preference. Read them with the helps that are now becoming available. I have mentioned earlier the help you can get in your reading.

*　　*　　*

The private interview is one of the most important parts of the work of a minister. Let me in closing show you just one picture. I think of a woman sitting in my room crying her

[1] Revelation 17³

heart out, her shoulders shaking with her sobs because two things had happened. She had committed a great sin and she had developed a terrible disease. She thought the second was due to the first. In my opinion, it could not have been so. It is often quite inaccurate, and it is so frequently unfair and unjust to argue back from an illness to some personal fault. As she argued that God was punishing her, I remembered the poor woman whose story is told in Luke 13$^{10-17}$, who thought as she did until Jesus said that her illness was the work of Satan. How could I help her? Was I to send her to the doctor for sedatives? I certainly do not despise that treatment. Was I to send her to the psychiatrist that she might understand her grief and get it in proportion? I greatly approve of that treatment. But in the end she only needed Luke 15. Look up the chapter when you get home. It is the story of a shepherd's search for his sheep, a woman's for her coin, a father longing for his son. Very quietly that afternoon God spoke to this woman. She found the release of forgiveness and the joy of reconciliation with God.

I can sum up the situation by saying that she had climbed the wrong mountain. You see, *her* God was the Old Testament God, a terrifying, vindictive, avenging, punishing, Monster who lived on the top of Mount Sinai and thought nothing of turning a terrified woman, like Lot's wife, into a pillar of salt, or visiting one of his devoted servants, like Job, with leprosy. *My* God is revealed on the top of another mountain called Calvary. The woman had forgotten that the Bible is a *progressive* revelation. God is not a vindictive Despot who hands out cancer to a woman because she has committed a sin. At the end of the afternoon we were both at the foot of the Cross and she found the real God, infinitely forgiving, utterly loving, endlessly longing for the response of a woman who had always been His dear child and who had never realised it. She was the victim of a heresy only too common. She had thought that His love depended on her goodness, but of course it does not, any more than her own love for her child depends on the child's goodness.

So go and read your Bible, but do not climb the wrong mountain, will you? There is nothing on the top of Sinai but storm and thunder and fog and commandments that all begin with "Thou shalt not". Christians do not worship in this mountain. Another mountain peak is the one to which they take their sorrows and from which they hear the new commandment. And on this mountain everybody who comes is received, everybody who longs to put things right is forgiven, and everybody is loved, whether he is good or bad, or, like most of us, both. You will find all you need at the top of Mount Calvary—infinite love giving itself in uttermost sacrifice to redeem us all. In a sense, the whole Bible was written to bring us there.

Prayer and Peril

(An Armistice Day Sermon)

O<small>UR</small> thoughts today are full of memories connected with war. Some of us can remember vividly the details of two world wars. For myself, I can even remember the Boer War and how my beloved Scottish father, when peace was declared, to the great annoyance of my mother, put out a flag from the bedroom window: annoyance, I should explain, because the flag kept the window permanently open to admit whatever dust was blowing down the street.

War always calls out a spate of prayer. In 1914 the churches were packed with people beseeching God not to let war happen. A Mission of Repentance and Hope, carried out by our Anglican friends, made hundreds of people pray.

We all remember the work of the beloved Dick Sheppard and his Peace Pledge Union. We remember the innumerable meetings held by our old friends Dr. Sidney Berry and the Rev. W. H. Elliott. They claimed that a million people were praying daily for peace. But prayer was not answered. On both occasions war broke out.

Not only on such a wide canvas must we paint the gloomy disappointments of men and women. In individual lives it was the same. "God let me down," said a young fellow to a friend of mine. "My brother was wounded in the war. I prayed to God that my brother might live. *Any decent person would have answered.* He didn't. My brother died. I don't believe in God any more."

I feel quite certain that there will never be again the horror of large scale war. Sanity, if not morality, is awakened, and certainly the word "win" would have no meaning. But the

101

occasion does challenge us to think together about prayer and other perils as well. Can we today straighten out some of our ideas about prayer?

* * *

Before we turn to this matter, however, I want to say first, and repeat it at the end, that in spite of our doubts, we must pray, for the simple reason that the very heart of prayer is communion with God. And do let us remember this, that there is no such thing as an unanswered pray-er. Prayers may not be answered. but pray-ers, persons who pray, will always be answered.

You have only to think of your own child clamouring for something from you. However silly it was, however impossible, however ridiculous, you would not in stony indifference avert your face and look the other way. Indeed, would it not be true to say that the more impossible or unwise the request from your child, the more you would gather him into your arms, love him and comfort him; make up for the disappointment of your refusal by an expression of the warmth of your love? There must be many occasions when our prayers are in God's sight silly, impossible, ridiculous, unwise. But the greatest heresy of all would be to think that, as it were, He looked the other way and passed us by in icy indifference, There are unanswered prayers, but no unanswered pray-ers.

* * *

Let us ask ourselves what sort of a God those who pray have had in their minds, and though I shall seem to speak negatively at first, it is only to clear the way for a more positive realisation of what God is.

So in what follows I want to say:

(1) God is not an insurance company.
(2) God is not a teacher who has favourites.
(3) God is not a magician.

Let us look at these three negatives for a moment.

(1) *God is not an insurance company*

The Jews in Old Testament times thought He was, and though I greatly admire many passages in the Old Testament, one of which I shall quote later, I do want to beseech you, if you have not done so already, to *stop living in the Old Testament.* Listen to this.

> "He that dwelleth in the secret place of the Most High shall abide under the shadow of the Almighty. I will say of the Lord, He is my refuge and my fortress; . . . . He shall deliver thee from the snare of the fowler, and from the noisome pestilence. He shall cover thee with His pinions, and under His wings shalt thou take refuge. . . . Thou shalt not be afraid for the terror by night, nor for the arrow that flieth by day; for the pestilence that walketh in darkness, nor for the destruction that wasteth at noonday. A thousand shall fall at thy side, and ten thousand at thy right hand; but it shall not come nigh thee. . . . For Thou, O Lord, art my refuge! . . . There shall no evil befall thee, neither shall any plague come nigh thy tent. For He shall give His angels charge over thee, to keep thee in all thy ways. They shall bear thee up in their hands, lest thou dash thy foot against a stone.".[1].

Men and women, it just is not true. Imagine a chaplain reading a psalm like that to some of the brave men who in the Battle of Britain gave their lives for our freedom. How could anyone say, "A thousand shall fall at thy side, and ten thousand at thy right hand, but it shall not come nigh thee"? What an insurance system religion would be and how men would rush—as some still mistakenly do—to pay the premium of unintelligent and selfish prayer!

The trouble is that modern men still live in ancient days. No one can blame the psalmist. His thought had not proceeded further, but the modern man who has listened to Jesus ought to know better. Yet, I, myself, heard a man in a prayer meeting pray during war-time, "Protect our sons, O Lord, under the

[1] Psalm 91[1-12]

103

shadow of Thy wings, for the bullet was never made that can pierce Thy wings." But a bullet pierced his boy's skull.

Listen to Jesus. *He* is the revelation of the nature of God. He supersedes all psalmists and prophets and poets, and He did not say to Peter, "Peter, follow Me! Your fishing business will always prosper. You and your family will be immune from disease. No evil shall come nigh your dwelling." He said to His men, "All the evil things that hurt other people will hurt you, and on top of that, men will persecute you. They will drive you from one city to another. They will kill you and think that they do God's service. But if you endure to the end, you will be saved." In other words, "if you can stick it out, you will find the way home, and then you will find that all so-called pain and loss is woven into a plan that is utterly beautiful and meaningful, so wonderful that nothing you have suffered will still be a liability. All will be asset."

If God were an insurance company, men would rush to pay the premium of a spurious piety in order to be saved from trouble, but God never says, "I will deliver you from the waters." He says, "When you pass through them, I shall be there too," and it is implied that *that will make all the difference to what the waters can do to you.* Paul says that "all things work together for good to those who love God". (Rom. 8²⁸). I like Prof. C. H. Dodd's translation: "With them that love Him, God co-operates in all things for good."

*　　*　　*

(2) *God is not a teacher who has favourites*

I have a great respect for the teaching profession and I am sure that what I am going to say is not true of anyone here, but if there is one despicable type of teacher, it is the one who *shows* favouritism. No doubt, a teacher may have in his heart favourite pupils. The boy or girl who does well is bound to be more attractive than the boy or girl who is lazy or stupid, but the teacher must not *show* favouritism. And how utterly revolting is the imaginary picture of a child who is set homework, sneaking round to the teacher's house, where, let us imagine, the teacher does his sums for him, while the other boys are left to do them by themselves. The teacher has achieved his highest end when, because his teaching has kindled the boy's own powers, the boy actually pushes the teacher's help aside and says, "Oh! I see how to do it!"

Yet men and women pray to God asking Him to show favouritism in a way which would be unworthy of God.

During the Great Plague in England in 1665, many Christian people must have prayed to God, "Lord, save my husband, save my child, save my lover from the plague!" But if God, in response to prayer, had had favourites, do you realise that *plague would still be with us?* Men would have thought that the way to treat plague was to pray. They would have put a prayer in the slot and drawn out a cure. The whole class—to carry out the teaching analogy—would never have used its resources to learn how to prevent plague and cure plague.

Do you not think we may be in similar circumstances now in regard to cancer? Let us pray, of course, because it is right for a child to pray to his Father about anything that is deeply concerning him, and when the whole class knows the answers we shall be able to cure the individual. We *can* cure him in some cases already by early surgery or by deep X-ray. But we must not lose our faith in a wise, loving headmaster who has the welfare of the whole class at heart and must not show favouritism to the individual. May I say this and, as it were, underline it? It is only very infrequently that one can trace any relationship whatever between character and calamity. You must not say that this happened to me because God punished me or willed this illness, as though God is the kind of person that will give a man cancer because he did not say his prayers, or drown a woman's baby because she did not go to church. It would be better to think of life as a football field. In the clash of bodies some will get hurt, and in the field of the world in the clash of wills, where ignorance, folly and sin affect others, some will fall. God knows about them. God is concerned about them. God's plan is not defeated by their temporary illness—temporary although perhaps fatal—but God will not leap out of heaven, as it were, to show favouritism. That would be unworthy.

I think I have an illustration near at hand which will amuse you. When the City Temple was burnt down in 1941, the Church Secretary of another church in London, and a very famous church, wrote to my Church Secretary and said, "The destruction of your church is a direct judgment of God. Surely you are not surprised with a heretic like Weatherhead in the pulpit." At my suggestion our Church Secretary made no reply, and indeed it was not necessary because the next week the writer's church was burnt down! We still did not reply. I can only hope that our silence was as eloquent as our feelings! Indeed, I noticed two angels nudge one another and giggle! No! God has no favourites.

* * *

(3) *God is not a magician*

Now here I must speak very carefully or you will misunderstand. I believe in miracles, but not in magic. I believe that everything that happens is within the realm of law, but not within the realm of law as we know it. Let me repeat an illustration which I used on the Brains Trust when I was suddenly confronted by the question, "What is a miracle?" Let us imagine a dog suffering from a wounded paw which threatens to become septic. On his doggy level of knowledge and understanding, all he can do is to lick it and lie up until it heals. But supposing man, from his superior level of knowledge and understanding, broke through on to the doggy level with penicillin. Then to *the dog* it would be a miracle. It is the use of law-abiding forces, but forces that operate on a higher plane than the dog knows or can ever know.

Now the miracles of Jesus were all activities within the realm of law. But Jesus was at home on a plane higher than ours, as well as being at home on our plane, and He used energies completely natural on that higher plane, but supernatural to us (not contra-natural, be it noted), and these are what I call miracles. I know that in some of His healings, we grope rather

106

blindly after Him, and in some situations achieve ends similar to His own. For instance, I have seen a man cured of a physical disease by accepting the forgiveness of God, much on the lines on which Jesus worked when He said, "Son, thy sins are forgiven thee." But many things that Jesus did, we have never done and may never be able to do. No one else has ever risen from the dead in the way Jesus did. Indeed, no one else has ever cured completely a raving lunatic in one evening of treatment, as Jesus cured the man amongst the tombs on the bluff above the lake of Galilee.

But do notice that God will not work magic. That is to say, He will not do things which would so make nonsense of law as to prevent our ever being able to learn laws at all. For instance, if fire burnt one child to death, but did not burn the flesh of your baby who had fallen into it, because you had said your prayers; if a nail driven into the palm of a hand was torture one day, but did not hurt one who was sinless; if God really did stop someone falling down a precipice half way and have him borne on angels' wings, as Psalm 91 suggests, then we should live in a chaotic and insane world of magic where no one could ever learn anything. You will remember that the Devil tried that particular idea about angels' wings on Jesus during His temptations. "He shall give His angels charge concerning thee, and in their hands they shall bear thee up lest at any time thou dash thy foot against a stone."—Jesus saw through the pretentious lie, and nailed it. He knew that one is as likely to be crucified if one is loving and selfless, as if one is a revolutionary or a brigand. He is reported to have said, "Thou shalt not tempt the Lord Thy God," and this is translated by some thus; "Thou shalt not put the Lord Thy God to the test." But that is surely what faith is urged to do daily. I think the sense of the passage is brought out better by our phrase "force the hand". "Thou shalt not try to *force the hand* of the Lord Thy God." In my opinion if Jesus *had* thrown Himself from the pinnacle of the temple He would have been killed.

We know perfectly well that if fire broke out, prayer is not relevant; water is. So it is more religious to use water than to use prayer. We know perfectly well that if a man's teeth give him trouble, he does not pray, he goes to the dentist. Dentistry is relevant; prayer is of far less importance. Why should man suppose that prayer is the best thing he can do for cancer when God is trying to teach the whole human family that if they spent less on nuclear experiments, their researches would soon find out the prevention and cure of cancer, just as men have found the prevention and cure of plague, or how to put a fire out, or how to stop a tooth? If I were a world dictator I would give far greater priority to the scientists, now criminally crippled by lack of funds, who would soon find out how to prevent and cure disease, than to the scientists who send meaningless sputniks blipping round the moon.

We must differentiate between what God no doubt *could* do— for instance, if He *were* an insurance company, if He *were* a bad teacher, if He *were* a magician—and what God *must not do*. He *could* cure your dear one. Has it occurred to you that perhaps He *must not*? The guard *could* hold up the train for an hour to let you, who had tipped him, catch it and get to your wife before she died. But he would be a poor guard. Others all along the line are counting on the train running to time. He *could*, but he *must not*.

In a million cases God *could* do what our prayers ask, but He *must not*.

Having criticised one part of the Old Testament, let me warmly praise another. There is not time to read to you the wonderful story of the three men thrown into a burning, fiery furnace. Read it yourself in Daniel 3, where those three brave men would have been let off the torture of the fire if they had denied the living God. The king, Nebuchadnezzar, we are told, was full of fury and treated those brave men with contempt, telling them that they could not really believe in the power of God or they would trust in His deliverance. Now listen to the answer—one of the finest expressions of Christian truth ever written down though written centuries before Christ: "Our God, whom we serve, is *able* to deliver us from the burning fiery furnace; . . . but if not," [that is, if He must not], "be it known unto thee, O king, that we will not serve thy gods, nor worship the golden image which thou hast set up." (Daniel 3^{17-18}). In other words, "God could deliver us, and probably He will, but perhaps He must not, and if He does not, we still believe in Him and we will not have anything to do with your golden image."

Let me finish where I started. In any case, let us pray always. Indeed, in severe sickness God often answers our prayers without magic or favouritism. The effect of the love and care of a praying group can alter the mind, even the unconscious mind, of a sick person, so that the balance between recovery and death is pushed down on the side of recovery. This is not magic or favouritism or insurance. This is one of the lessons the whole class is learning about prayer. But we will also say what the men said about the fiery furnace, "*But if not* we will still believe in God." I have said three things that God is not. It is more important to say that He *is* a Father.

But, men and women, can we really hope to understand all that a father does? Can a toddler, whose father is a surgeon, understand his father who makes people unconscious, lays them on a table and cuts them with knives? Can a child watching a building site, covered with cranes and cement and stones and rubbish, understand what the architect is going to do with it? Can a savage confronted with a batch of black dots on a sheet of paper realise that it is the music of Beethoven which will thrill the world as long as the world lasts?

But we will pray and we will pray for our loved ones in peril. We will even ask God to keep them safe. But then we will add, "If this may not be, may their faith in Thee remain unshaken, their courage be unbroken, their serenity be undisturbed to the last."

You may remember the words of the prayer which the famous padre, Studdert Kennedy, put into the mouth of a Cockney soldier:

> It ain't I 'opes 'E'll keep me safe
>   While the other blokes goes down,

It ain't as I wants to leave this world
   And wear an 'ero's crown.
It ain't for that as I says my prayers
   When I goes to the attack,
But I pray that whatever comes my way
   I may never turn me back.
I leaves the matter o'life and death
   To the Father who knows what's best,
And I prays that I still may play the man
   Whether I turns east or west.
I'd sooner that it were east, ye know,
   To Blighty and my gal Sue.
I'd sooner be there, wi' the gold in 'er 'air,
   And the skies be'ind all blue.
But still I pray I may do my bit,
   And then, if I must turn west,
I'll be unashamed when my name is named,
   And I'll find a soldier's rest.

The Case against God

SOMETIMES, when things seem uncertain and dark in our own lives and in the world around us, it is a good thing to face them, and even to state the strongest case against the goodness of God which these events seem to present. Lin Yutang, the Chinese philospher, said, "Peace of mind comes by facing the worst," and that wise, though neurotic, old philosopher, Thomas Carlyle, after a shattering diagnosis by his doctor, said to himself, "All right, so I am going to die. At any rate I will die courageously." He did not die—at least not then.

It may be that for some here, faith is likely to die. One of the ways in which it can be saved is to put down the case against God. Viscount Grey of Falloden, according to his biographer, G. M. Trevelyan, once said that the case against the Creator was "mountainous and watertight," unless one could believe in the Incarnation and that God Himself had thus come into the muddle of the world to redeem it.

*   *   *

Let us, then, look at some of the factors in the case against God, and if this part of the sermon seems dark and depressing, try to be patient in that it is against such a dark background that the light of truth shines more brightly. Scarlet looks brighter against a black background than against a pink one, and it is far from the truth to suppose that the modern scene is "pink".

When the Christian looks out on the world, he does see a very depressing situation, and we need not go into full detail about it. Russia seeks to dominate the turbulent Middle East, though the U.S.A. has a mind to contest the domination! Hungary is the victim of a ruthless aggression which has already overtaken other satellite countries. We move further West and find disunion in the Union of South Africa and fiercely divided opinions about apartheid. We move further West still and find in South America a Black-versus-White disagreement continually focussed in incident after incident. We move further West still until we come to what we call the Far East, and find displaced persons in comfortless camps, notably and terribly, for instance, in Hong Kong. The world, full of hungry, homeless, wandering and unhappy people, does not look like a world that is the protégé of a loving, powerful God.

When we come to events closer at hand, there are a thousand things that puzzle the thoughtful Christian. I still find that walking down the ward of a children's hospital is a most harrowing experience. Little children suffer pain that no-one can explain to them or justify to himself. When I was asked to broadcast an appeal for the Cancer Campaign Committee, I was sent particulars of this foul disease which kept me awake at night. I dare not have repeated them on the wireless. I had no idea that little children suffered to such a terrible extent from incurable cancer, and so far from the goodness of God being evident in the world, the sufferings of little children might suggest that a monster sat on the throne of the universe, for nothing that has ever happened in the life of a child can surely have caused such terrible retribution, and it is as though a fiend had set traps for unwary little feet in the dark, and then gloated over their incurable tortures. The matter has come home to some of us here within the last few days, for we know a young mother, with two little children, in hospital for nearly nine months, and then, after three operations, given up as' incurably ill and sent home to die.

We are counselled to prayer, and many Christian people most faithfully carry out the injunction to pray, but many honest Christians would say that it is still like talking to nothing, and they can see little result for their prayers. True, a strong case can be made out for private prayer. Nature knows nothing of an organism which has no correspondence with its environment, and if the soul and God are both realties, they surely must have communion. But prayer for others often seems barren. We here continually pray for the sick, but we pray in faith and we go on doggedly. Our continuance is not based on scientifically kept records which prove that prayer is worth while, or that it pays a dividend on renewed health. Let's be honest. Such figures alone would only prove that prayer was, in a high percentage of cases, a waste of time if the recovery of the patient is to be the test of the value of the prayer.

When we turn to Nature, even where it is completely free from man's possible intervention, we find suffering, fear and unhappiness. One of the hymns in our hymn book (No. 36) is, in my opinion, almost sheer nonsense. It begins:

> "Yes, God is good: in earth and sky,
>   From ocean-depths and spreading wood,
> Ten thousand voices seem to cry,
>   'God made us all, and God is good.'"

One verse tells us that

> "The merry birds prolong the strain,"

and another tells us that

> "The echoing sky and roaring seas,
>   All swell the chorus, 'God is good,'"

But without taking your time, it could be said that any school-boy who treated the birds as some of their own species treat them, would rightly be severely punished. The butcher bird or shrike gets little birds and spikes them alive on thorns to be devoured later. The robin, so the ornithologists tell us, is not pouring out a song of praise to the Creator; he is warning all other birds that this is his territory, and if any other robin dares to claim it, he will dispute the matter, if neccessary by a bloody battle. As for the roaring seas proclaiming the goodness of God, no-one who has travelled on them in a storm feels quite like that, and if he could penetrate into those depths and meet the octopus and the giant squid, the evidence that God is good might not seem so convincing as it may do when one is singing hymns in a crowded church on Sunday evenings.

Let me lighten the dark picture by reminding you that

> "There was a young lady of Ryde,
>   Who was carried away by the tide,
>   A man-eating shark
>   Was heard to remark,
> 'I knew that the Lord would provide!'"

Frankly, Nature seems one long attack of one species on another in an atmosphere of fear, and with much hostility by beasts, birds, fish, reptiles and insects against man, and with man ranged against them for supremacy in the world.

It is no wonder that the philosopher, John Stuart Mill, said that either God was good and not powerful, or He was powerful, but not good. If He is love, it is argued, He could not tolerate the agony that man suffers, unless it be that He is powerless to prevent it. If He is powerful enough to prevent it, He cannot be Love to allow it. We can sympathise with the apparent dilemma. Where is the sign of this power? We see examples of terrifying power in avalanche and storm and flood, but if God is a loving, omnipotent Spirit, can he not do more in His world than He does for those who are told to call Him "Father"? What a strong case there is against Him!

*　　　*　　　*

Now let us turn to the other side. Let us remember that God is still at work in His universe trying to make it according to His heart's desire. Jesus said so. If I may translate a text as Father Ronald Knox does, it runs, "My Father has never ceased working, and I, too, must be at work."[1] One Biblical writer, Jeremiah, likens the activity of God to a potter working upon clay. He has, of course, the right to use the simile and he makes it illustrate his point. But the image is not one that we can adopt for our purpose now, for when God works on humanity, He is working on clay which has a free will. He is working on clay that already possesses trends towards evil, for it is much easier to be selfish than unselfish. He is working on clay with a hereditary stress. He is working on clay which is affected and infected by other lumps of clay near it, and He is working on

[1] John 5[17]

clay acted on probably by evil intelligences, trying to use it for *their* purposes which are hostile to those of God.

In other words, the material on which God is working, perhaps in nature, but certainly in human nature, is as unlike clay as anything could possibly be.

Let us set down some things of which we are quite certain.

1.   For myself, I am convinced that the universe—including man—did not just happen without any purpose behind it and within it. My friend, Dr. Raynor Johnson, who is a Doctor of Science of London University,—not, you observe a mere parson who has an axe to grind—uses the illustration of the embryo within the womb: the way in which the cells in that embryo are differently determined, some to make nerves, some bone, some brain, some teeth, and so on. They go to their appointed places at the appointed time. They develop the right properties for carrying out the function of that part of the structure. Dr. Johnson is a first-rate physicist, qualified both at the Universities of Oxford and London, and he adds this: "If this is not evidence of purpose, highly intelligent purpose, I confess I do not know the meaning of the word."[1]

I entirely agree. I think it is indisputable that the universe bears marks of the purposefulness of a mind in some ways like our own, for if that purposing mind were not like our own, we should not perceive it to be purposefulness at all. May I, therefore, take that as acceptable to all of us, that while there is much in the universe that puzzles us, some things that seem meaningless, and other things that seem cruel or callous, there are at least marks of a Mind being at work? I call that Mind, God.

2.   The second thing of which I am quite certain is that our sense of values is in the main valid. If that sentence is difficult, I only mean that we *know* that love is *better* than hate, humility *better* than pride, unselfishness *better* than selfishness, and that personality is better than its opposite. To be "he" is *better*,—higher in the scale of being—than to be "it".

[1] *The Imprisoned Splendour*, p. 56 (Hodder and Stoughton, 1953)

Now man possesses those qualities and is also personal. At his best he loves, is kind, is self-sacrificing, is unselfish. Note the "he". If, then, the purposeful and creative Mind behind the universe does not contain these values, these qualities, then man is better than that creative Mind. In other words, man is better than God. It seems incredible to me that Mind does not contain all—and more than all—of the qualities in man which he himself regards as indubitably good, including personality. God must be supra-personal, that is more than we can possibly mean when we use the word "personal". My point is that He cannot be less than personal so we must call Him "He" and not "It".

Now this was the argument that Jesus Himself used. If ye, then, being evil, He says, would do kind things, and give good gifts to your children, how much more will God? If a good shepherd will go over the mountains to seek a lost sheep, do you think God cares less for you than a shepherd about his sheep? Jesus uses the argument again and again in various forms. For instance, in the story of the so-called unjust judge, Jesus argues that if a bad judge for a bad reason (importunity) will listen to a woman who has no claim on him, how much more will a good father for a good reason (love) listen to one who is His son?[1]

This is not only the argument Jesus *used*. It is the argument that Jesus *was*. It is clear that if God is supremely good, any man reveals God to the extent to which he is good. So a perfectly good man perfectly reveals God as far as God can be revealed within the limitations of human nature. So we find Him saying, "He that hath seen Me hath seen the Father."

I know this does not remove mystery, but it removes the charge of cruelty, or callousness, or carelessness against God. The argument does not dispel the darkness, but it suggests that the darkness will pass. The argument does not provide us with an answer to our questions, but it suggests that there *is* an answer.

[1] Luke 18[1-8]. Christ often used this "How much more" argument, e.g. The Friend at Midnight (Luke 11[5-12]), The Unjust Steward (Luke 16[1-13])

I cannot believe that Jesus Himself walked always in the light of assurance. There is plenty of evidence that He knew fear to the point of terror—in Gethsemane, for instance. He knew that horrible onrush of doubt. "If it be possible," He pleads,—He who had said that "all things are possible to God"—"let this Cup pass." He cannot immediately believe that His so early death—just when He was succeeding in implanting His teaching in the hearts of twelve wavering men—was the best way to that spiritual success which He craved in His Father's interests. Yet, though the case against God seemed, even to Him, I think, heavy, forbidding, terrifying, He did not go back on His faith in God's ultimate goodness.

We might suppose that in that terrible moment on the Cross when He felt deserted, He might have said to those gathered at its feet, "I was deluded. I was wrong. I hoped in God and I trusted God. But I fear He does not exist, or, if He does, He is callous, careless or cruel. I am sorry I asked you to follow Me. I was mistaken. Go back to your homes and forget all that I have told you about God . . . ." If He had spoken thus, there would have been a certain show of logic in the situation, for why on earth should a loving and omnipotent God let down His own Son Who had only sought to do His Father's will? Yet almost His last word was "Father, into Thy hands I trust My Spirit". And, of course, *that quality of faith*, though we may only possess it for brief moments, and in small quantities, is the answer to the case against God.

*   *   *

If you say, "Why does God allow evil so much scope and power?" I don't know the answer. If I were running the world, I would do many things differently! I would have removed Hitler as soon as he showed himself to be a fanatical monomaniac. I would have removed Stalin much earlier, and so on. I would either exclude cancer from my world, or I would rapidly show the men of science how to prevent it, as they have learnt how to prevent plague and other diseases. If I were omnipotent, I would throw my weight about. I would show them!

But seriously, men and women, how much easier it would be for God to do that! One is driven to belief in two important facts. One is that if He is love, as we suppose, He must in some ways suffer deeply and profoundly with all His children who suffer. "He that hath seen me" said Jesus, "hath seen the Father." God's revelation in Jesus assures us of this. "Surely He hath borne our griefs and carried our sorrows": not once at Calvary, but all the time. It is a solemn thought.

A second thought is that the very nature of power is not to rush at an end, whatever the means, but to achieve an end by worthy means, since the means accomplish more than the end in itself. It might be said that the aim of a football match consists in trying to put a leather ball into a net at certain intervals. But if that is all, why the struggle and fret? Why doesn't someone get up in the night or during the interval and put it there? Because the means accomplish more than the end! There is a value in all the toil and trouble it takes to get it there.

What is your definition of power? Mine is, "The ability to achieve purpose." We have discussed this point again and again, and I will not labour it now. A teacher with a difficult class could get on splendidly by excluding the lazy, tiresome and backward boys, but if her purpose is to educate them all, she must do so at the cost of keeping even the naughty and slow boys in the room. To use what we could call "overpowering might" and exclude difficult boys, would look impressive, but in fact would be an expression of weakness because it would defeat purpose.

I suppose the State could lock up everybody who was not only a criminal, but who might become one, or who was any kind of disturber of the peace, and that would be a show of power as impressive as the expressions of omnipotence which unthinking people want God to use. But if the purpose of the State is to make good citizens of all, it must take trouble over the difficult people and *appear* impotent in some situations.

Many people think that the omnipotence of God should cause Him, as it were, to rush to His end or goal by using the shortest possible means and by overwhelming might. But that would defeat His purpose. The means so often accomplish more than the mere attainment of the end. Indeed, the end could not thus be reached, for we are to be men, and neither passive clay nor machines, and we must be left not only the power of choice, but we must be left with all those pulls and trends of which I have spoken. We must be allowed to learn slowly and make mistakes and involve others in our hurt, so that the purpose of God may ultimately be achieved. We are made, like a good footballer, not by the goal, but by the manner of reaching it.

Men and women, I do not think we can hope in this life, at any rate, fully to understand. We have to say with Tennyson,

> "I can but trust that somehow good
> Will be the final goal of ill."

After all, we are very little children and what a little a child can understand!

Because we are little children we can do nothing but trust. The alternative would be to believe that the whole universe is a hideous nightmare, the creation of a malignant fiend or else a slobbering idiot. I believe that behind it is Someone not only like ourselves, but far, far better than we can ever conceive, utterly wise, utterly holy, utterly good and ultimately omnipotent.

If we can believe that, then the measure of what looks like unrelieved evil is at any rate the *measure* of purposed good, and—remember this, men and women,—unless God were as great and grand and good, as He must be, He would not dare to leave His children in a world that carries so strong a case against Him.

Does God Matter?

I SHALL at least *begin* with an irrefutable statement: either God matters or He does not matter! Either He is relevant to life and to every part of life, or He is an an outgrown conception belonging to the infancy of the race and now, in our maturity, to be cast away and thought of as many of us think of Santa Claus.

In that case, of course, Religion, the Church, the Sacraments and Services, Prayer, trying to love God, trying to love men, trying to follow Christ, go by the board. Ivy over a church tower may look pretty, but it does no good to the structure, and if it is cut at the root, it will loosen its grip and soon be a matter of dead leaves that do not even look pretty. This, some think is what is happening to religion. Modern science, and other axes have cut its root. More and more it is becoming dead leaves. The idea of God is banished as childish. The Church has had its day. These are the thoughts of many hearts.

*   *   *

We ought to realise, in passing, that if we decide that God does not matter, we automatically reduce man to a rather clever animal. With God, departs the soul of man. There is a vital and causative relationship between any living organism and its relevant environment. Ears perish if they have no relationship with sound. Eyes atrophy if they have no correspondence with light. Lungs soon wither if air be withdrawn. The mind out of relationship with truth is a mad thing. And the soul of man is dead if there be no correspondence between it and its relevant enviroment whose name is God. If God goes, so does the soul of man.

*   *   *

Is not this the point of danger which, in our life together, we are rapidly approaching? Taking a nation-wide view, the churches are deserted, few ever read the Bible, fewer pray with any sense that God matters. There is a polite, conventional recognition of God as of those who nod to one another across the street, or talk of Santa Claus in front of a child who still believes in him. But even those who, if pressed, would admit His existence, regard Him as a remote, impersonal, vague entity far removed from the life of the world. For most people in London He is one who does not count; one who does not matter any more.

*   *   *

Turn for a moment and look at the contrast to such an attitude which we find in the Bible. This library which is a library of almost every kind of literature, written by over a hundred authors and covering a period of over a thousand years, is made a unity by a fact which can be expressed in two words: God matters.

The first four words of the Bible give us the key. "In the beginning, *God*." We have no science as such in the Bible, but when the writers speak of such things as those with which science now deals, it is to tell us that God created them and owns them. The heavens and their contents, the earth and everything on it, the sea and everything in it, are called upon to praise His Holy Name. Listen to typical sentences! "The heavens declare the glory of God." "The earth is the Lord's and the fulness thereof." "The sea is His and He made it."

We have poetry and drama and myth and legend and parable and biography and prophecy in the Bible, but all are instruments to make men realise that God matters. We have history, but even accuracy does not matter to the writer so much as the desire to show the hand of God at work. And the Bible concludes with the strange dreams of a visionary, as hard to understand as some modern painting, but shining with the over-all authority of God reigning for ever and ever.

*   *   *

We have given all that up. We act as though God did not matter. We have substituted man instead. We do not really *mean* even at Christmas,

"Glory to God in the Highest."

With far more sincerity and meaning we sing with Swinburne,

"Glory to Man in the highest, for Man is the Master of things."

I am reminded of the old Danish fable which tells how a spider slid down a single filament of web from the lofty timbers of a barn and established himself on a lower level. There he spread his web, caught flies, grew sleek and prospered. One Sunday afternoon, wandering about his premises, he saw the thread that stretched up into the dark unseen above him, and thought, "How useless!" He snapped it. *But his web collapsed* and soon was trodden under foot.

I feel I want to say to you this morning, with all the power I can get from God, that the curse of modern life is man's decision that God does not matter, that man can manage, that man is the master of things. The most terrifying and sinister thing about modern life is that it is organised around Man, instead of around God. And the truth is that when we try to do without God, we collapse. When we cut the thread that holds us in living touch with the Unseen above us, we fall. God matters! God matters as air matters to lungs, and you, who are sensitive, must sometimes have heard already the choking of men, suffocating with fear and bewilderment, and purposeless, hectic hurrying, because they are trying to do without God. The assertion that God *is*, alone makes sense of life. The assertion that God rules, alone gives life purpose and meaning.

* * *

Let me remind you bluntly: The world exists for God, not us. It was created to fulfil *His* purposes, not ours, save as we cooperate with Him. You cannot bend its laws to fulfil merely selfish ends. Clearly, if it was created by God for His ends, then His ends are the only ones which it will finally serve.

What a queer expression we sometimes use! We talk about

"breaking God's laws". We say sometimes of a man who ignores the requirements of the body, or mind, that he has "broken the laws of health". On the contrary, the laws of health have broken him. His condition proves it. You cannot *break* law. You can be broken by defying law. "If," said Chesterton, "you walk to the edge of the cliff and keep straight on, you do not break the law of gravity, you prove it."

And let us remember that law runs through every part of the universe—the physical, the psychological, the psychical, the moral, the spiritual. This fact makes it a UNIverse instead of a multiverse. Miracles do not evidence broken law. They demonstrate its wealth and complexity. They point to the existence of laws we do not yet know. If miracle were a *breaking* of law, the fact would be a poor compliment to the wisdom of a God who apparently had overlooked all the possibilities which the original creation of law should have covered: as though God said to Himself, "When I made the world I never reckoned with such a possibility as this. Now I must work a miracle to put things right." No one ever breaks law. For example, no one ever sins and gets away with it. *Always* there is the come-back, either in consequence to body or mind or soul; either in illness, or sleeplessness, in bitter memories or in haunting terrors. Forgiveness restores relationship, but it does not obliterate all consequence. LAW REIGNS and it is God's signature on all things, for law is created by *God*. We merely discover the way He works and we call it Law, but it is His, not ours. Blessed are they who learn in time that fulness of life is for him who, on all levels of body, mind and spirit, co-operates with the law of God.

*   *   *

Does God matter? Let us contemplate those who want a better world, and, in their own field, are sincerely working for it.

The point I want to make was illustrated for me in a luncheon which I once attended here in London at the invitation of a Member of Parliament. After the meal we found that we had been invited because we were supposed to represent various fields of endeavour, and we were each called upon to say how we supposed that by our efforts the world would be made a happy place. A scientist spoke to us—but has science got the secret? Without blaming scientists, we must admit that their science of nuclear energy has made the whole world more terrified than it was before the Romans landed in Britian. Is this the "*progress*" of science? A medical scientist spoke to us of the effects of newly discovered drugs. I remembered that in America in 1956, thirty million prescriptions for tranquillisers were used compared with ten million the year before. Fifty thousand million tablets of one tranquilliser alone were swallowed in that one year in America. I have not seen the British figures for the same year, but barbiturate consumption in Britain in 1955 was estimated at forty-eight tons, that is twenty doses per head for every member of the population of Great Britian and Northern Ireland. Is this medical progress? Can the doctors make our world happy? A psychologist spoke to us of early analysis for everybody. Having found by experience over twenty years ago that a thorough analysis takes two hundred hours, I pass over that one! (An out-patient in Britain after waiting weeks and months, may get half an hour, often interrupted, once a week. A paying patient may be asked for five guineas for every session.) Educationists spoke to us as though the kingdom of happiness could be found in learning. I would not have thought university students were any happier than Teddy Boys. Sociologists spoke to us as though the people in Mayfair were happier than those in Whitechapel. I find the rich, by and large, much less happy than the poor, though, of course, if you are rich you can be miserable in comfort! The politicians, said it was a matter of changing the Government, but one could only remember the word of the beloved Studdert Kennedy: "When you change the Government, do remember that you only take one lot of sinners out and put another lot of sinners in."

More seriously, hear the word of Professor Toynbee, perhaps the greatest historian of our day, who has written certainly the most profound work of our time. At the end of ten volumes of historical survey, he says this: "The entire story of man on earth has no meaning at all except a religious meaning. There is no hope except in the vast increase of spiritual religion." He says another profound thing: the world, he tells us, has known twenty-one civilisations. Out of this twenty-one, fourteen have already disappeared. *They were instruments which God could no longer use!*

* * *

So what? Let one true story sum up my argument.

An American airman was shot down out of the sky and landed in the sea near a South Sea Island to which he made his way. He crept into the bushes to hide. And no wonder. Within living memory he would have been captured by savages, boiled and eaten. But not now. He was found and cared for, his injuries treated, and he himself nursed back to health. He wrote home to his parents. In his letter he said he had never been much of a Christian and had regarded many church-going folk as hypocrites. "But now," he said, "I have seen the real thing." In that island, once cannibalistic, where dark orgies were indulged in and sorcery practised, where dirt and disease abounded, and where men and women had lived like animals, there had been a transformation.

The airman had an interview with the Chief, who told him there had not been a murder during his lifetime. There was no jail. There was no poverty, no drunkeness, no divorce, no venereal disease, no brothels, and practically no disease. There was one doctor, "but," said the chief, "he spends most of his time fishing." Orphans were promptly absorbed into other homes. Honesty was taken for granted.

This is no made-up story. The name of the writer of the letter is given. But here is the point: when the airman asked the Chief how he accounted for this wonderful state of affairs, he looked reproachfully at his white guest and said, "You ought to know. Your ancestors sent us missionaries. We are Christians. *We have taken Christ seriously.*"[1]

* * *

[1] See *They Found the Church There*, Henry Van Dusen, p.81ff. (Student Christian Movement Press).

Oh, men and women, when shall we in this frightened, fevered, bewildered, selfish, materialistic west "take Christ seriously"?

We used to, you know. St. Bartholomew's Hospital here in the City of London was founded by a monk, Rahere. All the doctors were monks and the nurses were nuns. The Christian spirit permeated the hospital. Now, no one would raise an objection if a surgeon were an atheist; if a nurse were an agnostic. Our schools were all Church Schools. Nowadays your child may be taught by an atheist. Our dramas were first played in churches. There was a time when you could not be an actor unless you were a religious person. Now, drama and religion rarely go together. Our greatest music was set to religious words. When the soul of Handel was bursting with great music, the words he used to express it were taken from the Bible. Think of *The Messiah* and *Elijah*! Few great composers today would choose religious words to go with their music! The world's greatest paintings had religious subjects. Think of the great pictures of the Madonna! Our Courts of Justice were held in Church. The bar to which the bar-rister was called was the Communion Rail. The whole of life was organised around God. Now it is organised around man. God does not matter any more.

Oh, I know we have better hospitals and better schools and better theatres and better justice, but we have almost severed the thread that runs up into the Unseen. And it is a vital thread. If it is severed, we shall fall. However proudly we hold up our heads, they shall be bowed before Him at last and the proud West will pass to the limbo of forgotten civilisations like Babylon and Greece and Rome and Egypt and the rest. I have seen ignorant Arab peasants camping in the ruins of Babylon, once the centre of a mighty civilisation, and I have wondered whether one day men will dig and discover Piccadilly Circus, where, across the mud-flats on the banks of the Thames, a wind moans dismally in a great silence and only ghosts remain.

*   *   *

Let me conclude with a parable. Toscanini, the world-famous conductor, who was very exacting and almost tyrannical in rehearsals, practised with one orchestra the Ninth Symphony of Beethoven. First it was practised piece-meal, each group of instruments alone, and then, together, at full concert strength.

At last rehearsals were over, and master and orchestra were ready for the concert performance. When the performance was over, the first violinist said to the second, "If he scolds us after that I will jump up and push him off his platform." But Toscanini did not scold. He stood silent, his arms still outstretched, his deep eyes burning with an inner fire, the light of a great rapture upon his face and a spirit of utter contentment enfolding him. After a long silence he spoke: "Who am I? Who is Toscanini? Who are you? I am nobody! You are nobody..." The crowded hall was hushed. The master stood with arms still extended. The multitude waited in awed silence. Then, with the light upon his face of one who has seen a vision, he added, "Beethoven is everything—EVERYTHING!"

Does God matter? No one else matters. Nothing else matters. God is everything. EVERYTHING. . . . If you can only remember one sentence in all that has been said this morning, remember this and ponder it:

OUTSIDE GOD THERE IS NOTHING BUT DEATH

No! I have not forgotten the text. Take it with you as you leave. It is the Authorised Version of Acts 9[6]. When the Reality of God in Jesus Christ broke in on Saul of Tarsus, who became St. Paul, he said this:

"Lord, what wilt Thou have *ME* to *DO*?"

Is it a Sign of Intelligence to Disbelieve in God?

IT is always an advantage for a preacher to have certain topics suggested to him as likely matters for sermons. Lately, wireless and television programmes have brought before us a number of highly educated men who, rather by inference than by frank statement, have suggested that they do not themselves believe in the Christian faith. I have been asked whether it is a sign of increasing education and profundity of intellect to disbelieve in God.

This certainly is a live issue, especially with some of our students in colleges. There is a certain glamour for a young science student who greatly admires the masters of his subject, in taking up his masters' religious attitude as well. I can imagine some of these young people believing that religion is all very well for old fogies, for old women of both sexes, for simple-hearted, unintelligent men and women, but that to claim to be educated should lead one to disparage religion, and that it is a sign of intelligence to disbelieve in God.

Recently a correspondent sent me a cutting about the formation of a group of students at Cambridge. I quote the basis on which they worked:

> "The Cambridge Humanist Society was founded in 1955. The Society's premiss is that human problems can, and must be faced in terms of human intellectual and moral resources without invoking supernatural authority."

When we add to that Professor Julian Huxley's prophecy that "it will be as impossible for an intelligent, educated man or woman to believe in God, as it is now to believe that the earth is flat, or that disease is a divine punishment", then we certainly have evidence that in taking tonight's subject, we are facing some of the problems which are being discussed around us.

* * *

I think we might begin with the famous sentence of the Psalmist where he says, "The fool hath said in his heart, there is no God." I am quite sure, in my own mind, that anyone who made such a dogmatic assertion would merit the label "fool". I do not say this because I am prejudiced in the direction of the opposite opinion, but because anyone who invents a sentence containing such a universal negative, knows, if he thinks for a moment, how impossible it is of proof. Robinson Crusoe could say, "There are men on my island." He could never have logically said, "There are no men living on my island." He could not possibly know what existed behind every hill and every tree. He could not have searched every nook and cranny where a man might lurk, and if he searched successfully late last night, a man might have arrived this morning. It is a different matter when, seeing a footprint on the sand, he can say, "Here is evidence that there is someone beside myself on my island."

Similarly, apart altogether from religion, it is foolish, illogical and fantastic that a man can walk out of his back door on a starlit night, look up into the sky, and say, "In the vast universe, part of which is stretched before me, I can affirm dogmatically that there is no God." You may say, "I don't think there is." You may say, "I don't know whether there is or not." You may say, "The word 'God' has no meaning for me." But the complete, dogmatic, negative assertion you cannot make. If you do, then plainly such a lack of thoughtfulness, such an absence of logic, such an impossibility of proof of your assertion, renders you liable, even in the spirit of Christian charity, to the label "fool".

* * *

When we come to the agnostic—that is to say, not the atheist who says, "There is no God," but the agnostic who says, "I don't know"—I think we Christians must pause for a moment and learn something from him ere we pass him by. Some agnostics would go further than saying "I don't know". They would say, "Man cannot know," but that again, you see, is that same terrible, dogmatic, negative assertion which no one can prove.

Yet the attitude of the agnostic has much to teach us. It challenges our glibness; the smug complacency of insect men who are too apt to say they know, when they can only guess. It is not my business to point at any particular denomination or group of Christian people, but something is wounded in my own mind when men pray for guidance almost in the spirit of ringing up a friend, who can give you pat advice over the phone as to what you ought to do, or when they talk about God and the universe as though the latter were tied in a neat parcel of transparent cellophane, and offered to them by a God whose nature they can see through, as easily as they can see all that the parcel contains. To me the universe itself is an unending mystery, and the nature of God surely runs out beyond all human thought, so that there must be many things concerning which the humble student is bound to say, "I don't know." Some Christians by their attitude create agnostics who leave out God. It would be better if some agnostics created Christians, in whose minds room is left for reverent wonder and humble quest.

*　　*　　*

Men will tell us that intelligence makes faith deteriorate, and that, therefore, the intelligent disbelieve in God. But let us pause a moment. If faith deteriorates through the increase of science, may it not be that our faith is poorly based, or wrongly directed? Let me illustrate. If I once believed that the rainbow was a magic and pretty bow made in the sky by God merely to tell His people that He would never let it rain too heavily again, then, of course, the onset of science, which teaches me how the raindrops break up the rays of light into the glorious colours of the spectrum, destroys that kind of faith. But for myself, and surely for many others, that would be an oddly based and a strangely directed faith. Truth must always be welcome whatever it discloses, and my faith is directed to God and is quite untouched when I discover that God's method was not incomprehensible magic but scientific process. Nor is God excluded from a method when man can understand it. Every modern scientist, of course, accepts the scientific explanation of the rainbow, but it does not, *for that reason*, make it impossible for God still to speak through it and for the devout heart to be lifted up by its beauty and its promise.

What an old battle it is! Our great grandfathers were disturbed when the scientists talked of evolution, but no modern Christian allows his faith to be disturbed by such an explanation. Evolution does not explain God away. It only reveals God's method. It shows us the slow, patient steps He took to bring man to birth. Truth will never destroy faith, if faith is set free from verbalism and childish explanation and is based on truth and directed to God.

Surely, it is time that we learnt what we so badly need to learn from the scientists. They do not hug unreality to their minds. They do not chant the old formulae which no longer contain the truth. They are never eager to maintain traditional views when reality has gone out of them. They follow the star of truth wherever it leads them, and many of them have shown us that God is more wonderful than we thought and His ways capable of creating a reverence which the glib explanations of earlier days failed to evoke from reverent minds.

There is more of the spirit of true religion in the minds of some people who call themselves agnostic, and even atheist than in the minds of some people who call themselves orthodox and religious, but who cling to magic and recite falsehood, and not only allow, but persuade men and women to trust in a God who does not exist, and to believe that His promises will keep them from those dangers and trials which all the sons of men—including the real saints—have had to bear.

*   *   *

I must admit before you all that I love and admire many of these so-called agnostics. They are not fighting against God, but against false conceptions of God. They are doing us a religious service because what they are angry about is a caricature of God. They are not idolaters. What they destroy are false gods and false ideas about God, and we ought to welcome them.

What a terrible alternative to this attitude is seen in the famous book by Edmund Gosse called *Father and Son*. The father, even though he was a Fellow of the Royal Society, tries to make himself throw away the proved findings of science because he could not make them fit in with that narrow, orthodox idea of God in which he had been brought up. No wonder that the young Gosse, like thousands of young people in our own day, threw away the idea of God because the strictures and intolerance of the orthodox demand what is finally a disloyalty of mind, a demand for an impossible attempt to believe what can be proved false. If the mind could persuade itself to such disloyalty—and that would be the opposite of loving the Lord our God with all our mind—we should be betrayed and disappointed and find that we had believed a lie. If Christianity could be overthrown by a brilliant intelligence, it would deserve to be overthrown, and our wisdom is to welcome all truth and show that fundamental religion, which is belief in a God of love who is the personification of goodness, truth and beauty, and Who ultimately will win in the world, can never be overthrown by what have been miscalled the attacks of science.

When a man like Huxley says that in a hundred years people will no longer believe in God because they will be so wonderfully educated, I rather smile to recall that a similar thing was said more than two hundred years ago, and *yet men believe in God in greater numbers now than they did then*. The activity of a Huxley is valuable to cleanse our concept of God, so that we are not tied up and inhibited by thinking of God, for example, as someone who punishes an unbeliever in everlasting fire, sends a poor heathen or an unbaptised child to hell, or does a hundred of the unworthy things with which superstitious fools have credited Him, but which they themselves would condemn in any fellow citizen. Men like Huxley help us to clear our minds so that the real God can step out of the mists of superstition and sometimes orthodoxy, and reveal Himself fully to the hearts of His truly faithful people.

*   *   *

May we now briefly turn to another phase of our subject? It is so often supposed that increasing education based on reason makes our Christian faith deteriorate. Do let us remember the power of our emotional response to pretend that it is reason. Here I wish to make three brief points.

(i) You are perhaps a Congregationalist, perhaps a Methodist, perhaps a Presbyterian, perhaps an Anglican. If challenged, no doubt with your reason you would defend your position. But did reason determine it at the start? How many of us have examined those four denominations before deciding to which we would belong? Can we really say, "I have studied them all and here is the truth"? No! You were brought up a Methodist, or you were brought up a Presbyterian, and you made up reasons afterwards. I feel sure that if I had remained in the Presbyterian Church, where I spent my childhood, I should now be a Presbyterian Minister. I feel pretty certain that if I had been brought up an Anglican, I should be a Vicar. Indeed, I might be a Bishop!—Who knows? (I'm sorry you laugh, but I shall maintain my dignity!) If you had been brought up a Roman Catholic from childhood, I find it very hard to believe that many of you would have thrown over Roman Catholicism in your adult life at the pressure of intellectual opinions.

What does all this mean? Well, it means that it is not growth of intelligence that has influenced your religion, but emotional factors, some of them quite beyond your power to control. So many agnostics and atheists were brought up like that. So many great Christians have been lost for emotional reasons. Think of Gandhi being turned away from a Christian Church in South Africa by a devil in a frock-coat who was disguised as a deacon and who told him that black men could not worship there. What if Gandhi had been a fully pledged Christian!

I remember in my own experience at an earlier church, how a woman rushed into my home and declared that having thought out the matter, she had become an atheist. This turned out not to be a sign of growing intelligence, but of the fact that her brother had been turned out of the choir for inappropriate conduct. So much for reason bearing fruit in atheism!

Dr. Bernard Hart, in his book, *The Psychology of Insanity*, tells of a Sunday School teacher who went to his minister and said, "I have thought things over and I am giving up Sunday School teaching since I have become an atheist." Enquiry showed that a fellow Sunday School teacher had run off with the "atheist's" girl. His atheism was emotionally determined. Do not be too ready to suppose, then, that the atheism of Mr. Jones in your office shows that he is intellectually your superior. Not increased intelligence but emotional factors often make a person disbelieve in God.

(ii) The second point I would like to make is this. It is said by some that belief in God is merely wishful thinking, and that thoughtful, highly educated and intelligent people see through it and discard it, and this proves their intellectual advance. But what about the people who wish there were no God? Is that a sign of their intellectual feebleness? Let us remind ourselves that wishful thinking can work both ways, and it is no more feeble to believe in God because you wish there were one, than to disbelieve in God because you wish there were not one. Intellect may not come into either situation. Frankly, it is more likely to be manifested in the man whose belief in God is strengthened by his wishful thinking. After all, there is nothing in wishful thinking to deny that that which is wished, cannot *for that reason* happen. If I wish that my wife would recover from illness, my wishing does not make her recovery impossible. If I wish that I had a Father in heaven, my wishing does not make that impossible either. Indeed, in a world in which we observe causes and effects, the wish of the hungry man rather implies that there is food, if the universe is rational. Who would say to me, "The fact that you wish there were food proves that there is not any?" One would not say to a little evacuated child, separated from his father and mother by a ruthless foe, "Your wishing proves that they do not exist." Probably they do exist, and we who are evacuated on earth will, in my opinion, one day find the satisfaction of a rational hunger and find our Father more wonderful than our dreams of Him.

(iii) When men say that the more intelligent you get, the less you will believe in God, I know that it is no good my quoting brilliantly clever men who are Christians, and supposing that that answers the argument. I should like to quote such men as Father Ronald Knox, Dean Inge, William Temple, Professor Butterfield, Professor Coulson, Professor Hardy, Sir Oliver Lodge, the late Dr. Barnes, and one could go on into the hundreds. But I know that you would turn round and say, "What about Huxley?" and a list of others whom you could readily name.

When we have finished swopping names, I do have a feeling that if Sir Julian Huxley spent as much time on the bases of religion as he has spent on his biological enquiries, he might come to a different conclusion. If you say that that is a speculation, I would remind you that C. S. Lewis was once an atheist. I regard him now as the most skilful apologist alive. I would remind you of Frank Morison, sitting down to tear up the evidence for the Resurrection, and finishing by writing its most convincing defence. I would remind you of Joad, for twenty-six years a militant atheist, dying as a convinced and communicant member of the Church of England. I would remind you of Bertrand Russell who, on his eightieth birthday, after half a century of atheism, was asked what he thought was the most important asset he thought a man could have in this life. Let me quote you his actual words: "The root of the matter," he declared, "is a very simple and old-fashioned thing, a thing so simple that I am almost ashamed to mention it, for fear of the derisive smile with which wise cynics will greet my words. The thing I mean—please forgive me for mentioning it—is love, Christian love. If you feel this you have a motive for existence, a guide in action, a reason for courage, an imperative necessity for intellectual honesty . . . and although you may not find happiness, you will never know the despair of those whose life is aimless and void of purpose." Fancy that from a lifelong atheist who once told us that the only place at which we could take our stand was that of "unyielding despair!"

To these distinguished names I would add this comment which I have never seen made or contradicted. Whereas it is common to find men who have spent years in atheism or agnosticism, turning to a warm faith in God, I cannot remember half a dozen distinguished names of men who, having had a warm faith in God, turned, after deep thought, to the conviction that God does not exist or that nothing can be known about him.

*   *   *

Finally, I wish to offer you, if you are not too tired, a chain of incredibles which I once drew up for myself when my faith needed some undergirding. If you find a flaw in this chain, please write and let me know. Show me the flaw and why it is a flaw. Before I give it to you, I wish to state that I cannot myself accept the view that the universe is endless and had no beginning. If it had always existed, there would be no radioactive matter in it, for it would all have become dead unless some new source of radio-activity could have been provided, and that, of course, gives me my point, for it would have been a point of creation. Now listen, if you will, to my chain.

1. It is incredible to me that the universe "just happened" accidentally and fortuitously. If someone flung in the air a handful of tiny cards each bearing a letter of the alphabet, it is incredible to me that any of them would fall on the floor arranged as words, much less sentences. If, on turning my back, I found even one sentence, I should deduce that a mind

136

had been at work. Much in the universe is meaningless to me, but there are a few "sentences" or marks of purpose, as, for example, the way the cells in a human embryo seem differently determined, some to make nerve, some bone, some brain, some teeth, and go to their appointed places at the appointed time, "develop the right properties for carrying out the function of that part of the structure. . . . If this is not evidence of purpose, highly intelligent purpose, I confess I do not know the meaning of the word."[1] So I find the marks of a mind in the universe.

2. It is incredible to me that this mind is not in some ways like my own mind. If it did not in some ways work like my own, I should not perceive what I call "purpose" or "orderliness" to be thus. What seems disorder to me may be order to a higher type of mind, as algebra is disorder to a savage but order to a mathematician. But what seems order to me cannot be disorder to a higher mind. All phenomena do not seem orderly to me, but some do and they prove a mind like my own. So I find a kinship between the world-mind and my own.

3. It is incredible to me that my sense of values is all wrong: I regard love as *better* than hate, kindness as *better* than cruelty, humility as *better* than pride, self-sacrifice *better* than egotism. It is incredible to me that beastliness is *better* than loveliness. Hitler a *better* man than Jesus, a cosh-boy *better* than St. Francis.

4. It is incredible to me that the creative-mind asserted above does not possess and express these values. (I now give the word "God" to this creative-mind). If God does not love, and is not ultimately good, then I am *better* than God, unless my sense of values is utterly misleading, and if *this* be so it is no use thinking at all. No mental processes are reliable if hate is a *better* thing than love, etc.

5. It is incredible to me that this creative-mind has no personality; that God is "it", but not "he", a thing, not a person,

[1] Raynor Johnson, M.A., Ph.D., D.Sc., *The Imprisoned Splendour*, p. 56 (Hodder and Stoughton, 1953).

since personality (by which I mean a self-conscious centre of thinking, feeling and willing) is my greatest asset. I recognise that God must be far more than I have words to describe, and can be supra-personal, but it is incredible that He is infra-personal. He may be far more than I mean when I use the word "personal". It is incredible to me that He is less.

6. It is incredible to me that this powerful, creative, personal Planner has no purpose in humanity. If I find purposefulness in any part of His creation, I should expect to find it where other *persons* are concerned. Even I have a purpose in the lives of my children who owe their creation to me. If God has no purpose in men's lives, He is less good than I. I plan for my children's highest well-being as I conceive it. Does God do less?

7. It is incredible to me that God has done nothing about sin and suffering, since sin is the greatest hindrance to the success of His planning, and suffering the greatest stumbling-block to man's belief in Him. Sin seems due to the misuse of man's freedom of choice in moral situations, a freedom which was the only alternative to a mechanical morality which would be no morality at all. The evil which follows is shared by the whole human family which gains by the family assets and loses by the family liabilities, so that the innocent suffer with the guilty. The alternative would deny to the individual the family assets. The fact that man so often misuses his freedom and chooses evil may be due to the hangover from his animal ancestry (e.g. promiscuous sexuality is amoral in the jungle, and only becomes lust when man sees a higher way of life). Evil—which I distinguish from sin which is a personal thing—may also be due to the invasion of man's personality by evil psychic entities (e.g. the Devil or other evil spirits), or by the possible consequences of man's activities in an earlier incarnation. (There is nothing in Christianity to deny the basic idea of reincarnation.)

8. It is incredible to me that God has not *disclosed* His purposes, since, by His own ordaining, they can only reach

fruition by man's conscious co-operation. Man's Christ-enlightened conscience, his standard of values, his insight, his reaction to the words and lives of others help him to read God's purposes. The Bible comes in here. To the Christian it contains the supreme revelation of His nature and purposes.

9. It is incredible to me that Jesus Christ never lived or that He was mentally unbalanced, or wholly misreported, or hopelessly mistaken when He claimed to stand in a unique relationship with God, or that the early Church and the saints were wrong when they saw in His death and resurrection and life after death facts importantly relevant to the redeeming purpose of God, i.e. that God was pledged to end sin and suffering and use both for the highest welfare of mankind in a plan beyond our present power of understanding. Those who feel intensely the "problem of suffering" may find suffering a "frozen asset" which later events may unfreeze to their great enrichment and the confounding of their doubts.

10. It is incredible to me that man does not survive death. The nature of God, the nature of man, the rationality of the universe, the faith of the great mystics would all be indicted if man does not survive. As the babe in the womb has ears and eyes and lips for a life which begins at birth, so all men have embryonic qualities which only become meaningful in a life that begins at "death". No man at death has exhausted his possibilities. The evidence of psychic research is impressive, and in a rational world an all but universal hunger implies its satisfaction.

11. It is incredible to me that Christianity is false or irrelevant to man's problems. One only knows a few really good Christians, but they claim that Christ has changed their lives. No one can doubt that it would be a wonderful world if all men were like them. Christ never demanded from anyone mental adherence to intellectual propositions, but He lived, revealed, and invited men to enter, a way of life which, if widely entered, would answer most of our problems. What problems would remain if all men were like Him?

12. It is incredible to me that the Mighty Planner we call God can finally be defeated. Ignorance, folly and sin can temporarily defeat His will and bring suffering, sorrow and frustration to men. But omnipotence, while it does not mean that everything that happens is His intention, does mean that in allowing it its power, God knows He can use it for a higher purpose, namely man's ultimate welfare and blessedness.

These things make me want to dedicate my life to Him and to be used, however humbly, in the working out of such a mighty plan.

*　　　*　　　*

I hope you will not believe any longer that disbelief in God is a sign of a greater intelligence than that of the humble Christian. I suppose for most of us the really convincing evidence is what God has done in other men's lives and in our own. I shall never forget hearing at Cambridge a very brilliant scientist beginning his lecture to us by saying, "Before my lecture I want to tell you something. I am a Christian. I was brought up in a Christian home with my brother, and the two of us were the closest pals. We were both at the university together. My father and mother were deeply religious. My brother and I had no time for religion. We thought that religion was all right for old people, but we were scientists and we thought we had found our way through by what we were pleased to call scientific methods. Then my brother was killed. My father and mother had resources, and with their resources they could meet that shattering loss. But I had no one. I had no resources at all. One night, broken-hearted and with all my proud science in ruined uselessness at my feet, I knelt down. I did not know how to pray. I had scorned prayer, but I put out my hand"—and then in deep emotion the lecturer went on—"*and I found it was grasped.* I knew that Someone was coming to my help and somehow I knew it was Christ. I have been a Christian ever since and no one, nothing, will take Christ from me any more."

My friends, I invite you to find your answer in experience.

Let the scientists say their say, and let us welcome it. Let the philosophers have their word, and let us receive it. Then let us put down our intellectual pride, and let us no longer imagine that the only road to certainty is that of the intellect and let us look quietly at Christ. If we keep on looking, He will do the rest, and, wise or ignorant, intelligent or foolish, I believe we shall find true Reality at His feet.

The Limitations of Reason

THE text is in the prophecy of Isaiah, chapter one, verse eighteen: "Come now, and let us reason together, saith the Lord; though your sins be as scarlet, they shall be as white as snow; though they be red like crimson, they shall be as wool."

Ewald called that grand first chapter of Isaiah the great assize, or the great arraignment. The picture is one of God as both Judge and Plaintiff. The Jewish nation, Israel, is the defendant. The witnesses are the heavens and the earth. "Hear, O heavens, and give ear, O earth, for the Lord hath spoken."[1] "Hear the word of the Lord, ye rulers of Sodom; give ear unto the law of our God, ye people of Gomorrah."[2] The charge is one of brutish stupidity, blind rebellion, meaningless ceremonies, damnable hypocrisy. I wonder if anywhere in literature there is such scathing sarcasm as we find in this chapter, and I cannot refrain from reading again some of those passionate sentences:

"To what purpose is the multitude of your sacrifices unto Me? saith the Lord: I am full of the burnt offerings of rams, and the fat of fed beasts; and I delight not in the blood of bullocks, or of lambs, or of he-goats. When ye come to appear before Me, who hath required this at your hand, to trample My courts? Bring no more vain oblations; incense is an abomination unto Me; new moon and sabbath, the calling of assemblies—I cannot away with iniquity and the solemn meeting. Your new moons and your appointed feasts My soul hateth: they are a trouble unto Me; I am weary to bear them. And when ye spread forth your hands, I

[1] Isaiah 1[2]
[2] Isaiah 1[10]

142

will hide Mine eyes from you: yea, when ye make many prayers, I will not hear: your hands are full of blood. Wash you, make you clean; put away the evil of your doings from before Mine eyes; cease to do evil; learn to do well; seek judgment, relieve the oppressed, judge the fatherless, plead for the widow. Come now, and let us reason together, saith the Lord: though your sins be as scarlet, they shall be as white as snow; though they be red like crimson, they shall be as wool."[1]

Now that last sentence, which is our text, is badly translated. Every preacher on the prophecy of Isaiah goes first to its greatest exponent, Dr. George Adam Smith. He translates in this significant way. "Come now and let us *bring our reasoning to an end.*" It is as though there is the great unanswerable indictment, so that the defendant is utterly crushed and overwhelmed with the charge brought against him, but immediately there follows the offer of the great forgiveness, "though your sins be as scarlet, they shall be as white as snow; though they be red like crimson, they shall be as wool."

1. The first point that I want to make is that, without doubt, reason and argument have their function, but *reason always stops at an unsatisfying place.* Let us suppose that with every justification you argue with a person who has done you a wrong. You hurl your criticism at his face. You feel that reason is on your side. To use a colloquial, but vivid, phrase, you make him "eat his own words". To use another, he "hasn't a leg to stand on". You prove to the hilt that you are right and that he is wrong. Even then, as one of God's children, you feel that you must go further. He is wrong, you are right: so what? What an unsatisfying place to leave matters!

When we turn to our Lord's attitude, we find Him rarely engaging in what would be called now a logical argument. He seems to seek to give men insight rather than to convince the intellect by means of an argument. He paints vivid pictures that men may *see.* I think there are one or two places in

[1] Isaiah 1[11-18]

143

the gospels which we could label "arguments", but He never seems to leave the situation with His victim—if one may use such a word—almost disabled in mind by the authority brought against him.

When a woman is brought to Him who was caught in the very act of adultery, Jesus might have said, "Well, you have only got yourself to blame. You knew that the penalty for adultery is to be stoned to death. You were caught in the act. The evidence was overwhelming. You brought it on yourself. It serves you right . . ." Instead of that He says, "Neither do I condemn you. Go in peace and sin no more." Not, of course, that He thought of that sin, or thinks of any sin, as of no consequence, but He knew that the woman had condemned herself already. When we condemn ourselves, a just and loving God does not add salt to the wound, but oil. The woman is in no doubt about the wrong that she has done. Therefore, as primarily a lover of souls He does not further argue. It is at this point that love goes on and offers pardon. "Let us bring our reasoning to an end; though your sins be as scarlet, they shall be as white as snow."

We do not need to go far away from home to find the kind of illustration which lights up the matter. Few of us can have entirely escaped domestic rows. Perhaps you have been forced to listen while an angry altercation takes place between husband and wife. There may come a moment when the husband says, "But, darling, do be reasonable." If he says that, I for one, am quite sure that he has lost his case, for "darling" never has been reasonable, and "darling" never will be reasonable, and the more he proves that "darling" is wrong, the more resentful "darling" will be. Indeed, the measure of her resentment will probably equal the measure of his convincing proof that she is wrong! This is the place for love to say, "Let us bring our reasoning to a close." They may be able to talk matters over in a calmer atmosphere, but a quarrel never ends satisfactorily at the place where it is left by reason. *There is no healing in reason*, and it is much more important for the man to prove that he loves his wife than to prove her wrong. He will get a very barren victory in the latter case, but a wonderful victory in the former.

Men and women, it is no good our arguing against God. We are sinners and we are convicted sinners, and we are in the dock, and the sentence is utterly just and entirely reasonable. But, thank God, He brings His reasoning to a close and offers forgiveness. This is what we must jump at and accept, pushing our pride away, and this is what we must do for other people, and they must accept it, pushing *their* pride away.

*   *   *

2. The second point I want to make is this. *Christianity is a reasonable religion, but this does not prove to be the strongest case of those who proclaim it.*

For myself, I am deeply happy to think that Christianity is intellectually respectable. In its essentials it does not affront the reason. Were there time and opportunity you would want to challenge me on what the essentials are, and I should shock you by some of the things I should regard as unessential. Things of which the Church makes much, but of which Jesus said nothing—like the Virgin Birth, for instance—I cannot regard as essentials, for how can any matter be essential in a religion if the Founder of that religion never mentioned it? But we must leave that attractive and provocative country.

Sometimes men of science say to us, "But you cannot prove your Christianity." It all depends, of course, on what you mean by "prove". I will claim here three very simple points.

(a) The historicity of Jesus Christ can be as conclusively argued as the historicity of Plato. I never heard any sceptic say that he did not believe Plato ever lived. From non-Christian historians and from extra-Biblical evidence the proof that Jesus Christ lived and taught and died, yes, and the evidence that He rose again, is to my mind incontrovertible. It may be that after forty odd years in the ministry I have overlooked some important point there, but I have never found any flaw in the evidence which can be set forth to prove that Jesus Christ lived and died and lives again, and that the important facts about Him related by four separate evangelists, of differing outlooks, are, broadly true.

(b) I claim that Jesus was not mad, or misreported, or mistaken. If this is madness, it is more attractive than our sanity and widely copied would bring sanity to a mad world. If He is misreported, it is by a strange and incredible collusion of liars and deceivers, and if He was mistaken about God, one can only say that in a similar way Shakespeare was mistaken as to what is a sonnet, Chopin and Beethoven as to what is good music, Turner as to what is a good picture, and so on. For here, to put it at its least, is the Expert on his own subject, the nature of God, which He not only taught, but, the Christian believes, He reveals. Christ not only claimed to be in a unique relationship with God, but He accepted the worship of man. For myself, I would say that He was all of God that could be poured into a human life without disrupting its perfect humanity; that He believed He had the clue to the meaning of life, and that if given a chance He could change men's lives. Unless you say that He was mad, or misreported, or mistaken, I think His case is unanswerable.

(c) The third point I want to make here is that the Church is a growing fellowship. It is encouraging to read the latest report of nine million churchgoers in America. Fancy nine million cultured Americans following a madman! And it is certainly encouraging to hear that there are six hundred million church members in the world—more than a quarter of the entire human race. The world is growing in culture, education and scientific discovery. In every possible way humanity is thrusting out its arms, the arms of reason, and bringing more and more areas within its purview and within its grasp, and yet at the same time this religion is becoming the religion of more and more people. I feel that this is very strong evidence that Christianity is a reasonable religion. As the world becomes better educated more people become Christians.

But again let us say, "So what?" I doubt if anyone has ever been converted by reason. I know it has played a part in the conversion of very thoughtful men like C. S. Lewis, Frank Morison, C. E. M. Joad and a few others, but one of those three I can personally vouch for as finding feeling a more convincing thing than argument. Supposing you prove Christianity reasonable. You have not done your work with another human being, however ready he may be to be convinced. Christianity has been brought to men and they have accepted it, not merely because they are convinced it is true, but because they have had insight. They have seen in it something that they long for, and please God, if they have been lucky they have seen other people whose lives have been changed by it.

What an interesting comment on all this is St. Augustine's tribute to St. Ambrose! St. Ambrose brought Augustine to Christ. The two of them argued endlessly. What a mighty intellectual feast that must have been to listen to! But notice Augustine's comment, "I began to love him not first as a teacher of the truth, but as a fellow creature who was kind to me." I love to picture those two men arguing hammer and tongs, both of them of brilliant intellect, calling to their use all their knowledge and all their dialectical skill, and then Augustine, at the close of some day of heated argument, writing down the words I have just quoted.

My friends, may I warn you from my own failures that while you will be of immense help to the cause of Christ by being able to defend its intellectual position, you will be a ten thousand times more potent missionary if you exhibit a life that Christ has changed, if you show in your nature those fruits for which all men hunger, if you have that quiet serenity, that endless goodwill, that deep joy and that passionate purpose which are amongst the important marks of a nature surrendered to our Lord.

* * *

3. Thirdly, note that it is alleged that reason brings the truth home to us. I wonder . . . Truth is a word too loosely used, and we sometimes forget that truth is of two kinds. We speak of the truth of a matter when we mean information about

147

it conveyed from without. But more importantly truth rises from within the soul, and finds terrific power over personality when from this unconscious or half-conscious depth it arrives in consciousness.

Let me illustrate what I mean. The outward kind of truth can certainly be arrived at by reason and argument. Let us call it ascertainable truth. The astronomer tells me that this star is ten million light years from that star, and I suppose if I had the ability and the time and could follow the steps of the argument, I could arrive at the same degree of certainty as he possesses. It is ascertainable truth. It can be conveyed to my mind from outside.

If that argument sounds profound and difficult we can take a humbler one. If your friend says, "My Aunt Lucy weighs fourteen stone," I may look at her and kindly say, "I doubt it." You may say, "Come with me!" We produce the scales, and if she is willing, we persuade her to mount them. We test her weight on another scale, and on yet another, and behold the unpalatable truth is proved—Aunt Lucy weighs fourteen stone! It is ascertainable truth.

What I want to interest you in is the other kind of truth for which a different word should be reserved. I would choose the word "insight". It is an inner certainty concerning something that hitherto has been secretly known and is now revealed. I wonder if you know what I mean. Sometimes I preach a sermon that I have a wicked pride about because I think it is original. Someone is sure to come up and say, "Thank you so much for your sermon. I have always thought that." They even say, "I have always *known* that." It was a buried knowledge, or a half-buried knowledge, which has got a new power because it has become more fully conscious, and, joking apart, I love to hear them say it.

I am quite sure that our minds go to incalculable depths and join up with other minds, and ultimately with the universal mind, and the truth that is not science so much as wisdom, and is not so much outwardly conveyed as inwardly revealed, is of far greater importance.

Now here we must listen to Browning. This is from "Para-celsus."

> "Truth is within ourselves; it takes no rise
> From outward things, whate'er you may believe.
> There is an inmost centre in us all
> Where truth abides in fulness; and around,
> Wall upon wall, the gross flesh hems it in,
> This perfect, clear perception—which is truth.
> A baffling and perverting carnal mesh
> Binds it and makes all error, and to *know*
> Rather consists in opening out a way
> Whence the imprisoned splendour may escape
> Than in effecting entry for a light
> Supposed to be without."

You will remember that when Jesus preached, the people did not go home looking puzzled, saying, "Well, no doubt He was very clever, but it was all over our heads." Their faces shone and "the common people heard Him gladly". "He speaks with authority," they said, and it was the authority of something perceived to be true because in a sense it had always been part of the truth possessed by the deep mind. They *recognised* truth through insight.

Beauty has the same kind of appeal. If I took you to the Alps at dawn on a summer's day and showed you the sunrise over the snow, you would not want ten reasons for believing it is beautiful. You would be impatient of one. There is so much beauty inside you already that it recognises its own nature in the outward world and you are speechless and reason is miles behind.

So it is, of course, with music. What is the good of my giving you twelve reasons for believing that Beethoven's sonatas are good music? I might prove their perfect form to you. That is knowledge conveyed from outside and in its sphere convincing, but either you would say to me, "I get nothing out of it," or you would be almost speechless with delight. The music in your own heart would have been made conscious by Beethoven, and you would need no reason, for insight would have taken you far beyond its pedestrian, feeble, staggering steps.

So Jesus does not try to prove God's Providence. He says, "Behold the birds of the air." And He does not say here are ten reasons for thinking of God in terms of beauty. He says, "Look at the lilies!"

Again and again, men have had experiences like that of Sidney Lanier, the American poet, lying prostrate, broken, defeated and in despair, and then beholding a single violet and saying afterwards, "A violet saved me from despair." So Tennyson, holding a flower in his hand, says:

> "Flower in the crannied wall
> I pluck you out of the crannies.
> I hold you here, root and all in my hand,
> Little flower!—but if I could understand
> What you are, root and all and all in all,
> I should know what God and man is."

Says Pascal, "The heart has its reasons which the reason knows not."

* * *

So let us bring our reasoning to a close. It has its place, but our first point was that it is a very unsatisfying place. Christianity is a reasonable religion, but in the second place do not let us suppose that that will convince another. Reason is supposed to bring the truth home to us, but it stops far short of insight. In your dealings with others, do not stop when you have proved them wrong. Love them into the right. Do not think that when you have allayed their doubts, you have allayed their fears. Your courage is a higher card in your hands than your intellect, and never think that reason brings men to the place of truth unless also you can make them see.

Let me finish with this true parable. During the second World War there was a transport vessel carrying hundreds of troops and four chaplains—a Roman Catholic, a Jewish chaplain and two Protestants, an Anglican and a Methodist. The father of the Methodist chaplain has preached for us in the old City Temple. You can possibly imagine what sort of arguments those four chaplains had had in their spare time during the voyage. I must say that for myself I should like to have joined in.

But one dark night in a cold, northern sea the transport ship was torpedoed and began to sink. Life-belts were insufficient. Each chaplain unfastened his own and gave it to one of the men. Finally those four chaplains joined their hands together and went down with the ship. Oh, what a sermon on Christian unity and Christian love was there, my friends! Not one of them ever preached such an eloquent sermon as that. When they stopped arguing and revealed love they all did their best work for their Master. Come and let us draw our reasonings to a close, and let us look with insight on the Cross. For there Love goes on beyond all reason. There Love convinces beyond all argument. There Love brings home the truth to us, until, all doubts and questions silenced, we only want to kneel and worship and adore.

Is Christianity the Only Way to God?

(A Missionary Sunday Sermon)

AMONGST my letters recently there was one which puts a question we all ought to face, and it is peculiarly appropriate to the Sunday we call Missionary Sunday, when we consider the world-wide kingdom of Christ. Here is the paragraph:

"Can the tree of truth have Christianity as one of its branches? Can other world religions be also branches, or must all other outlooks be changed for ours in name as well as in spirit? We" (meaning the writer and her husband) "have deep friendships with Indians, and whereas we find unity of outlook in our ideals, we see little hope of making them active Christians in their own country when they return, partly because they think of it as a political link with the West. We are convinced that they are as near to the truth as we are, but Christianity does seem to impose very exclusive terms. Are these necessary, or is it possible that Christ speaks directly, even under another name, with those who are not recognised by fellow Christians?"

It may be said at once that some branches of the Christian Church are quite exclusive; so exclusive that they would not like to be called "branches". The Roman Catholic Church does not talk about other *churches*, but of other "bodies." It regards itself as the only true "church". Its only idea of unity is absorption. It demands complete conformity to its doctrines and ceremonies, so that if I were a Roman Catholic, I should have to tell members of other religions to renounce them and come over entirely to the Roman Catholic way of life and thought.

But a great many Christians in other denominations feel

sympathetic with the writer of the letter. They feel enormously drawn to those attractive Indians and Chinese and Africans who live exemplary lives but who do not adopt the tenets of Christianity. Yet I think such Christians have twinges of loyalty to Christianity which make them wonder whether their tolerance is not too far reaching. Loyalty to Christianity seems to call them to exclusiveness, but loyalty to their own inner light makes them wonder if such exclusiveness is really Christian!

Let me this morning be, at any rate, entirely honest. To my mind Christianity is certainly not the only way to God. Who can suppose that Billy Graham's latest convert, a youngster with an imperfect knowledge of, and an untested faith in, Christianity, is in any sense "saved," to use the old-fashioned phrase, while a devout Buddhist or Hindu, who through a lifetime has meditated on truth and reality and practised the highest way of life he knows, is, by a just, loving and holy God, excluded, or in any sense finally shut out from the fellowship of the saints?

*   *   *

Let me here bring before you two texts. Acts 10^{35}: "In every nation he that feareth God and worketh righteousness is acceptable to Him"; and again in Acts 14$^{16-17}$: "God suffered all the nations to walk in their own ways, but left not Himself without witness."

When we ask whether God can be found in other religions, we do not need to turn to Mohammedanism, Hinduism, or Buddhism. Let us turn to Judaism. That is not the Christian religion. Yet when we read that "Enoch walked with God," that "Abraham was the friend of God", that "Moses communed with God", that David lost even his fear of death through his sense of the divine companionship, how can we possibly say that they were all deceived because they were not Christians; that since Christ had not come, they could not possibly have access to God? Such a claim would be nonsense. Surely, then, in other religions, those who have sought the light and have longed for fellowship with God, have found

153

something real, even if we think it incomplete. We should never, by our superior attitude, pretend that they are excluded from the all-embracing love and care of God.

* * *

Having said that, I want to go on very quickly and add that I have never discovered, or read about, any religion which fills the word "God" with such glorious meaning as does Christianity. Perhaps that is another way of saying that, in my opinion, no other path up the mountain of truth leads towards the summit so directly, or comes so nearly to its goal as Christianity.

This, I think, is true not so much because of the profound truths that Jesus taught. In the mere teaching of truth, other teachers do not fall so far below Him. Jesus we regard as in a different category, for we regard Him as divine, and for our purposes this morning I mean that this Man was filled with the spirit of God more than any man, and indeed was as full of God as man could be without his humanity being disrupted.

We notice the difference at once when we compare Him with teachers like Isaiah, who point away from themselves that we may see something of the glory of God. Christ, in such a striking and significant way, points to Himself. "*I* am the Light of the world." "*I* am the Way." He can even, it is reported, say, "No one cometh unto the Father but by Me." If these were not His exact words they represent a view of Him held by a reverent mind which had loved Him and possibly known Him. The Old Testament had often likened God to a father, but had likened Him also to a tyrant and a despot and a jealous tribal God. It is as though Jesus is saying, "You will find from Me that He is never anything but a Father, and that all ways of viewing Him which contradict My revelation must be considered false." It is, of course, a unique claim and a unique revelation, and if both be accepted, then surely there can be no more direct way or means of proceeding further towards God than is implicit in Christ.

It was because we believed this in India that forty years ago some of us supported an experiment which drew much criticism and, I fear, stopped some subscriptions! Hindu professors were invited to speak on Hinduism to our Christian students in Madras. Many critics raised their voices: "You were sent out to teach Christianity. What do you think you are doing?" But what a poor Christianity it would be if Hinduism could be shown to be a better way to God, to hold up higher ideals, to reveal a better God altogether. One could not help thinking of the man who at Darjeeling asked where the Himalayas were, and someone pointed to the foothills and said, "There they are in front of you." But when the sun had dispelled the mists, he beheld the glories of Everest and Kanchenjunga. We believed—and I still believe—that when the exponent of another religion has painted his faith in the most glowing colours, it lies on the horizon, beautiful, it is true, as the purple foothills are beautiful, but Christianity rises like Everest with its unstained snows and peerless splendour far above the foothills, let alone the fever haunted jungle and scrub at the bottom of the valleys. Instead of excluding others on their way to God, we should rather welcome the pathways they open up, for some of them lead to truths we have not yet received. But then we may point to Christ and His revelation, as one who enjoys low-level glories, delights even more at sunrise to raise his finger and point to the snow.

I have often meditated on the pregnant words of an old Hindu of thoughtful mind and devout character who, having heard about Christ, said this: "I have known Him all my life and now you have told me His name." It is as though the old man had dreamed of the snow, and even caught glimpses through the mists, and then saw it in unveiled splendour and learnt the Name above every name.

Professor E. L. Allen, who is Head of the Department of Divinity at King's College (University of Durham) at Newcastle-upon-Tyne, was a missionary in the Far East for more than five years. He told recently of a Japanese Buddhist, "for whom," he says, "the word 'Christlike' was the natural epithet." Then he adds this, "A Japanese woman, head of a school in Osaka, told me that she had become a Christian through contact with him." Dr. Allen adds: "We can do no other than see in it the will of God and a rebuke to our shortcomings. It almost seems as though our witness of Christ is so pitifully inadequate that He can speak to the hearts of some men better if they remain in their tradition than He could if they abandoned it for ours." Yes, we could put that more popularly by saying that there is more likelihood of revealing the nature of Christianity by being a good Buddhist than by being a bad Baptist, though some narrow-minded people would exclude the former from the kingdom of Christ and include the latter in it.

*　　*　　*

A third point that I want to make is that our own interpretation of Christ may be enriched by the teaching in other faiths, for all these other faiths contain truth. Truth is one and Christ is truth. Says Dr. Allen in words which command my entire agreement: "I never entered a Chinese village for evangelism with the sense that I was taking Christ there for the first time, but always as one convinced that He had been there before me." Then he adds: "There is a latent Christ in the hearts of men the world over. In India and China and Africa He walks the Emmaus road with them, even though they do not perceive who it is who is by their side." I agree, and we must allow these unconscious Christians to show us Christ as they have seen Him through their intuitive insights and their experiences of life.

I have every sympathy with the little Indian girl who wept a little when, having heard about Jesus, she saw a portrait of Him with a very white face and golden hair. No Indian is like that. "I didn't think He would be like that," she sobbed, and in a sense He isn't like that. It is as though the true portrait were a composite one. The practical West may paint His hands. I would let the Indian paint His eyes. I would invite the African, who knows so much about bearing burdens, to paint His shoulders, and I would let the Chinese and Japanese paint His feet. But we shall never really know the fulness of Christ, or what Christ is really like, until all the nations have brought the treasures of their thought and insight to the final and complete revelation. Christ has revealed God, but who shall reveal Christ? In this task all nations must play a part, not *merely* the practical West with its materialistic values, and its too often repeated attempt to thrust its home-made Christ on other peoples of the world.

* * *

I hope no one present will say, "Well, if these other religions contain so much truth, and if there are many other ways up the mountain besides the Christian way, why don't we leave these native peoples to their native religions? Why do we bother to send the gospel to them?"

It is incredible to me that anybody can have followed the sermon so far and feel like that, for we have so much more to give, as I have tried to show. Further, it may be said that the test of a religion is not the ideals that are printed in its sacred books, but the way it works out in the lives of the people who follow it. Aldous Huxley can write a beautiful book by culling scraps of philosophy and idealism from a score of sources, but I have seen Hinduism at work.

Now do not turn round on me and say that Christianity has nothing to be proud of in Christian countries; that the Indian, for example, can watch life in our own country and say "Why do you bring your religion to my country? It hasn't done much for your own. Look at this evil and that!" Where evil is done, Christianity is thereby denied. But there are situations in which it is true to say that in India where evil is done, *Hinduism is being expressed*: in the treatment of little prostitute girls in the temples, for instance.

I do not know any religion that works out in terms of living with greater happiness or fulness of life than Christianity as Christ taught it and lived it. There will still be much sorrow, but there will not be hopeless despair, and Christ's joy—one can say without fear of contradiction—has no counterpart in any other faith in the world.

* * *

157

Let me remind you, as we close, that the mental concept of a missionary has immensely altered in the last fifty years. It used to be of a man in clerical dress standing under a palm-tree holding a Bible and demanding that his listeners give up everything in their old faith in order that they might receive his version of his own, and often it was a narrow, fundamentalist, intolerant version at that.

A modern missionary goes out to learn as well as to teach. He still hears Christ saying: "I came not to destroy, but to fill full with meaning; to take truth a step further than your teachers have been able to do."

Secondly, the missionary goes out to witness, not to exclude. He offers what seems to me an unanswerable argument for Christian missions, for he says, by his deeds as well as by his words, "I have found Someone Who means so much to me that I want others to know Him too. I want them to know the light and joy and peace which He has brought to my heart. He has revolutionised my life and He can do the same for you."

No one can possibly object to meeting a new Friend for Whom such claims can be made and indeed substantiated, for the greatest argument for Christianity can be put in one sentence: If people will take Jesus Christ seriously, He can and does change their lives.

So, my friends, you will be invited to pray and serve and give so that the world kingdom of Christ may be extended. Let us be sincere in this matter. Be careful that you are not paying for others to be offered what you have rejected. I can leave this matter of overseas missions with you. If you have no Christian experience, you will not be missionary minded whatever I can say. If you know Christ, you will want others to know Him too. In religion it is what we have ourselves experienced that we want to pass on.

Some Meanings of Pentecost

(A Whitsuntide Sermon)

MOST Christians believe in the doctrine of the Holy Trinity. They think of Father, Son and Holy Spirit, three Persons in the unity of a Divine Being. This is indeed a difficult conception, but then we should expect that the nature of God is far beyond our comprehension. Indeed, I do not know anyone who pretends to understand the nature of man, let alone the nature of God. Perhaps the idea of the Trinity is the least erroneous way in which man can speculate about God. Sometimes I think it is too clever to be true! Sometimes I think it is not nearly clever enough to be true and that it is absurd for little man to think that with his puny mind he can put a measuring tape around the nature of that august Being we call God.

The point that I want to make first this morning is that whether we think of the Father, the Son or the Spirit touching our lives today, *in experience* there is no difference. God the Father does not draw near to us in a different way from God the Son or God the Spirit. *In experience* there is no distinction. In the fourth chapter of Acts, at verse eight, we read that Peter was "filled with the Holy Ghost and spake unto the people". In verse thirteen, we find that the deduction of his hearers was that he had been with *Jesus*. Both statements were true. There is no difference in experience.

We saw last Sunday—Ascensiontide—how the risen Christ performed a ministry, during forty wonderful days, in which He planted a sense of His Presence in the unseen. In other words, He taught men to appreciate that Presence without the need of their physical senses. That He succeeded is abundantly proved in that when He did disappear from their sight, they felt no sense of being deserted. When we say "Goodbye" to a beloved dear one we are sad. But we read about the Ascension that when He departed from their sight, they "returned to Jerusalem with great joy," and proceeded to preach and to teach, conscious of that ever-present Friend still with them.

Then came this tremendous experience which we celebrate today. They had been told to wait for an experience of power —"Tarry ye here until ye receive power"—and then the amazing thing happened which is described in the second chapter of Acts already read to you.

For myself, I am convinced that the experience of Pentecost was not predominantly for the Apostles the coming of the third Person of the Holy Trinity, but rather the experience of their beloved Master convincingly in their midst once more. Had He not promised to do this very thing? Let us turn to some of His own words. "I will not leave you desolate; I will come to you."[1] And again, "There be some of them that stand here which shall in no wise taste of death till they see the Son of man coming in His kingdom."[2] He told them that they should not have gone through the cities of Israel until the Son of man be come.[3] He told them that *they* should *see* the Son of man coming with great power and glory.[4] No distant "coming" could fulfil these words. Pentecost meant their fulfilment. They had only made a beginning on the cities of Israel, and not one of them had tasted of death save Judas, and here Jesus was with them in power and glory, as He said.[5] I do not mean to deny that this was a coming of the Spirit, but it was also a coming of Christ in the power of the Spirit, and there can be no difference, I repeat, *in experience*.

*   *   *

One hesitates to criticise any branch of the Christian Church, but I have never quite understood why the Second Adventists

[1] John 14[18]   [2] Matthew 16[28]. Luke 9[27]   [3] Matthew 10[23]   [4] Mark 13[26]
[5] Matthew 24[29-31]; Mark 13[24-27]; Luke 21[25-28]

are still awaiting the fulfilment of a prophecy which was fulfilled at Pentecost. I have no doubt that human history will have a worthy climax; that the prayer which Christian people offer every day—"Thy kingdom come on earth"—will be answered, and that the consummation of all things will be in a true sense a "coming" of Christ. But one does not need to be a psychologist to realise that no mind can hold at the same time two contradictory ideas, and if a branch of the Church is focusing on a future "coming," it is the more difficult to focus on a far more important truth, that Christ is here in our midst *now*. His promises are already fulfilled, and the hope of a future "coming" should be translated into the realisation of a present power.

* * *

I think we shall not get the best out of our meditation on Pentecost if we concentrate our minds too much on the phenomena, on the fire and the winds and the supposedly foreign tongues. I sometimes wonder if the wind and the fire do not illustrate the impossibility of conveying to others a great experience. I may be quite wrong in this and perhaps psychic research will one day interpret for us the two words "wind" and "fire," for certainly the blowing of a strong wind is the concomitant of many psychic experiences. But there may be a much simpler solution. Men have said, "I felt on fire with the Presence of God," or, "I felt as if a great wind were sweeping through the place and cleansing us all?"

As for the tongues, I find it difficult to believe that simple Galilean peasants suddenly began to speak in foreign languages. For one thing, there was no necessity for them to do so, since Hellenistic Greek was the world language, understood and spoken by all those whose countries are mentioned in the second chapter of Acts. Peter could not even speak his own language without a brogue that gave him away. Did he suddenly start talking Italian without understanding himself what he was talking about? It doesn't sound like him to me, nor does it sound like evidence that God was with him. Further, Babel, where there was a confusion of tongues,[1] represented to the Jews the *disapproval* of God. It would be difficult for Jews to regard foreign tongues as a symbol of the Divine favour. Further still, there *were* no specific languages belonging to the Cretans.[2]

I am in no doubt myself that what happened, and what so surprised the multitude, was that Galilean peasants, who normally spoke with a strong brogue and in dialects as different from one another as Scottish is from the brogue of Somerset, were all found to be speaking clearly in eloquent Greek.

This point is illustrated for me by an experience that happened to a friend of mine, Professor J. Alexander Findlay. He tells us[3] that when he began his ministry, he was sent direct from Cambridge to a colliery village in Durham. He found it difficult to understand a word of the dialect spoken by his flock. But he tells us of a Durham miner, whom normally he could not understand, who, when he prayed at a prayer meeting, "poured forth a flood of beautiful language without a trace of dialect." Dr. Findlay writes, "If I could have copied down his prayers in shorthand and published them, I am sure they would have been recognised as classics of devotion. They were not simply a patchwork of verses taken from the Bible or the hymn book. They were his own and yet not his own. I asked him once to let me write them down, but he could not reproduce them. I have always thought this a supernatural gift and have met no psychologist who could explain it to my satisfaction. There was no evidence that he had ever met anyone capable of teaching him such prayers, or that he had ever read them. Incidentally he was the greatest saint I have ever known . . . and when I try to visualise the face of Jesus, that of Isaac Hewitson at prayer comes to my mind: he was lit from within." Dr. Findlay continues, "The secret of power is to be possessed by the Spirit of God; this involves no mere enhancement of a man's own faculties; it is a supernatural endowment."

[1] See Genesis 11[1-9]

[2] Acts 2[11]   [3] *British Weekly*, November 26th, 1942

So we have the story of a sense of the power of the risen Christ which *intoxicated* these men. I use the word carefully, for they were charged with being drunk, and I can never escape the feeling that Peter had a great sense of humour in the answer he gave to the charge. When those in the crowd said disgustedly, "They are filled with new wine," Peter did not seem at all offended by this attack on their respectability. He merely pointed out that being only nine o'clock in the morning, the pubs had not yet opened! "These are not drunk as ye suppose, seeing it is but the third hour of the day." Tonight, in our service, the Choir will lead us in the chanting of the General Confession and we shall pray that hereafter we may live "a godly, righteous and *sober* life." But I wonder sometimes if we are too sober. The impression made by the Apostles was that they were drunk; intoxicated with God.

To read the book of Acts is to read a book which is at once thrilling and depressing. It is thrilling to read the story of these men full of power and full of joy. They went out through the known world, preaching, teaching, healing, inspiring, and, in spite of opposition, hostility and persecution, they won men and women everywhere to the new way. Nothing could stop them, not even the might of imperial Rome, and is there in literature a more thrilling story than the story of that radiant Christian witness, of that infectious Christian living, of that unquenchable enthusiasm?

But the book of Acts is depressing also, for we make comparisons and wistfully look around us at church life in our own day. Conversions are rare, few are added to the Church, fewer still are healed. We criticise one another's methods and maintain our denominational walls. Five out of six churches could be closed without the neighbourhood noticing any loss of spiritual impact, and in some areas six congregations could get into the one church left open. We have more public support than the Apostles, more money, beautiful buildings and lovely music. We are supported by distinguished people, praised even by politicians, regarded as part of the State, and now many, even of the scientists—with some condescension here and there—acknowledge that there may be something in religion. But we have completely lost anything that could even remotely be called the wind and the fire of Pentecost. As a Methodist friend of mine lamented, "We have got into the House of Lords, but we have lost the hallelujahs from the front pew!" We have developed the most amazing organisation, but is it not rather like building more and more machinery when we haven't enough current to drive the machinery already installed? Is it like putting a heavy gold chain on to a five-shilling watch that won't go? Many of us attend more meetings than the divine plan can ever have contemplated, until I, at least, am reminded of the steamboats that used to take us up the River Tigris in the first World War. When they blew the whistle, the ship stopped, there being insufficient steam for both at the same time. We blow the whistle loudly enough, but we are not making much progress upstream.

*   *   *

What can we do? I should like to point out three things that preceded Pentecost in the lives of the Apostles, and I think we must pay attention to these three things before we can claim the power of Pentecost.

1. They had been with Jesus

This sounds very easy, but if you had been reading the Gospels wrongly, do try to get the picture straightened out in your mind. Maybe you have imagined these men sitting down on the green grass and watching Jesus, in a spotless white robe, preaching the Gospel in the open air, or stretching out healing hands over a patient suffering from some invisible illness. You may have imagined how lovely it would have been to have been with Him. He certainly was never really poor, for Judas kept a bag and a committee of women in Jerusalem kept it filled. You would not have felt much risk in being with a person who could feed five thousand people from half-a-dozen sandwiches, and you would not have feared enemies in the presence of one who could raise the dead. But I would ask you to correct the picture. The disciples continually were physically tired out. On the Mount of Transfiguration they fell asleep on the warm heather as soon as He gave them a chance by going yet further up the steep crags of the mountain. In the Garden of Gethsemane, although they loved Him dearly, they fell asleep and brought upon themselves His pathetic reproach, "Could you not watch even one hour?"

Mentally He must have strained them to the utmost, for we have been discussing His words for two thousand years and still find some of them most difficult to understand. Spiritually He took them into a new continent of experience and feeling. Again and again, they must have wished that He were a little more conventional, or easier to understand and to follow. Do not forget, when you think how nice it would have been to have been with Him, that many turned back and followed Him no more. But a few did stick to Him, and that stiff training prepared them to receive power.

*　　*　　*

2. THEY HAD BEEN WITH ONE ANOTHER

and one feels sure that that was not as easy as it sounds. Use your imagination a little and you will see what I mean. Peter, for instance was a fisherman with a dialect or brogue or accent, as we say, that you could cut with a knife. Indeed, it was his Galilean brogue that gave him away when his Master was taken prisoner. You will remember the words of the girl who said, "Thy speech betrayeth thee." He slurred his syllables, we are told, and could not disguise his accent. I wonder also if his clothes smelt of fish, and whether he boasted, as fishermen do, of the size of the fish he had taken! Think of Judas not in terms of his alleged defection, but in terms of his political fanaticism. He was the Sinn Feiner of the party. How would you Conservatives like a man who would not stop talking Socialism, and how would you Socialists like a fanatical capitalist always attacking your political theories? Then we must think of James and John who, Dr. Barclay tells us, were the cousins of Jesus, and who used their relationship to try to secure the best places in the kingdom. "Grant that we may sit the one on Your right and the other on Your left, etc." How would you get on with these sneaking little seekers for pride of place? And do not forget Simon, the Zealot, for, being a Zealot, he was pledged to drive his knife into the back of anyone who took money from patriotic Jews and handed it over to Rome. How did Simon feel when Matthew walked into the upper room for the first time? Matthew did this very thing every day. You can nearly hear Simon saying, "Oh! Surely not Matthew! An impossible person!" This is ridiculous! Jesus really can't expect us to have him in the team!

Yet, you see, they became one. They really did become a fellowship. Just as some metals in a fierce heat become an alloy stronger than any one of the separate metals, so in the blazing heat of the love of Jesus, these differing personalities became a unity in unbreakable loyalty to one another and to Christ. We have a long way to go, haven't we, before that is true of the modern Church? Even in this place I have heard A describe B as "impossible." I have known C withdraw from this fellowship because D entered it. And what of our attitude to other denominations? How the Devil must love the present attack on Rome by some members of the Church of England, and the sneers with which some members of the latter regard what they called recently "Nonconformist sects", to one of which, the Church of Scotland, Her Majesty the Queen belongs as soon as she crosses the Tweed on her way to Scotland!

I repeat, we cannot expect the power of Pentecost until we keep the conditions of those who had lived with Jesus and, by His grace, learnt to live with one another.

* * *

3. THEY HAD BEEN IN CONTACT WITH THE NEEDY SOULS AROUND THEM

That is an important condition of power. If in this pulpit I stood on a thick mat of dry india-rubber, I could lift up my hand and touch a live cable carrying one thousand volts

without any harm to myself, for the simple reason that elec-
tricity will not come in unless it can go out. The same is true
of the power of the Holy Spirit. If I try to make my religion
a soul-saving smug little bit of self-satisfaction for myself; if I
say my prayers and read *Daily Light* or *In His Steps* or even the
New Testament, only to save my own soul, my devotion will
become so self-centred and stagnant that I shall be self-
poisoned. Power comes in when it can get out.

You must forgive my talking like this, for you have every
reason to say, "Well, it's all very well for you. You are paid
to preach and teach and help others." But I can only challenge
myself and you that until our lives touch others in Christ's
name, they remain insulated from the very power that they
need. You could write a letter, lend a book, bring someone
to church, visit someone with healing sympathy, say the right
word at the right moment, and do a score of things which
would carry the current of God's love not only to others, but
induce it into your own heart.

* * *

You may say to yourself as we meditate on Pentecost, "Ah!
But these men received a *gift*." Here again must we not pause
to remember that so many of the gifts of God can only be taken
and used by those who undergo a discipline. Without such
discipline, many "gifts" are valueless. We may say of the
poet, "What a gift he has!" But if you care to study the original
of Tennyson's "In Memoriam," you will find that there is
hardly a line that has not been altered as this painstaking
poet disciplined himself to correct and re-correct word after
word.

We have all been thinking of Elgar lately, for it is just one
hundred years ago since that great composer was born. Let
me quote to you from one of his letters to his publisher. "I
don't want to send you the manuscript until I have been
through it again and again and again and again, and after
that once more."[1]

[1] *Letters of Edward Elgar*, Percy Young, p. 82 (Geoffrey Bles)

I suppose his most famous composition is "The Dream of Gerontius," published in 1900. We are told that he took twelve years to write it.[1] When next you hear it and rejoice in God's gift to Elgar, remember those twelve years. At the end of the score in the original manuscript, Elgar wrote these words: "This is the best of me. For the rest, I ate, I drank, I slept, I loved, I hated as another. My life was as a vapour and is not. But this is what I saw and know. This, if anything of mine, is worth your memory."[2] When a friend praised "The Dream of Gerontius," Elgar said simply, "Well, that is my religion." *After twelve years' discipline*, you perceive, he could use what was a *gift*.

Let us not then just be content to bleat hymns full of the phrase, "Come, O Holy Spirit," without realising that the men who received the gift endured a discipline. They had been with Jesus, had been with one another in real fellowship, and had made contact with the pagan world around them.

* * *

Can we do these three things?

1. In his book, *The Gates of New Life*,[3] Dr. James Stewart reminds us of an incident in the life of Napoleon:

"There was a day in Napoleon's life when disaffection and mutiny had broken out among the men of the Old Guard, and the risk was great. But Napoleon knew how to meet it. He sat alone in a little room in his palace, a room which had two large apartments opening off it to right and left; and in the hall to the left the members of the Guard were assembled. Each man was summoned alone to Napoleon, and, as he entered, the door was shut. Not a word was spoken; but Napoleon clasped the man's hand and looked him full in the face. Then each passed out again by the door on the right, until the whole of the Guard, one by one, had passed through. And when all had passed, the disaffection and the

[1] *Elgar, O. M.*, Percy Young, p. 317 (Collins)
[2] *Edward Elgar, His Life and Music*, Diana McVeagh, p, 129 (Dent)
[3] P. 101 (T. & T. Clark)

168

mutiny were over. The silent look and the handclasp had done their work: every man of them was Napoleon's now."

In the same way our Master calls us to renewed loyalty.

2. Can we practise fellowship? Do we not all know families where there is something approaching hatred, where there are unkind silences, critical words, bitter dissensions? I can think of elderly people miserable because they feel in the way; young people miserable because they are not understood; husband and wife keeping together for convention, but icily aloof in spirit. It is the lack of fellowship that brings divorce; the lack of fellowship in industry that brings strike and lock-out; the lack of fellowship amongst nations that means war. Let us always be bridge-builders, fellowship makers.

3. Let us remember that spiritual contact with others is not just the preserve of the minister of religion, but the condition of spiritual power in every one of Christ's followers. Every day every one of us can drop seeds of kindness, understanding, sympathy, love.

I read recently of Dr. Leslie Hunter, once Archdeacon of Northumberland and now Bishop of Sheffield, who told of a dream. The dreamer entered a spacious store in which the gifts of God were kept, and behind the counter was an angel. In his dream the would-be purchaser said, "I have run out of the fruits of the Spirit. Can you restock me?" When the angel seemed about to refuse, the dreamer angrily burst out, "In place of war, injustice, lying, hate, tyranny, I want love, joy, peace, integrity. . . . Without these I shall be lost." But the angel behind the counter replied, "We do not stock fruits. We only keep seed."[5]

I would like you to go from our Whitsuntide worship with the words of an old Gaelic saying ringing in your ears: "I, too, will turn *my* face to the wind and cast *my* handful of seed on high."

[5] I owe this reference to a sermon preached by the Rev. Howard J. Clinebell, Minister of the Methodist Church, Great Neck, near New York.

The Religion of the Dawn

IN that excellent monthly publication, "The Reader's Digest," I read in a recent number an article called "You can't hold back the dawn." The writer, Clarence Hall, tells of a journey he made some years ago to the Holy Places of Palestine. He very much wished to attend the Sunrise Service on Easter Morning held at the Garden Tomb, one of the two traditional places of Christ's burial, and, as I think, the more likely. The night before seemed endless. He was restless and could not sleep. Querulously he turned to the Christian Arab, who had promised to be his guide, and asked him if the night would ever pass. He writes, "Abdul's face in the candlelight rebuked me, 'Never fear, my friend. The day will come. You can't hold back the dawn.' Two hours later at the Garden Tomb, the service began. The minister read from the Bible with the aid of an electric torch and the choir sang Easter anthems. Then, with dramatic suddenness, the sun burst over the horizon, banishing the gloom and flooding the sky with light. I remembered Abdul's phrase: 'You can't hold back the dawn.'"

*   *   *

I call Christianity "The Religion of the Dawn" because, if I may so put it, it has a Dawn-Answer for every situation. It does not pretend that there is no night. Nor, though here we must desert the figure, does it counsel that nothing can be done to hasten the dawn. But it is a religion of unquenchable faith and hope and patience; unquenchable because it believes that the permanent thing is light and the passing thing is darkness; that however long the night, whether it be in world affairs or the poignant private world of the human heart, the night will pass. "You can't hold back the dawn." All affairs, private and world-wide, are in the hands of a God who is in complete and final control and who has decreed the entire conquest of all evil and the final emergence of indescribable good.

*　　*　　*

I think my description of Christianity, "The Religion of the Dawn," is not ill-chosen, for Christianity was born in the most wonderful dawn in the world's history.

Cast your mind back, if you will, to early beginnings. Watch those young men whom Jesus called to Him,—Andrew, Peter, Matthew, John and the rest. I suppose we shall never be able to enter into the darkness of the night that overwhelmed them when they shivered behind shut doors on the night when their Master was taken and on the next day when He was brutally put to death. They had heard His words of new life. They had watched His marvellous deeds. They had seen Him raise the dead. Who would have thought He would let Himself be taken, tortured and murdered by a handful of Jews? Was He not in command of supernatural forces? Had He not spoken of legions of angels ready to do His bidding? And now it was all over! He was dead and they were disillusioned. Where were all His promises about a new kingdom and their privileged places in it? What now of His talk about the whole world responding to His message?

And then, at dawn on Easter morning the Resurrection! After the great darkness, this amazing dawn! Within seven weeks they—the hunted, frightened fugitives—had become flaming missionaries and willing martyrs ready to lay down their lives rather than deny the truth of His risen glory and His transforming power. Christianity was launched on its world mission. From the East the dawn-light spread across the skies of the world. The religion of the dawn!

*　　*　　*

But there was a second darkness. They thought He would return in their own lifetime and that that return would be the end of the world they had known. Some of His own words lent credence to this. St. Paul preached at one time this very message. Men actually left their work. It seemed silly to go on making pottery that would never be used, or ploughs that would make furrows for seed that would never come to harvest. It seemed feeble to slave for a master when *the* Master would soon return and open a new era on a new plane of heavenly existence.

But He came not. What did come was persecution. The first epistle of Peter was written against a background of the terrible persecution of A.D. 65 when saints were martyred, not delivered, and when to confess Christ's name meant certainly a new life in one sense, but a quick death as well. Says the letter to the Hebrews (11^{35ff}) : women were tortured, mocked, scourged. Men were stoned, sawn asunder and slain with the sword. "They went about in sheepskins and goatskins; being destitute, afflicted, evil entreated of whom the world was not worthy, wandering in deserts and mountains and caves and the holes of the earth."

What sort of new day was this? They were happier before it dawned.

One is reminded of a story told by Hilaire Belloc. With a friend he set out one evening to climb in the Pyrenees. They were caught in a terrible storm and the night came on. Thunder roared and lightning flashed. Rain drenched them and the tempest all but dragged them from their hold on the rocks amongst which they sought to shelter through the long and terrifying night. Belloc's friend was new to the experience. "Isn't this terrible?" he shouted to his friend. "It seems like the end of the world." Back came the reassurance of the more experienced traveller. "This is how the dawn comes in the Pyrenees," he said.

And again and again in Christian history, both widespread and personal, the dawn has seemed born of storm and tempest, danger and horror, tears and death, but it has come, and its light has spread across the world.

*   *   *

Is it merely wishful thinking to suppose that Christianity is really like the dawn? Is it as certain? Is it as all-conquering?

I think we may say that it is not merely wishful thinking to believe in its power when we consider three points.

1. *What Christianity has done.*

Admittedly it has been the cause of much quarrelling, strife and bloodshed, of cruelty, persecution and intolerance. But it has always fought evil, when it was recognised to be evil.

It tackled slavery and overcame that darkness. It tackled the evils of disease and suffering, and while it did not originate the hospital, it immensely enlarged the scope of tackling disease. The very names of some of our oldest London hospitals—St. Bartholomew's, St. Thomas's, St. Mary's, St. John's and St. Elizabeth's—testify to the support of religion. It tackled ignorance. The first schools were church schools and the Church kept the torch of education alight through the darkness of the dark ages. It tackled injustice. The phrases we still use reveal the part the Church played. Justice was first of all administered in church, and the "bar" to which bar-risters were "called", was the communion rail. The judge sat below the high altar and the bow of the advocate is a relic of the earlier bow, not to the judge, but to the crucifix above his head.

As Christianity has been like a dawn, dispelling slavery, disease, ignorance and injustice, it will, as it is promoted and extended, banish class-distinction, colour bars, prostitution, married unhappiness, poverty, industrial strife and war.

*　　*　　*

2. *Where the dawn of Christianity cannot yet banish darkness, it shines in judgment upon evil.*

Look for a moment at this imaginative picture. "Here is a great banqueting hall in ancient Rome, on the tables is every possible thing to eat and drink; round the tables are noblemen and women, wearing wonderful robes and glittering dresses, enjoying themselves to the full. Imagine the scene to be full of pagan splendour, with wonderful music stealing through the room. Imagine that feast going on and on through the night, an orgy of eating and drinking and making merry. Then imagine that through the windows facing the East, there rises the slow, majestic, steady, certain light of dawn, until the guttering candles seem an insult to its glory. As the sun rises higher in the sky, what a dejected, vulgar, dismal scene it is, with men drunk and woman dishevelled, with candles guttering and people stupid with wine! Yes, when the Dawn comes, all other lights fail and *all false ways of living are betrayed*."[1]

In the blessed dawn-light of Christianity, how mean and sordid, how shabby and meretricious, unworthiness looks! No one, since Christ rose with a glory like the sunrise, will ever be satisfied with things that belong to the darkness. Where Christianity has not banished evil, it has made us ashamed of evil. "This is the judgment that the light has come."[2] And as men cannot pluck the sun from the summer sky and push it back so that the night that is past once more overcomes the day, so no one will ever live as though Jesus Christ had never lived.

Christianity is a Dawn Religion and you can't hold back the dawn.

> "Whatever clouds may veil the sky,
> Never is night again."

*   *   *

3. *The third factor we must remember is that of the character of God.*
It is this that makes the dawn certain. As we *know* that the dawn will come tomorrow because of those unalterable majestic laws by which God governs His universe, so we may *know* that that same omnipotent hand is on man's affairs, yes, on every man's life, and on them for good, to banish all that is evil and to establish all that is good.

If the history of the world ended in a welter of atomic wars and the incredible horrors of which we have been warned; if cancer and polio, pain of body and madness of mind, frustration of personality and unredeemed disappointment, if these things of the night had the last word, then, indeed, there would be at the heart of the universe either nothing at all or a feeble and

[1] I have quoted here a passage from my earlier book *Over His Own Signature*, pp. 85-6 (Epworth Press).

[2] John 3[19]

174

purposeless obscenity instead of a loving, wise and finally omnipotent Spirit. We might as well sing in such a case, a new Nunc Dimittis—"Lord, now lettest Thou Thy servant depart in tears, for mine eyes have seen hell."

Our certainty about the dawn is firmly based on the character of God.

I heard, many years ago, a sad but true story. Try to picture the scene. It was Christmas Eve in a middle-class home. There was no poverty, no real need. Three children had gone to bed. But they were much too excited to sleep. They did not believe any longer in Father Christmas, but they did believe in Daddy. Their mother, too, had given them reason to hope. Daddy had promised that when he was up in town he would get the presents which were to fill their stockings.

Then, very late, there was the sound of unsteady feet and a rough voice which they hardly recognised. Daddy was drunk. He had spent all his money on drink. He had completely forgotten his children. When he got home, it was too late to do anything about it, and he was much too fuddled, even if a shop here and there had still been open. The mother could do nothing. The next morning three little stockings were empty. The children crept together into one bed and wept out their disappointment under the bedclothes. Having dressed, they loyally tried to keep back further tears, tried to behave as though nothing had happened, tried to love the one who had brought such disappointment to their home. They had hoped, they had had reason to hope, but the character of the person concerned, the character which was the basis of their hopes, had broken down. All through the night they had hoped that the dawn would bring happiness, but he on whom all depended let them down.

For us, the character of God is the supreme assurance of the blessedness of a satisfying dawn.

*   *   *

I dare not leave my message there however. We must remind ourselves of two facts, one challenging, one comforting.

1. God uses men to bring light to them that sit in darkness. "Ah," you say, "your imagery breaks down there, for God does not require man to help Him make the dawn." But God often wants men to tell their fellows that the dawn is in the sky. How many times have great men pulled up a blind that men may see what God can do; aye, what God has done! How many times have wise men opened a door and urged their fellows to turn their backs on darkness and turn east towards the dawn light! Moses told Israel that the dawn was in the east and they found the light of liberty, and so we could go on through the great names of the world—Augustine, Luther, Wilberforce, Lincoln, Wesley. They pointed to a new dawn in religion.

Congregations misunderstand the preacher's use of famous names. They think, "Yes, but I am not great like that." But the preacher uses these names because he has access to these lives. Everybody knows about them. But you and I can visit a lonely heart, a sick soul, an unhappy spirit and carry the Dawn-Religion in our eyes, our handclasp, our gift of flowers, our simple word of love. We can say, "You are facing the wrong way. The dawn is in the sky."

2. So I come to this last word of comfort. Because I believe in God and because I believe in the character and might of God, I believe that for everyone, *everyone*, EVERYONE, life is working out towards an indescribable good. Nothing less than this would satisfy the God I believe in. He is such a good Shepherd that He will never be content if a sheep be lost. He will search and search "*until He find it*", as Jesus said. (Luke 15⁴).

There will come, after however long a night and dark a road, a sense of being safe, of being secure, of utter well-being. God is good beyond our dreams, and the universe is finally friendly to all that we value most. The values we cherish like love, beauty. truth, humility, unselfishness, will triumph over every force of evil, however blatant and powerful that evil may seem to be. All things work together towards an indescribable good, to all who do not finally close their hearts against God, and surely no one will *finally* do that; see the splendour and beauty and meaning of Love and repudiate it. Oh, yes! I too believe in Hell. But there is not a word in the Bible which proclaims that it is endless. We may suffer in the next world. I think we shall as we realise how our sins here have hindered God's Kingdom, hurt other lives, hampered our usefulness and retarded our progress. We shall all suffer the pains of discipline and remorse. But we shall still be free to turn to the light and all men will do so at last, however distant that "last" may be. The alternative is a God who has failed and is eternally mourning His lost sheep and is eternally deprived of the fullness of joy.

Every man and woman, whatever trouble they may be facing, may say with utter conviction—feeling as sure as they are sure of the dawn—this will not only pass, but be woven into a pattern of indescribable beauty. Sorrow, diasappointment, physical pain, mental anguish and spiritual desolation, these things are of the night and the night will pass. The joy of all men is finally absolutely certain.

Now having listened so long you deserve to hear the text! It is in Psalm 30, verse 5: "Weeping may tarry for a night"—the Hebrew word, "tarry" means, "spend the night as a lodger";— "but *joy cometh in the morning*", and the morning is CERTAIN.— And joy comes not to "tarry", "to spend the night as a lodger", but to stay for ever, enthroned in every heart. Ours is the Religion of the Dawn.

The Quality of Mercy

I ONLY realised the other day that although I have been preaching for over forty years, I have never preached a sermon on the mercy of God. Let us meditate on the theme this morning.

Mercy could be defined as goodwill on the part of one person towards another over whom he has some advantage. One thinks of the successful duellist, whose victim is disarmed and on the ground and—as we say—entirely at his mercy. One thinks of the man who cannot repay a loan of money and is at the mercy of his rich lender. One thinks of the man in one parable who lay in the ditch until the Good Samaritan turned from his own superior advantage of health and security, and had *mercy* on his fellow.[1]

* * *

We can often see the value of a virtue by glancing at its opposite. Clearly the opposite of mercy—mercilessness—is a terrible sin against a loving God. Men in a position of advantage, who have others in their power, do not always show compassion and goodwill. Through motives of pride or selfishness, or sometimes through sheer ignorance, they impose hardship on others.

I remember a headmaster, whom I knew, who made it a rule to thrash every boy who was late for school, without asking if there were an explanation. One morning, after he had thrashed a little fellow who had never before been late, he found that the boy had only that morning heard news of a colliery disaster and on the way to school had gone to the pit-head to gather news, only to find that his elder brother had been killed. I hope the headmaster felt remorse for that terrible, ignorant mercilessness.

[1] Luke 10²⁵ff.

I remember reading of a society girl taking a luxury cruise on a famous liner. The chef was a man with original ideas and he would often fashion an ice-cream pudding into various shapes to please the passengers. On one day the ice-cream would resemble a statue, on another an animal, on another the ship itself, and so on. One day the girl complained to the captain that the ice-creams were not as "cute" as they used to be. She said the chef had grown slack and she asked the captain to rebuke him. She did not know that far away from those sunny seas, where the passengers idled in deck-chairs, the chef's wife was lying ill in a little home in Liverpool, and that on the day the girl reported him, he had had a wireless message to say she was dead.

How often we, who are in a position of advantage for the time-being, fail to be merciful, to show goodwill to those who are in our power, in our power at least in the sense that we *had* power to show love, patience, sympathy, understanding, restraint!

The best example of our theme is Christ's story of the unmerciful servant read to you in the second Lesson (Matthew 18[21-35]). I will not stay to do justice to the whole story. I have tried to do that elswhere.[1] There is in the story the humour of exaggeration, in which, I think, the Master often indulged. A servant owed a king ten thousand talents. That sentence of our Lord must at once have made His hearers smile. Ten thousand talents were worth two-and-a-quarter million pounds. The exaggeration is intended. All the gold on the ark was only worth thirty talents. Why, the annual taxes of all the provinces of Palestine only amounted to less than a thousand talents. The whole revenue of Herod the Great was only nine hundred talents a year, and he was a rich man. Here is a slave saying to his master, "Have patience and I will pay thee all."—A debt ten times Herod's annual income! It is like a little maid-servant offering to liquidate the National Debt. It is an illustration of our Lord's humour.

But the story darkens. The servant was treated with great

[1] See *In Quest of a Kingdom*, p. 211[n].

mercy and forgiven this vast sum, but when another servant got into his power, who only owed him a hundred pence or three pounds ten shillings, he would not show mercy, but cast him into prison. A terrible punishment followed such mercilessness.

*   *   *

You will remember the Beatitude. "Blessed are the merciful for they shall obtain mercy."[1] We are not to think of that saying as a kind of bargain either between man and man, or man and God. It does not mean, if I show mercy to A, B will show mercy to me. Life does not work out like that. Neither does it mean that if I show mercy to another, God will show mercy to me. We cannot bargain with God like that.

Surely we can see the meaning of the Beatitude more clearly if we drop the word "mercy" and substitute "goodwill". Blessed are they who show goodwill, for they obtain goodwill *from the person to whom they are kind.* That is where they "obtain mercy".

Blessed are the merciful because they do not just condemn what is wrong. They make sure that the bond of fellowship is unbroken, so they receive back goodwill. They win gratitude. To show mercy is to do a thing that wins a thank you. This, I am told, is the origin of the French word for "thank you", "*Merci!*"

When I think of those who, in difficult circumstances take trouble over their relationships, I think of my own father, and I hope this personal reference may be forgiven. My father was engaged in business, and it was sometimes his painful duty to dismiss an employee. Such dismissal was sometimes demanded by those at the top. But how it distressed my father! I can remember his visiting the home of the dismissed person and never ceasing to be concerned until other work had been found. Blessed are those who show goodwill. They get goodwill from those to whom they are merciful. Blessed are the merciful, for they shall obtain "*Merci*".

What a lot of merciless criticism and condemnation flies

[1] Matthew 5[7]

180

about! I often wonder whether in personal affairs much good is done by condemning even what is wrong, if by so doing a gulf is opened between the condemner and the condemned. We are not to condone evil, but we are to separate it from those who do it and try to understand them. How often we should halt the reproachful word if we knew all that the wrong doer had had to overcome, all the distortions created in his childhood, all the wounds his soul had sustained!

*   *   *

So we come to contemplate the mercy of God to ourselves. How unutterably He is above us in His holiness and love, and how our dirty, little sins and loveless deeds must hurt Him! How He must hate them! And yet He loves us. He shows boundless mercy to us and tries to maintain the love-relationship. No gulf is opened by Him because of our sins. That is the miracle of the everlasting mercy. He never casts us off.

Mind, we cannot put this relationship right with deeds. We cannot *buy* His mercy and goodwill. That great hymn of Luther which we have just sung, contains a profound truth.

> "Our pardon is Thy gift; Thy love
> And grace alone avail us;
> Our works could ne'er our guilt remove,
> The strictest life would fail us.
> That none may boast himself of aught,
> But own in fear Thy grace hath wrought
> What in him seemeth righteous.
>
> And thus my hope is in the Lord
> And not in mine own merit . . ."

It is a truth in line with Christ's own words. "Many shall come to Me in that day and say, 'Lord, did we not prophesy in Thy name and in Thy name cast out devils and do many mighty works?' Then I will profess unto them, 'I never got to know you. You would not come into the love-relationship with Me'."[1]

I have related previously the true story of the little girl who had done wrong, and who went to her mother eager to put

[1] Matthew 7[22-23]

matters right, and said, "Mummy, would you like me to run any errands?" "No, thank you dear." "Would you like me to dust down the stairs?" "No, thank you!"—"Mummy, isn't there anything I can *do* for you? . . . " And then, prompted by her good angel, the little girl flung her arms round her mother's neck and said, "Mummy, forgive me. I'm so sorry." Yes! First the relationship right and the goodwill restored, and the mercy granted. And then the deeds are not *attempts* to buy goodwill. They are an expression of the goodwill alread re- stored.

Let no one suppose that serving God by doing good deeds is to be despised. But we cannot buy God's mercy with them. We cannot say, "But, Lord, you *must* forgive me and show mercy to me. I was a churchwarden, or door steward, or society steward, or I sang in the choir. I was in the ministry, I visited the poor, I wrote many books . . . " In that sense "our works are nothing worth".

No, we are to fling ourselves on a mercy that is free.

> "The quality of mercy is not strained,
>   It droppeth as the gentle rain from heaven
>   Upon the place beneath:"

and in the same way, it is offered freely to all. It cannot be deserved, or bought, or bargained about. We can no more square accounts with God, or atone for our sins, than a He- brew slave could repay two-and-a-quarter million pounds, or a servant girl pay up the National Debt. But "the mercy of the Lord is from everlasting to everlasting". It is infinite and as vast and as cleansing as the sea.

*　　　*　　　*

In one of his later books—and I think his best—called *The Secret of Radiant Life*, Dr. Sangster tells us about the sludge vessels which are such an important part of the sanitary system of London. Sewage is not a pleasant subject, but it is an apt illustration of sin. The Master Himself used it thus.[1] London has four sludge vessels. On every weekday tide two of them, each carrying fifteen hundred tons of unusable sewage, travel

[1] Matthew 10ff

182

down the Thames to what is called the "Black Deep," a great hole in the bed of the ocean, fifteen miles off Foulness. The valves are opened and the whole horrible cargo runs out in twenty minutes into the salt, aseptic sea. "A dark stain spreads over the wake of the ship, but so wide is the ocean, so deep the declivity, and so cleansing the sea, that within an hour, samples of water taken from the surface, or from the bed of the estuary, prove to be completely innocuous. The sludge has gone, devitalised of all evil power, never to be seen again."[1]

What a parable of that loving, forgiving, vast mercy which swallows up our sins! So John Wesley wrote:

> "O Love, Thou bottomless abyss,
>   My sins are swallowed up in Thee!"

and Whittier wrote:

> "There's a wideness in God's mercy
>   Like the wideness of the sea."

In the world-famous, twenty-third Psalm which I read to you, I am quite sure, in my own mind, that the goodness and mercy mentioned in the last verse are the shepherd's dogs that follow the flock. While the shepherd goes ahead and leads the sheep, the dogs follow. "Goodness and Mercy shall follow me." The Hebrew word for "follow" means follow like a dog. Indeed, it was reading that last verse of the Psalm in that sense, and meditating on it, that led Francis Thompson to write his poem, "The Hound of Heaven."

May the thought of God's infinite love and everlasting mercy keep us in the right track as the dogs did for the sheep in Palestine so long ago; may they press us closer to one another in fellowship, as they kept the sheep together; may they press us nearer to the Good Shepherd who leads us, and who, if we follow Him, will bring us home at last.

"Goodness and Mercy shall follow me—dogging my footsteps —all the days of my life, and I will dwell in the house of the Lord for ever."

[1] *The Secret of Radiant Life*, p. 186 (*Hodder and Stoughton*, 1957).

No Private Harvest

(A Harvest Festival Sermon)

1 Corinthians 12 [26-27]: "When one member suffers, all the members suffer with it; and when one member is honoured, all the members rejoice with it. Ye are the body of Christ and severally members thereof."

ONE of the facts of life, with which we must come to terms, is that we depend on one another. We may speak of a gentleman or lady of independent means, but *someone* is getting up early on foggy mornings to make the dividends from which he or she draws income.

A man may grow wheat, but he needs the miller and the baker, and even then man cannot live on bread alone. He needs meat and fruit. He may make a fortune growing apples, but probably he will only eat a few himself. He needs what others produce.

Before the end of breakfast this morning—as has often been pointed out—you were in debt to half the world. A Frenchman, maybe, gave you a cake of soap, a Pacific islander a sponge, a Turk a towel. Your linen may have come from an Irishman, your suit from a Tweedside Scot. You sit down to breakfast and need an Indian or Chinaman to pour out your tea, a Scot or Mr. Kellogg to give you your cereal, a Berkshire farmer manages your bacon and a Guernseyman your fried tomato. A Spaniard passes you the marmalade and a West Indian your banana.

How now, my ladies and gentlemen of independent means!

How the Harvest Festival brings our dependence home to us! Supposing we had nothing to eat save what we ourselves could

184

procure. We should be hungry even in a wheatfield. There is no life that is independent, no life that is private. We cannot live on what we make for ourselves. There is no private harvest. I must share to live. I must borrow or die.

*　　　*　　　*

Seeing clearly how much we depend on one another, let us note how essential it is to get on with one another.

In olden days this was easier. For one thing, the so called "natives" of far off lands were more amenable. The sugar industry was built on slave labour. I met an old man last February in the West Indies, who could remember slavery. His grandfather was a slave. I will not repeat all he told me. He showed me the foul hovels in which slaves were huddled and locked for the night. A slave belonged to the master. The slave-owner could rape the young girls. He could flog any slaves at will. He could beat them to death, and often did. So we got our sugar. Thank God it is different now. The young nations are growing up and insisting on being brothers as God meant them to be. This is progress. And the Little Rock snobs of Arkansas and the South African apartheid merchants, who think they can hold back that progress, might as well take out their brooms and buckets and try to stop the tides of the sea.

Furthermore, the world is shrinking and this means that the far off lands are only next door. In olden days men sent us coffee and sugar and rubber from distant countries, and we knew little of the senders, and cared less. We gaped at magic lantern slides of African "natives" and hardly thought them as human as ourselves. Their lives did not impinge on ours. So life was easy. Now we must all live together and that is more difficult.

An illustration clears the matter at once. If difficult Aunt Jane lives in Scotland, I can get on with her splendidly. I send her a present at Christmas—something that the Jones' gave us last year and we don't want—and she sends us two pink china dogs which we put in the attic, and all is peace! But if she comes and lives next door . . . and certainly if she comes and lives with us, we need a far deeper and stronger basis of understanding. Life without love—a love that means tolerance and endless goodwill—is going to be hell.

Into this hell the world has fallen. Our national relatives lived a long way away. China was a land almost of myth and legend. What Russia did was a remote matter. We did not always remember even the name of the American President. But now the name Eisenhower is mentioned every day, and if he plays only nine holes of golf instead of eighteen, we realise that he really must be thoroughly frightened, and we share his alarm. If he goes sick the money market goes crazy. And as for Russia, she is not remote. She lives next door. We do not mind her use of her sickle, but her hammer is another matter. She hammers on the wall when we want to go to bed, and sets off satellite toys blip-blipping round the world and disturbing our sleep.

Men and women, isolationism is dead. We may try to ignore our interdependence, but it is the policy of the ostrich hiding its head in the sand. No man can live to himself on his own little private harvests and no nation can. We must learn to live together or we shall die together. No-one in this atomic age can deny that truth.

And just as our grandfathers wakened up to the iniquities of the slave system, the world is waking up to the present reproach. You may say, "What reproach? Is not this the welfare state?" *But we must work for a welfare world.*

It is not for me to say how. That is for the statesmen and the economists. But look at a few of the facts. In a world of two thousand five hundred million people, half do not get enough to eat. In some areas, one of which is the Middle East, four out of five live on the edge of starvation. What can that spell but unrest? Yet so badly do we run this world-family that one fifth of all the food produced in a year is wasted, and that waste would feed for a year one hundred and fifty million people, namely the entire population of the African continent.

We speak and think of God as Father. Imagine the father of a family seeing what God sees. God looks down on a human family in which some of His children are burning wheat and coffee, throwing fish back into the sea and pouring milk on the fields, when *someone is dying of hunger every five seconds*. This service will last at least an hour and a quarter, seventy-five minutes, four thousand five hundred seconds. So while we have been sitting here at our harvest festival service, looking at food, nine hundred people will have died of starvation.

My friends, the bill will come in for all this. We cannot have a private harvest and eat it ourselves while our brothers are starving. Someone has said that Asian 'flu broke out amongst starving and destitute people. If so, we are all paying for our neglect of starving and destitute people. Disease—all admit— would be lessened immensely if all men were fed well, clothed well and happy.

It seems a grim fact that if we are not moved by Christian love to share our well-being with the unfortunate, they will share their diseases with us. For the world is a unity. If we will not give them our food, they will give us their 'flu.

Christianity has always taught that God's plan for the world is to make one great family. It envisages all nations bringing their treasure into the kingdom of God, all members of a family whose father is God, where the assets of one are shared by all and give joy to all; where the liabilities of any are the concern and the burden of all. Just as it is in the ideal Christian families in our homes, so God's plan is that it should be in His world. Each must serve the welfare of all. All must be at the disposal of each.

* * *

But I should like to mention another phase of our theme.

There is no private harvest of goodness or of evil. I spoke some time ago of two farmers in India, whom we will call A and B. Their land was adjacent and underneath both their farms there was a big underground lake. For them the problem of water supply—often so difficult in India—was easy. They had but to sink a well and fresh water bubbled up. But—for the sake of the argument—supposing A put arsenic in his well. He would poison the water B and his family and cattle drank. Supposing he put vitamins in his well. He would—let us imagine—enrich the water that B drank.

Now life is like that. No man liveth to himself. I cannot live even one day cheerfully, joyfully, optimistically, buoyantly, forgivingly and lovingly, without enriching others. I cannot be gloomy, grumpy, pessimistic, bad tempered and negative, without influencing the water of life which others drink. And if I *sin*, however secretly, I poison the public reservoir. I lower the spiritual health of the community.

Some time, I would like to offer you the support for this theme that comes from psychology, with its insistence on the collective unconscious—the underground lake—and the unity at a deep level of all minds. I would like to show you how psychic research supports my theme, with its overwhelming evidence of the fact of telepathy, the uncommunicated impact of mind upon mind. But that must not be now.

Do, however, accept the fact. There is no private harvest. He that soweth to the spirit is joined by other reapers delighted to find such a harvest; the whole world is enriched by his sowing. Alas, he who soweth to the flesh, infects others with his own corruption.

Private lives are not as private as we once thought. Someone has said, "We may desecrate human relationships, but we cannot destroy them." You cannot live to yourself. We only become persons by our fellowship with others. If we help others, our own lives share the harvest. If we injure others, we may remember with Coleridge that

> "In His vast family, no Cain
> Injures uninjured."

*   *   *

For myself, I believe this whole matter can be taken further still. I cannot see that there can be any *final* heaven for anybody unless all are gathered there. If you say, "This is not good theology," I could argue the point. The shepherd goeth over the mountains to seek the lost sheep *"until he find it"*. He "willeth that all shall be saved", and finally His will is surely done. Human nature will always be *able* to say "No" to God, but finally, perhaps after much suffering, and possibly after many lives yet, surely every soul which contains the divine spark will see the beauty of the spiritual and the glory of love and long to be one with God.

Will it be heaven for you if your dear one is excluded? And if not for you, will it be heaven for those who love you most dearly and nearly? And if not for them, for *their* dear ones—so for any of us? I can imagine no final heaven unless it includes all.

*　　*　　*

We must leave the matter. But clearly we are to go out from this place to love our neighbour, and all men are our neighbours. We are to say the Lord's Prayer with greater sincerity, for never once does it say "I" or "me" or "mine", but OUR Father Who art in heaven. Give us, *all of us*, our daily bread. Forgive us our sins and deliver us *all* from evil.

And we might add another famous prayer—the lovely prayer of St. Francis of Assisi:

> "Lord, make me an instrument of Thy peace;
> Where there is hatred, let me sow love;
> Where there is injury, pardon;
> Where there is doubt, faith;
> Where there is despair, hope;
> Where there is darkness, light
> Where there is sadness, joy.
>
> O Divine Master, grant that
> I may not so much seek
> To be consoled as to console,
> Not so much to be understood as to understand,
> Not so much to be loved as to love.
>
> For it is in giving that we receive,
> It is in forgiving that we are forgiven,
> It is in dying that we waken to eternal life."

From such a sowing comes the universal harvest of God's desire, the perfect fulfilment of His holy will.

189

The Nature and Use of Freedom

(A) "THE BONDAGE OF THE 'FREE'"

W E are to discuss today a subject which is peculiarly appropriate as we remember those who have suffered and died for our freedom. We are to think together about the nature and the use of freedom, and the text both morning and evening is found in 1 Peter 2[16] , where Peter says that Christians are to be "free, not using freedom for a cloak of wickedness, but as bondservants of God." The Greek word for "bondservants" is the blunt word, "slaves," and within the paradox of the text, I hope we shall find together the very essence of the true idea of freedom. Christians are to be free because they are the slaves of God.

*   *   *

Freedom is one of the hardest things in the world really to understand and enjoy, and I can only hope that at the end of this day—if you are able to come tonight as well—your ideas about freedom may have been clarified. Not only is freedom difficult to understand, but it is a matter of immense importance. If we misunderstand freedom, and live according to our misunderstanding, we inevitably find ourselves in a new bondage. I hope, as I talk to you this morning, that you will realise how many people, seeking freedom, have only exchanged one bondage for another. This morning we will talk about "The Bondage of the So-called 'Free'" and tonight we will talk about "The Freedom of the So-called 'Bound'."

I note that in our midst is a large number of young people who have recently come up to London to begin either a course of study or a new job, and I am going to talk to them especially today about freedom. I am going to imagine a young man up from the country, who has been rather strictly brought up in a conventionally religious home. In imagination, I hear him saying something like this: "Now I have freedom to live my own life. I shan't have to go to a church when I don't want to. I shan't be nagged about the books I read or the friends I make. I shan't have to heed my father or mother saying, 'Be sure you are in by ten, Bob,' and 'I wish you wouldn't smoke cigarettes in bed. You will have the house on fire one of these days.' I shan't be told, 'You shouldn't attend this or see that show.' Now I can do what I like. I am free at last. One is only young once. One only has one life to live. To hell with all those stuffy old conventions of my parents. Youth has a right to freedom. . . ."

I feel very sympathetic with these sentiments. I came up to London University as a young student many years ago, and I felt exactly the same, but as one who has made many mistakes, do let me offer youth a warning. Unless you realise what freedom is and under what conditions alone it can be enjoyed, you will find yourself, in the name of freedom, merely exchanging one bondage for another.

* * *

Think, for example, of convention. Granted you have lived what you now think of as the stuffy and cramping conventional life of the home in which you were brought up. But would I be wrong in suggesting that many of you have already joined another set of people whose conventions can prove just as cramping? I am not sneering or jibing at the cocktail party set, or the music-hall going set, or the card-playing set, or the Bohemian, arty-crafty, Sunday-smashing set. I am only warning you lest the new set-up impedes real freedom by its conventions which you may come to dislike and feel just as cramping as the set you have left. You, who now are rejoicing in the escape from your home conventions, may soon be saying secretly within yourself, "I should really like to do this and that; to take life more seriously; to serve the community in this way or that, to attend church as I used to do at home. But what would my new companions think of me? What would George say and what would Phyllis think?" Conceivably, since you are here today, you may want to go to church, and yet you may, through loneliness, get into a set where that will be ridiculed, and you will be too shy to brave criticism and ridicule. You think you are on the way to freedom. You rejoice that you have left Little Puddleton behind and entered the life of this great London. Have you found freedom, or are you already in the toils of a new tyranny, more likely to crush what is beautiful and splendid than the conventional tyranny you left behind?

* * *

Let me remind you of another kind of tyranny—that of conscience. Let us imagine that you have come up from the country to London and that there are things which in your village you would not dream of doing, partly out of respect for your parents, partly because of the censure of others, who, in a village, watch everything you do, but partly for conscience' sake. I wonder if on occasion you have said, "I am free. In London no one will know, no one will tell my parents, no one will censure me. They will not *think* critically, let alone *say* anything." So you did this and that. Then do you remember one night when you could not sleep? At two o'clock in the morning you were still twisting and turning in bed. You were still arguing and saying, "I don't think it is really wrong." At half past two you said, "In any case my parents will never know anything about it." At three o'clock you said, "Nobody can possibly find out." At four o'clock you said, "Other people do it." At half past four you said, "I shall get over it and forget all about it." What a lovely night you are having! Do you call that freedom? I think I would rather have a form of captivity that allowed me to sleep.

Do let me tell you, from the point of view of psychology, as well as from the point of view of morality, that the tyranny of what is called "conscience distress" is one of the worst prisons in which to land yourself. If this were a lecture on psychology, I could give you the cases of people who have become physically ill largely because they were trying to escape the tyranny of conscience distress. Better the limitations of Victorian parents than this new captivity of an outraged conscience. And let me remind you that often conscience does not listen to reason. You can reason with yourself and others, until you are blue in the face, that this and that action is right, but reason does not on that account let you out of prison. The truth is that reason is not one of the sentries at the door of the soul. You have misunderstood freedom. You have only exchanged one prison for another.

*　　*　　*

Think of the same kind of thing in regard to another prison —that of habit. You came up to London free from certain habits because your parents had brought you up in a certain way. Then you said to yourself, "Now I am free. I shan't have to follow their wishes any more. I can do what I like." I do beseech you to see what a heresy it is to regard freedom as doing what you like. So you did a certain thing, quite secretly perhaps, and when you did it the first time, something lovely in you shrank from it as unclean and unworthy and you were a little bit ashamed. But it was easier the next time, and when several other occasions had taken place, the voice of conscience grew fainter—as, of course, it does—and you thought, "Now I can do it without any ill effects at all," and, of course, you thought, "I can stop whenever I like. I am free to break this habit if I want to."

Hear the parable of the eagle! One bitterly cold frosty day, high above the Niagara River, a great golden eagle stood perched upon a pinnacle of the cliffs. It saw in the foaming water below it, the carcass of a bullock floating down the Niagara River a few miles from the famous Falls. This was a find indeed for the hungry bird, so it spread its glorious wings, circled round and swooped down on the bullock. It drove its claws into the carcass, and then its beak got busy and it began to satisfy its hunger. After a time it could hear the rush of the water as the river went over the Niagara Falls, but it thought, "I am free. I can rise at the last minute when the carcass goes over the edge. I am free to fly back to my mountain home." So, when the carcass got to the edge of the Falls, the eagle spread its mighty wings . . . *but its feet were frozen into the carcass.* It could not rise. It was carried over the edge and it perished.

Note this! During the whole time when the bird was saying to itself, "I am free," the bondage was becoming more inescapable, the icy grip on its feet was becoming tighter.

Does that parable touch you? Are you saying about a newly acquired habit, "I can break it any time I like: I am still free?" But are you free, or has the habit got you? See what has happened! In the name of freedom, you acquired a new habit which is a bad habit, and you have not found freedom. You have exchanged one form of tyranny for another.

*   *   *

Look again at what used to be called "free love," and what some have called "the new morality." It is not a good title, for it is not new. It is as old as humanity, and, even by the loosest standards, it is not morality. Its teaching roughly runs like this: "Why should not a man be free of moral restraints? Why should he take any notice of words that he said in church to a woman at the dictation of a parson? Why can't he follow his instinctive desires and be free from these stuffy, ecclesiastical restraints? If a man becomes tired of his wife because she is not quite so nice-looking, does not take such care with her dress, and perhaps becomes burdensome and irritating to him, why shouldn't he find some little bit of fluff and go off with her for a week-end and enjoy himself? Let them both express their instincts and find freedom."

To certain people in certain moods, it can all be made to sound not only attractive, but reasonable. I can only give my witness. I have been in the ministry for over forty years. I have spent, I suppose, thousands of hours talking to people in trouble. I have spent many hours talking to people in this kind of trouble, I have met many people who tried "free love" and

194

"the new morality"; people who rushed up the roads that were signposted, "This way to liberty," or "Find freedom for your instincts," and I can only report that the liberty promised is never delivered. The so-called freedom turns out to be a new bondage. Men and women can rush up a particular road that is alleged to lead to a life of freedom, but only two things happen on that road. One is that men notice a warning that says, "No thoroughfare this way," and they turn back in time, and begin, often late in the evening of life, to find another road. The other thing that happens is that they go over the precipice at the end of the road. What is the good of following a road, however broad and attractive, if it does not bring you out where you want to be? Men and women, it is no good softening down the gospel message. To refuse a course of evil is not just to be dictated to by a Victorian committee of elderly spinsters, who sit down on one bright afternoon and say, "What rule can we make today to stop people enjoying themselves?" Many so-called conventions are the rules of the game of living, discovered after much trial, suffering and error, to be the best rules to follow for those who want to get the best out of the game. To follow a course of evil and not to turn back, is to land oneself in an indescribable captivity for which the New Testament invented the word "hell."

For those who travel far on that road and then turn back in the evening of their lives, that evening is rather grim. Miserable old men and women find themselves cursed with a disturbed and unhappy conscience, with bitter and unforgettable memories. They cannot find peace of mind. One hears a man say, "If only somebody had warned me. If only I had known that my old age would be full of regret and remorse and inescapable feelings of guilt . . . if only I had been told" . . . All right! I am trying to tell you this morning. Be careful that in a search for freedom you do not exchange one tyranny for another.

(B) "THE FREEDOM OF THE 'BOUND'"

Let me state now the conclusion to which I hope you will come. The only way to enjoy freedom is voluntarily to accept a bondage. That is the meaning of the text. St. Peter says that the Christian is to be free because he is the slave of Christ. You have been singing about the same theme:

> "Make me a captive, Lord,
> And then I shall be free."

Let us look closely at this paradox.

* * *

First of all, it fascinates me to think of the freedom of some great souls in history who have been grievously bound. We think, for example, of Bunyan lying bound in Bedford gaol, and then we rejoice in the freedom of his mind. His body lay in prison, but his soul was out on the road to the Celestial City with Christian and Hopeful and Faithful and the rest.

In more modern days you may have read a book called *The Roadmender* by Michael Fairless. For years I thought he must be a wonderful naturalist, with a style of poetic prose that helped one to revel in the glories of nature. I can remember the awe and wonder in my heart when I learnt that "Michael Fairless" was the pen-name of a sick woman who was dying. She lay in bed in a tiny bedroom, and with her left hand wrote the book on a pad propped up against her breast. There is not a moan or a whimper in the book. When you read it, you cannot hear anything but the singing of the birds, the whisper of the wind in the trees, the chatter of a brook down the hillside and the murmur of bees on a summer evening. Her body was bound by disease; her mind was gloriously free. Here is perhaps our first clue to the meaning of the phrase, "the freedom of the 'bound'."

A prisoner of war wrote some lines that express the same theme:

> "Freedom is and ever must remain
> Spiritual, not physical, and they are free
> Who can rise spiritually above their pain,
> Their minds uncrippled by captivity.
>
> More free by far than any bird that flies,
> My mind is free to climb amongst the stars;
> My soul is free to wander o'er the skies.
> Only my body lies behind the bars."

Let us thank God for the freedom of the so-called bound, and though their bondage was not voluntary, they prove the fact of freedom within bondage.

* * *

Have you ever noticed that in realm after realm of human activity, ability depends on bondage? Bunyan would never have been famous if he had never been in gaol, for he would never have attempted his book.

When you think of the great musician and envy the way in which his fingers can wander over the keys with such freedom as he extemporises, you realise that his freedom is due to the bondage of self-discipline. The singer who seems so free to reach those glorious top notes, has spent hours of disciplined practising. The footballer who seems to have such freedom in his movement and in his power over the ball, is the product of self-discipline. The doctor is free to heal because of the bondage of his six long years of training. I can remember a newly-qualified doctor saying, "Now I am free to be a doctor." Yet even the qualified doctor is soon hampered and restricted if he throws off the discipline of continual study, and the effort to keep abreast of modern discoveries. His freedom to be an efficient doctor depends on his bondage to his continued studies.

* * *

All of this, I think, helps us to realise that in the Christian life those are free who voluntarily accept the discipline of Christ. "Ye shall be free as bondservants of God."

Francis Thompson puts our theme into unforgettable lines in his "Ode to the English Martyrs";

> "Hardest servitude has he
>   That's jailed in arrogant liberty;
>   And freedom, spacious and unflawed,
>   Who is walled about with God."

If you still think that freedom is ability to do what you like, try driving your car on the wrong instead of on the correct side of a two-way street. You will probably find captivity by tonight in the local Police Station!

I am reminded of the captive tennis ball my children and I used to play with many years ago. It was attached to a length of elastic, and we were *free* to hit it because it was *bound*. When the elastic broke, one could not have the same freedom. If we tried to exert it then, the ball found captivity in the gutter of the house next door or in the jaws of a neighbouring dog. We were only free because of the bondage.

You might imagine a curve in a road alongside which runs a railway line following the same curve. If you say to the motorist, "You may take that curve at fifty miles an hour," and if he obeys you, he will find the captivity of the ditch. But the train is *free* to take the curve at a high speed because it is *bound* by the rails. The car is not similarly held by the road.

Rabindranath Tagore, in one of his poems, has a lovely illustration of our theme. Without quoting the whole poem, let me give you its message. The poet picks up a piece of catgut and finds that it is a violin string, but as he holds it between his finger and thumb, it is all but useless. It is free at both ends, but no music can be made from it in that state. When he fits it to his violin and binds it at both ends and turns the peg until the violin string is taut, then, because it is bound, it is free to sing.

Youth is looking for freedom. If you interpret freedom as doing what you like, you will probably land yourself in a greater bondage because you have not disciplined yourself yet to like the things in which freedom is found. Someone has said, "You can do what you like in heaven because they make sure of what you like before you get there." But we are not yet ripe for heaven. Think, then, when you quest for freedom and ask this question: "What do I want to be free to do?" I think you will find that if it is freedom to do a worthy thing and to make the most of your life, you will need to accept what St. Peter called "the bondage of Christ." The violin string that is bound is alone free to sing.

Somebody recently asked Derek Ibbotson, the runner, to

join in some orgy of drinking, or smoking, or feasting, or something of the same kind. I do not remember the details, but I noted his answer. "I am not free," he said, "to do what you ask. For if I did what you ask, I should not be free to run." By voluntarily accepting the bondage of self-discipline, he is free to run. What do you want to be free to *do* in the world?

I think St. Paul knew a great deal about our theme today. When he wrote to the Philippians he was in prison at Rome. It is supposed that he was chained by one ankle to a staple in the wall and by his left wrist to a Roman sentry. Outside the door another Roman sentry paced up and down. Paul's body was bound, but his soul was free, and hear what he says: "The peace of God which passes all understanding, shall stand sentry over your hearts and your thoughts." No wonder he thought of the word "sentry"! The peace of God is a good sentry to post at the door of our lives. If the sentry has to be gagged, or stunned, or killed, or evaded, then our personalities are invaded by factors which will cause final unrest and the bondage of a great unhappiness. The peace of God is a grand sentry of the mind.

Do let me suggest to the young man up from the country, or the young woman far from home, that you post that sentry today outside the door of your heart, so that you, too, may know freedom within captivity; "as free because ye are the bondservants of God."

*   *   *

Jesus Himself, of course, says all that needs to be said on our theme. In His first sermon, He announced that He had come to bring "release to the captives and liberty to the bruised and bound."[1] Yet, as He offers freedom, He says to those who would find it, "Follow Me!" When He has bound them in loyalty to Himself, they find the glorious liberty of the children of God, and Jesus is an authority on our theme. He was willing to be bound in our flesh that He might be free to be our Saviour.

[1] Luke 4^{18}

*   *   *

199

Let me conclude with a parable. Can you imagine a mariner setting off to sail the seas in a sailing vessel, and saying to himself, "I am not going to take any notice of this conventional chart, or this compass, or indeed of the stars in heaven. I am free of them all. I am going to do what I like. I am going to sail my vessel as I like and where I like. These old, conventional, stuffy rules about navigation, what are they to me? . . ."

How grimly the stormy seas would laugh at him and how soon he and his ship would find the bottom of the ocean! It is when he accepts the discipline of the chart, the advice of the compass, the tyranny—if you like—of the eternal stars, that he finds at last the harbour. Let me remind you of that old proverb which says: "He who will not heed the stars, shall heed the rocks." "Ye shall be free as the willing servants of Christ."

Do not be, therefore, as the young mariner who, in the name of freedom, throws off restraint. There is not only a chart and compass and stars. There is a Pilot. Take Him on board today, follow His guidance, obey His direction, become His willing slave, and you will find freedom now, and, at eventide, the only true harbour of the soul.

There is a lovely promise in the Psalms which seems to me only true of Jesus: "So He bringeth them at last into the haven where they would be."

The Power of the Bible

Isaiah 55[11]: "My word . . . shall not return unto me void,
but it shall accomplish that which I please, and it shall
prosper in the thing whereto I sent it."
Dr. Moffatt translates: "It carries out my purpose."

LET me begin with a confession that is at least honest. I am
amazed at the power of the Bible! I hold in my hand a copy
of the Bible common enough amongst schoolboys. This is the
Bible I myself had in my teens, and it is the kind of copy, which
a schoolboy has to purchase, along with his other books, in
order to study Scripture as a subject for examination. It is
bound, as you see, in dull, black cloth. It has no illustrations.
It is printed in small print and in parallel columns. It has no
explanatory notes. It has a few maps at the end which show
the curious movements of Abraham, and then Palestine in the
time of Christ, and then a plan of the Temple in Jerusalem.
Lastly comes a map illustrating what I always used to regard
as Paul's over-enthusiastic missionary journeys!

If I open this book at random, I may find the story of a
massacre carried out by Joshua at what he claimed to be the
command of God. He not only massacred his male enemies,
but their wives and children, "as the Lord commanded him."
We read the dreadful sentence, "Joshua drew not back his
hand wherewith he stretched out the javelin, until he had
utterly destroyed all the inhabitants of Ai."[1]

I turn over the pages of this so greatly praised book which the
devout are invited to read every day so as to enrich their
spiritual life, and I find a bloodthirsty Psalm like number one
hundred and thirty-seven, where the poet invites his brethren

[1] Joshua 8[26]; cf. 10[40]

to take the innocent little children of Babylon and dash their brains out against the rocks.[1] This, we are told, will make the perpetrator happy.

I turn more pages and find prophecy with place names that I cannot identify and with language that I cannot understand.[2] Even in the New Testament I find a strangely uninspiring argument which Paul had about circumcision,[3] and when I get to the last book in the Bible, I find what is to any modern reader meaningless nonsense, as, for instance, the sentence about "a scarlet beast, full of names of blasphemy, having seven heads and ten horns."[4]

Where, indeed, could you find a book containing so much unattractive, unrewarding matter, a book so likely to be set aside, a book so dull and so confusing, so hard in so many places to understand, and often completely irrelevant to the life of modern man? We can understand someone saying, "Why on earth do the parsons invite us to read a book of this kind every day?"

*　　　*　　　*

But now turn and look at what has happened! Over a period of a thousand years, more than a hundred people, of different education, outlook and temperament, have contributed to this library of books gathered together under circumstances of immense difficulty. Parts of this book were written on material made from the skins of animals. Other parts were written on material made out of the dried reeds growing in the mud at the river's edge. Later, Biblical manuscripts were copied laboriously by loving hands and hours were spent on the illumination of a single capital letter at the beginning of a new chapter.

As for the Bible in English, it was translated nearly six hundred years ago and printed and read in situations so dangerous that we can scarcely credit the stories that have come down to us. Yet there is little doubt that those stories are true. Englishmen were burned at the stake with their Bibles tied round their

[1] Psalm 137[8-9]　　　　　　[2] e.g. Isaiah 47
[3] Romans 4[9ff]　　　　　　　[4] Revelation 17[3]

necks. The Church hunted to their death those who possessed this book. John Wycliffe, the famous translator, was fortunate in that he died a natural death, but in futile, ferocious revenge, his body was dug up and burned and the ashes scattered, presumably to defeat any hope of resurrection.

A hundred years later, Tyndale, a man of only thirty years of age, crossed to the Continent, in order to found an underground movement for the printing of the Bible. He became an exile never to see his homeland again. He shipped his Bibles to England hidden in bales of cotton, in bundles of flax and in bags of flour. The books were eagerly bought, although the Church did everything she knew to destroy them, punished those who were found possessing them and tried to stop their import. Finally, Tyndale himself was imprisoned near Brussels and subsequently strangled to death and his body burned to ashes. Four hundred years ago this young man of only forty-two laid down his life so that we might have the Bible in our own tongue.

This, of course, was not the end of the story of sacrifice, heroism and devotion. Few books can have a record like this one. It took sixteen hundred years to make and it has exerted a unique influence for eighteen hundred years more.

* * *

The publication figures of the Bible are frankly fantastic. This library—as the word "Bible" means—has been given to every race under heaven. It is translated into over a thousand dialects. "The world circulation of the Scriptures has reached the staggering figure of twenty-three million copies a year. . . . In Brazil alone, for the two-year period 1951–53, three million Bibles, New Testaments and portions of Scripture were sold, and even then the supply did not meet the demand. In *two months*, four hundred thousand Gospels were sent to Brazil and almost immediately sold out."[1]

[1] I owe these facts to an essay by the Rev. Robert McVeigh, Chairman of the Northern Ireland Branch of the British and Foreign Bible Society, in *The Irish Christian Advocate*, 6th November, 1953.

I heard only last week of a schoolboy who said to his father, "I have got to have a Bible for my school work." The father could not find one, whereupon the boy said, "I think I can get one for a bob, and at the end of a year I can sell it to another boy." No doubt the schoolboy just regarded it as another dull lesson book. But does it not kindle the imagination to think of the sacrifice gladly made to put it into our hands? And what do these fantastic circulation figures mean? They mean that the Bible does something to people, and since we, here, in this comfortable church, take the Bible for granted and have lost all sense of its dynamic and amazing power, let me tell you three true stories that will challenge us to ask whether we have not missed something. Surely if men laid down their lives year after year for the Bible . . . surely if twenty-three million copies are sold in a year throughout the world, we, who find it hard to lay our hands on a Bible, or who leave one at our bedside for weeks together without consulting it, must have missed something.

* * *

(1) Dr. Chirgwin tells of a Japanese criminal, Tokichi Ishii, who had sunk to the lowest depths of crime and degradation. One would imagine that in him all fine feelings had been obliterated. Anyone who stood in his way, whether man, woman or child, was ruthlessly murdered. Finally, this bestial criminal was captured and put into prison under strong guard. There he awaited death. He was visited in prison by two Canadian Christian women who tried to talk to him through the bars of his prison cell. He glowered at them like a savage animal and would make no reply. Defeated in their effort to speak with him, they gave him a Bible in his own tongue, which he flung across his cell in a paroxysm of rage. But when the ladies had left him, bored and having nothing else to do, he read it. Providentially he did not start at Genesis, nor did he hit on a brutal massacre or a revengeful Psalm. He started with the story of the Crucifixion. When he came to the words of Christ on the Cross, "Father, forgive them for they know not what they do," he stopped. "I was stabbed," he said

afterwards, "as if pierced by a five-inch nail. Shall I call it the love of Christ? Shall I call it His compassion? I do not know what to call it. I only know that I believed, and that henceforth my heart was changed."

Later, when the jailer came to lead him to the scaffold, they found, instead of a surly, brutish man, one with a great light upon his face and a composure and serenity that surprised everyone. In the last hours of his life he had been born again through reading the Bible.[1] The power of the Bible!

*   *   *

(2) Mr. McVeigh, from whom I have already quoted, tells of a Japanese woman whose husband died and left her with three children. She longed for comfort and turned to a priest of her own religion, which was Buddhism. He did his best and suggested that she made a pilgrimage to a special shrine in a sacred city. This she did, but nowhere could she find comfort. One day a schoolgirl brought her a grubby, little pamphlet, and said, "I found this in the street. Somebody must have dropped it. I read it. There is a wonderful story in it of a Man Who helps those who are unhappy. I thought of you. It might do you good."

The woman took the booklet. It was St. Luke's Gospel. She read it right through from the beginning to the end. She not only found her heart comforted, but her whole life changed. Immediately she began to seek out Christian people and asked them to tell her more. One day, in the market-place of a neighbouring town, she heard a missionary speaking about the same Jesus of whom she had read. She waited and spoke to the missionary and asked him to come to her village. He did so and in a few months, after careful instruction, she was baptised. Months later there began to grow up in the village a little community of Christians who found a new way of life because a village woman had read St. Luke's Gospel! The power of the Bible!

*   *   *

[1] This story is quoted by Dr. William Barclay in his *Commentary on St. John*, Vol. 2, p. 109.

(3) I like the true story of the little boy who was asked to put a penny in a missionary box, and who objected, saying in his own way that he had no proof that the penny put in that dull, brown box would ever reach a missionary in a foreign land. To please the child a minister offered to sell the boy a New Testament for his penny, and also to tell him the name and address of a missionary in India to whom he could post it himself. So the boy bought the New Testament for his penny, wrote a simple message on the fly-leaf and added his own name and address. Then he posted it. The missionary in India duly received it and gave it to an English-speaking Indian who had walked miles through the jungle to try to persuade the missionary to visit his lonely village.

Twenty years later another missionary, on a tour of villages which he supposed were quite untouched by the Christian message, noticed in one village congregation that his words were causing excited delight   Pausing in his preaching to ask questions, the preacher found that it was true that *no missionary* had ever preached there, but the Indian, who twenty years earlier had received the English New Testament sent out by a schoolboy, had read it aloud to his fellow villagers, translating for them as he went along. So many were interested that they formed a little Christian group which met together for reading, prayer and discussion. The Testament concerned was produced. The missionary made a note of the boy's name and address and he wrote home to England. The boy, of course, by now had grown up. Recently he took the Chair at a missionary meeting in England, told this amazing story and claimed, quite rightly, to be the founder of a Christian community in India, although he had never been out of England. The power of the Bible!

*   *   *

So you see, this dull, old school book, that has to be mugged up to pass Scripture examinations, cannot really be so dull after all, and, I repeat, stories like this, sacrifices such as we have recalled, and the immense circulation figures, challenge us to go on a step further and say, "What is this power? Can it be that we smug, complacent, English Christians, who just take the Bible for granted, and who listen to it being read in church without ever taking in what is being read, have missed something tremendous?

As I have thought about the power of the Bible, I have come to feel that reading it does certain things to the reader who is prepared to come to its message with a fresh and alert mind.

1. THE BIBLE REVEALS A GOD WHO CARES

Unless the witness of the whole book is merely wishful thinking, we are all in the hands of someone very wise, very loving, very strong, who cares about each one of us. How providential that that Japanese woman should read St. Luke's Gospel, the Gospel which is notably tender and sympathetic towards women, and the only Gospel that contains the story of the lost sheep, the lost coin and the lost, or prodigal, son! "Of course," she would argue, "God *must* be like that. He *must* feel like that about each one of us." And, men and women, what a tremendous thing it is—what strength, what comfort, what re-assurance there is in the thought that God cares! "He loves *me*," we can imagine the poor Japanese woman saying: "He cares about *me*."

The Bishop of Winchester tells a grand story of two officers who were lying badly wounded in a war hospital. One said to the other, "Well, I really don't care whether I get through or not. It is a world hardly worth living in. I have got no job to go back to and it will be impossible to get one anyway. What is there to live for?" "Well," said the other officer, "I feel rather like you, but with me it is different because I have got someone who very much cares whether I get through. . . . There is a girl up in Scotland and she cares." If this were a psychological lecture instead of a sermon, I should bring in some other evidence at this point to show that the physical resistance to disease of the second officer was immensely greater than that of the first. At times of strain, our minds find both anchorage and sustenance from the caring of another person. How much more does the caring of God mean!

* * *

2. THE BIBLE REVEALS THE PURPOSEFULNESS OF GOD

What a need of mind and heart that message meets! One of the reasons for the present disquietude of mind is that so many of our fellows have an awful fear that perhaps, after all, life is meaningless. We go on day after day, forcing ourselves to carry out a round of duties or pleasures, or both. Does anything mean anything? Have the day-to-day lives of ordinary people any significance?

Now the Bible teaches that every man's life, including the detail of every man's life, is important and significant in the eyes of God. In a lovely Easternism—if I may so call it—Jesus says that the hairs of your head are numbered. Jesus says that God cares for the sparrows, and He added, "You are of much more value than many sparrows."

Even the things that happen to us which God does not intend, things like disease and frustration, bereavement and sadness, are being woven into a plan, and both small details and vast disasters finally carry out His purposes. As St. Paul said, "With them that love Him, God co-operates in *all* things for good."[1]

Now if I can live my life believing that each day's life, whether it includes the trivial round; or, may we say tonight, a tragic railway disaster; whether what happens is due to God's loving intention or due to the ignorance, carelessness, folly or sin of man; if everything can be woven into a plan—even though that plan be too vast and wonderful to be understood this side of the grave—then at least I can live my life quietly, humbly, trustfully, lovingly, and be delivered from the horrible nightmare of meaninglessness which has descended like a fog on the thoughts of so many of our contemporaries.

[1] Romans 8²⁸ C. H. Dodd's translation.

In a word, God can make all things serve Him—evil things and good things, little things and big things. The Bible reveals the purposefulness of our God.

*　　*　　*

3. THE BIBLE REVEALS A GOD WHO CANNOT BE DEFEATED

I have made fun of the last book in the Bible and certainly it is very hard to understand and in many places appears to be talking nonsense. I think we may be forgiven when we laugh at the beasts with several horns and many eyes, the dragons and the lake of fire, and so on. But, of course, we ought to remember that this book was written to the members of an underground movement, and to preserve their safety it had to be written in code. The truth is *we have lost the key to the code*. When the writer stops using code language we have many passages which are unspeakably beautiful and infinitely precious, such as: "Behold, I stand at the door and knock: if any man hear My voice and open the door, I will come in to him, and will sup with him, and he with Me."[1]

Now the book of Revelation is fond of using the word "throne" and the imagery connected with it. The infant Church, persecuted as it was, expecting, as some of our contemporaries expect, the imminent end of the world, was certain that God would win. "He that sitteth on the throne says, 'Behold I make all things new.'" This enthroned Christ possessed the keys of death and hell.

What a message this is for our day! It means that in spite of appearances, in spite of the sway of materialism, the attempted domination of the world by an atheist state, the feeble influence of the Christian Church on men's affairs, the appalling energies which modern science has unleashed, yet God is the supreme Ruler of His own world. Man will not be able to defeat Him. If man co-operates with Him, a glorious victory of truth and righteousness will be realised. The New

[1] Revelation 3[20]

Testament is certain that Christ "must reign", that "all His enemies shall be under His feet" and that "before Him every knee shall bow".

So I can go on believing and trusting, praying and loving, knowing that one day I shall understand, one day I shall find my faith and my sense of values vindicated, and one day I shall find that my life has been guided, its detail and its disaster over-ruled, and nothing of value finally thrown away. What a message!

* * *

4. FINALLY THE BIBLE REVEALS A GOD WHO END-LESSLY SEEKS TO BE THE FRIEND AND GUIDE AND SAVIOUR OF MEN

Right through this priceless library is the message that God is with us. In the first few pages we hear of Enoch, who walked with God; in the first few chapters we hear of Abraham, who was the friend of God; of the great leader Moses, whose strength lay in the fact that God was with him. We hear a Voice say to Joshua, "As I was with Moses, so I will be with thee." David feels he can walk through a shadowy path because God is with him. And then, as we celebrate at this time of the year, the Son of God Himself comes to be with men and to be with them for ever. Almost the last verses of the Bible —and here I *can* use the imagery of the book of Revelation— tell us that "the tabernacle of God is with men, and He shall dwell with them, and they shall be His peoples, and God Himself shall be with them, and be their God: and He shall wipe away every tear from their eyes; and death shall be no more; neither shall there be mourning, nor crying, nor pain any more. . . . There shall be no night there; they need no light of lamp, neither light of sun, for the Lord God shall give them light: and they shall reign for ever and ever".[1]

Almost the last verse invites men into a fellowship with this God Who is ever seeking to be their Friend. "The Spirit and

[1] Revelation 21³⁻⁴; 22⁵

the bride say, 'Come' . . . He that is athirst, let him come: he that will, let him take the water of life freely." That is the grandest message of all. Whatever you have been, whatever you have done, whatever you believe or do not yet believe, however tangled and difficult your life may be, however frustrated and feeble you feel, all the way through this library of books the message is "Come, for the God Who is like Christ will receive you, befriend you and never desert you."

Turn back to the old book. Read it in a modern translation. Join the Bible Reading Fellowship. Read one of Dr. Barclay's fascinating expositions of the books of the Bible, published for only a few shillings, and obtainable from the Church of Scotland Publications, George Street, Edinburgh. Whatever you do, do not miss the food for which your soul is hungry. In the Bible are stories of men and women who have passed through every possible kind of experience and they have been brought through by the power of God. Your experience, you know, is not unique. It has all happened to others. It is all recorded here. If they have come through victoriously, why not you? You too, are precious to God. Your life, too, has meaning. Your God cannot be defeated and God is calling you to come to Him. He understands you. He loves you. He wants you. He will receive you. He will tell you what to do next. Why not begin again tonight with God?

This Child was Different

(A Christmas Day Sermon)

Hebrews 1¹: "God having of old time spoken unto the fathers in the prophets . . . hath at the end of these days spoken unto us in His Son."

THIS great book, the letter to the Hebrews, or, as the word implies, to the "pilgrims", was written in Greek to a small group of Aramaic-speaking Jews living in Rome, for the purpose, says the late Principal W. F. Howard, of preventing them from turning their backs on Jesus and returning to the synagogue. The authorship of the book has been a problem to scholars. It is clearly not by St. Paul, they say, for its style is entirely different from his, and, from a literary point of view, inferior. Origen gives the matter up and says, "God alone knows who wrote it." Tertullian in about A.D. 200 ascribed it to Barnabas. Luther ascribed it to Apollos. Later scholars, notably Harnack (the Kaiser's librarian) in Germany, and Peake, Rendel Harris and James Hope Moulton in England say it was written by a woman, probably Priscilla, wife of Aquila.

It opens with the tremendous assertion that God, Who had formerly spoken through the prophets, had spoken to the world a final word in His own Son. How different is that Word from any uttered before or since!

I wish to meditate with you on three differences:

      (i) He was different from the beginning.
      (i) He was different in what He became.
    (iii) He was different in what He did for the world.

*   *   *

(i) *He was different from the beginning.*

How significant and even sinister seem some of the stories that cluster around the birth of Jesus if we try for a moment to see them with a freshness which their familiarity may have destroyed! Was Herod, a powerful king, so afraid of a tiny baby that, without awaiting developments—which surely he could have dealt with—he had to murder all the other male children in Bethlehem? What a sinister significance lies in the last line of Mary Coleridge's verse!:

> I saw a stable, low and very bare,
>> A little child in a manger.
> The oxen knew Him, had Him in their care,
>> To men He was a stranger.
> The safety of the world was lying there,
>> *And the world's danger.*

And how strange were the gifts of those three astrologers at the end of a long, tiring and dangerous journey which must have taken them, even by the swiftest available transport, two full years through robber-infested mountains and across scorching deserts! Gold, the symbol of royalty, frankincense, the symbol of worshipful divinity, and myrrh, the symbol of the bitter suffering of humanity—what strange gifts to bring to a child! I do not mean to be in the least irreverent, but did no one give Him a soft, woolly, cuddly toy, the ancient equivalent of a teddy-bear? Did no one give Him a rattle? Did no one treat Him as a little baby thing? Was He *so* different from the very beginning that a star shone over His humble birthplace? And did the hills round Bethlehem echo the voices of angels which filled the moonlit night with song? I am not going to discuss these things, but they seem to point to a difference from the very beginning.

Of course, orthodox Christians believe that His birth was quite different from all other births in that He had no human father. We must not now debate the theory of the Virgin Birth, but I would say three things about it and pass on.

(*a*) It is not to be regarded—in my opinion—as essential to the faith of a Christian. There were many good Christians in the early Church who had never heard of it. Further, I cannot see how a belief can be *essential* to a religion if the Founder of the religion never said a word about it. No tenet is fundamental to a faith if it is not part of the missionary message of its first exponents.[1] The fact is that the early Church never mentioned it. The earliest Gospel, Mark is silent about it, St. Paul's missionary message was not built on it.

(*b*) The Virgin Birth theory does not safeguard the divinity or sinlessness of Jesus. Divinity is not established by a remarkable birth, but by a quality of adult life. As for sinlessness, we men are a bad lot, but the sins of our children are not more due to their fathers than to their mothers. How can the fact of having no father make one either divine or sinless?

(*c*) I would, however, ask you not to miss the evidence of the very beauty of the story. Clearly, Mary was expecting a child. Equally clearly Joseph was shocked and was "minded to put her away privily", "being a righteous man and not willing to make her a public example".[2] Unless he were a consummate hypocrite, the reference to his righteousness rules out pre-marital intimacy. Besides, if the child were his, Jewish Law would have demanded his care for Mary and her unborn child. He would not have been allowed to "put her away privily". Indeed, it would not have entered his head to do so. Whence, then, came Mary's pregnancy? Can we suppose that some village rascal was responsible for her condition? I hold that the beauty of the peerless story rules this out. Read again the first chapter of St. Luke's Gospel and imagine a village maiden of sixteen or so, after some mystical experience beyond the power of any pen to describe, saying quietly, "Behold the slave-girl of the Lord; be it unto me according to Thy word!"[3]

[1] The word "virgin" in both testaments simply means a mature young woman.

[2] Matthew 1[18-19]

[3] Luke 1[38]

If we are asked to believe that that incomparably beautiful narrative is a "cover up story" for some sordid sexual relationship in a back street in Nazareth, we are being asked to believe in a psychological miracle which strains credulity more impossibly than does belief in the physiological miracle of the Virgin Birth. What genius made up that story? And how did he hush up the facts? No, that certainly will not do.

I do not ask you to accept the Virgin Birth if it offends your intellect. I do not ask you to reject it as impossible. Hold it, if you like, *sub judice*, awaiting further light. But do not dismiss the evidence of the sheer beauty and innocence of the Gospel narrative, a narrative which seems to me to support my first point—He was different from the beginning, and, as you meditate upon the birth of Christ, give a measure of reverence to the girl-mother,

> "Who with a sweet thanksgiving
> Took in tranquility what God might bring,
> Blessed Him and waited, and within her, living,
> Felt the arousal of a Holy Thing.".[1]

* * *

My second point is more important:

(ii) *He was different in what He became.*

Jesus and John the Baptist were cousins and boys together. The latter grew to be a prophet "and much more than a prophet",[2] but he only called men to repentance that *God* might forgive them. His cousin *forgave* them, "that ye may know that the Son of Man hath power on earth to forgive sins, He saith to the sick of the palsy . . ."[3] John the Baptist *taught* the nature of God. Jesus *revealed* it.

We remember the young Isaiah almost crushed in the temple by the awe-ful majesty and splendour of God, so that he could only cry, "Woe is me for I am undone; because I am a man

[1] F. W. H. Myers, *St. Paul.*
[2] Matthew 11[9]
[3] Mark 2[10]

of unclean lips . . . for mine eyes have seen the King, the Lord of Hosts,"[1] but Jesus stands upright in the Holy Presence of the Infinite Creator and says, "I and the Father are one."[2] This is different. And what a difference!

All the saints have felt that the nearer they got to the white throne of God the blacker their own hearts looked. The comparison became intolerable. But this Man says, "Which of you convicteth Me of sin?"[3] All men pray for forgiveness, but when He teaches them to pray, He says, "When *ye* pray, say, 'Forgive us our sins'."[4] "On every page of the Gospel," says Professor H. R. Mackintosh, "we encounter such imperial demands for obedience as well as gracious promises of help and pardon, as it would have been an enormity for a sinful man to utter."[5]

All the religions of the world could be said to have as their aim the search for light, the light of the truth about God. Here is One who says, "I *am* the Light of the world." In all religions men seek for God. "Seek ye the Lord!" is their cry. But here is One who does not say, "Seek God," but, "Come unto *Me*," and who is reported to have said, "No one cometh unto the Father but through Me."

All honest and sincere men would repudiate being worshipped. I remember that when my wife and I parted from a gardener, who had been in our employment in India for six years and of whom we were very fond, he prostrated himself on the platform of the Madras Central Station, tried to hold our ankles and used words which were the language of worship. He persuaded his girl-wife, who was with him, to do the same. I shall never forget the sight of them both completely prostrate, with their hands on our shoes. I do not think I have ever been so embarrassed in my life, and though we loved them both dearly, our first act was to raise them to their feet, shake them warmly by the hand and say that though we should always remember them and find our hearts warmed at thought of

---

[1] Isaiah 6[5]   [2] John 10[30]
[3] John 8[46]   [4] Matthew 6[12]
[5] *The Doctrine of the Person of Christ* p. 36 (T. & T. Clark).

them, they must never, never regard us as any different from themselves, fellow Christians treading the upward way. We read in the Acts (14[11ff]) how when Paul and Barnabas were taken for gods, they were distressed so that "they rent their garments," and cried, "We also are men of like passions with you." It seems to me that no one who was not divine could be worshipped without protest. Yet *Jesus accepted men's worship as His right.* And when Thomas cries, "My Lord and my God,"[1] no one rebukes him for blasphemy. However exact or inexact a report that is of an actual occurrence, its inclusion in the New Testament demonstrates men's current thoughts of One who was quite different.

The saintly John Wesley lay dying, and loved followers bent over him to hear the last words of one who had given the better part of a century of arduous service to his Lord. They hear these words:

> "I the chief of sinners am,
> But Jesus died for me."

How different from passage after passage that we could quote of the words of Jesus! "Ye are from beneath; I am from above; ye are of this world; I am not of this world. I speak the things which I have seen with my father . . . I came forth and am come from God."[2]

Man can never put into words this difference of which I speak to you today. As Hooker once said, "Dangerous it were for the feeble brain of man to wade far into the doing of the Most High, whom, although to know be life, and joy to make mention of His name, yet our soundest knowledge is to know that we know Him not as indeed He is, neither can know Him. Our safest eloquence concerning Him is our silence when we confess without confession that His glory is inexplicable, His greatness above our capacity and reach. He is above, and we upon earth, therefore, it behoveth our words to be wary and few."[3] At the same time, as we bow before the cradle of the Christ child and

[1] John 20[28]   [2] John 8[23] etc.
[3] *Ecclesiastical Polity*, Book 1, Chapter 2, Section 3, p. 201.

remember the full grown man, we can say, with awe in our voices and a hush in our hearts, "God of God, Light of Light, Very God of Very God . . . Who for us men and for our salvation came down from heaven." For, of a truth, He was different!

*　　*　　*

(iii) More importantly still *He was different in what He has done for the world*.

Before Christ, man was ever the seeker. What a transformation has been wrought by this Man who was different. For man now knows himself to be the sought. Christ is the Shepherd and His search for us puts our half-hearted search for Him to shame by its inconstancy. Again and again in our lives we seek the help of those whom we think could help us in our difficulties. We seek *them*. We want *their* help. Maybe we hear of some wise physician who can deal with our infirmity, or some learned lawyer who can give us advice, or some wise counsellor who will give us guidance. We seek *them*. But what a transformation of the whole situation it would be if we found that, for some unimaginable reason, they wanted us, yes, and longed for communion with us far more than we wanted them. That is the situation in religion. This Man is different. He is seeking us.

Furthermore His coming spells the initiative of God. Theologians have sometimes discussed what they call in Hindu theology the monkey and the cat theories. The baby monkey clings to the mother and his safety depends on his clinging. The kitten is grasped by the cat and his safety depends on his surrender. Both truths have their place in the Christian view of things. Man is required to do his bit of clinging, but by far the more important truth is that *God* acts.

> Let me no more my comfort draw,
> 　From my frail hold of Thee;
> Rather in this rejoice with awe,
> 　*Thy mighty grasp of me.*

This man is so different from all others for the divine nature is revealed perfectly in Him and the divine values find in Him

218

their permanent expression. Do you not feel at Christmas time that the situation is as if a woman should go to a drawer and take out some piece of jewellery, dust it and wear it today and tomorrow, so that all might see its glory and enjoy its beauty, and then put it back into the drawer until next Christmas?

I cannot believe that today anyone in these islands who has ever really felt the spirit of Christmas active in his heart could be mean, or cruel, or unkind, or hard-hearted. We are all wearing the jewels called the Christian values: humility, goodwill, unselfishness, tolerance, kindness, love. But by the time the holly is taken down, or even by the time the cracker-papers are gathered up and burnt and the paper caps are thrown away, the jewels will be back in the drawer and—is it too hard a saying?—Scrooge will be himself again. But this Man who was different wore those jewels always. They were the only jewels He had.

Think of this! You can imagine—perhaps you know of—one family of parents and children where there is perfect Christian harmony and goodwill. Little children may have to be guided and advised and even disciplined, but nothing ever happens— let us suppose—that could be called cruel, or suspicious, or underhand, or unworthy, or mean. There is no *fear* in the atmosphere. Now imagine two homes like that, twenty, two hundred! There are communities like that. Read a little book by Henry Van Dusen of New York, called *They Found the Church There*. It is published by the Student Christian Movement. You will read of South Sea Islands where Christ has won, where the missionary message has been taken seriously, where a Chief on an island, which fifty years ago was cannibal, can say to an American airman who had to bale out of a burning plane over the island, "We have no jail, no divorce, no vice, no venereal disease, no poverty. We all help each other and care about each other. Your own missionaries taught us! ... "

Yes, this Child was different. That is what He could do for the whole world. That is what He *will* do for the whole world as soon as the world takes Him seriously. For He came to save the world. He is the Redeemer of the world. And He is God.

And the Lord God omnipotent reigneth! The triumph of the spiritual is assured to those who, with seeing eyes and understanding hearts, bow in worship before the lowly cradle of the child who was different.

*   *   *

Do you remember how Edward the First surprised the Welsh people into subjection at a difficult moment? He secured the assurance of their loyalty by promising them:

(*a*) The son of a king.

(*b*) One born in their own country.

(*c*) One in whose character no one could find a flaw.

He then offered them as their ruler his own son, newly born in Caernarvon Castle in their own beloved Wales, and too young to have commited any fault.

So God comes to us this morning with a yet more wonderful offer. He offers to us, to be our Ruler and King, His own Son, born in our own world, in whose character, through all the centuries, none has ever found a flaw.

We may feel that there is little we can do to bring peace to a distracted world and to extend God's kingdom of goodwill. But we can all start this morning with ourselves:

> "Reign over me, Lord Jesus;
>   O make my heart Thy throne.
> It shall be Thine, my Saviour,
>   It shall be Thine alone.
> O come and reign, Lord Jesus,
>   Rule over everything.
> And keep me always loyal
>   And true to Thee, my King."

The Dynamic Personality of Christ

FROM time to time I am sure it is a good thing to spend part of a service in what I call 'looking at Jesus'; for the heart of the Christian religion is our personal relationship with Him, and thus it is of supreme importance that we see Him as clearly as we can and from time to time look at Him from a different angle.

Let us go back to the origin of Christianity. Let us imaginatively do away with a lovely building like this, the architecture of which has the one aim that men shall be helped to worship God and to listen to Christ's message. Let us wash out imaginatively all the aids to worship, the comfort and warmth of this place, the lovely music, the book in front of you which contains a thousand hymns, the language of the prayers, some of them sanctified by centuries of use. Let us imaginatively see twelve young men who companioned with Jesus. None of them is highly educated or socially important. To us now they would look like a group of uncouth young fellows, little more than boys.

I want you now to make a mental picture of your fishmonger, the man who last Friday wrapped up some cod in a newspaper and handed it to you! Don't think I am criticising fishmongers. Ours is a friend. But if on the way home somebody said to you, "Do you know that the man who wrapped up your fish today will one day be known by his Christian name to every educated person in the world? The most influential cathedral in the world will be named after him and he will write words that will be read in every church for two thousand years. In some people's minds he will not only be called a saint, but be regarded with the deepest reverence. People will not only revere his statue, but kiss its toe?"—would you not laugh and say, "Don't be so ridiculous"? But all this is true of Peter who wrapped up in leaves, parcels of fish and sold them to men and women in Gallilee. And what was the transforming power that changed Peter, the fisherman, into Peter, the most famous apostle in the world? The answer is the dynamic personality of Christ.

You may remember that when you returned from the Continent, a dull and rather stuffy little man, who peered at you through thick glasses, made you open your bag at the dock and declare what your luggage contained. If somebody said, "He will one day be a world-famous saint and his words will be read and revered throughout Christendom for all time," you would find it hard to believe. But, you see, Matthew, the customs clerk, met *Jesus*.

Luke was only an ordinary general practitioner as far as we know, but nobody else recorded the parable of the Prodigal Son, or the detailed story of the Way to Emmaus, or the parable of the Lost Coin and the Lost Sheep. You see, Luke, the doctor, wrote about *Jesus*.

Pilate was only a very ordinary governor of a very ordinary province, in a very ordinary country at the wrong end of the Mediterranean. But every time an Anglican says the creed, he speaks the name of Pontius Pilate. Pilate's name would long since have been forgotten. But one of his prisoners was *Jesus*.

As for the half-crippled, probably epileptic tent-maker, of whom we read that "his stature was unimpressive and his speech contemptible",[1] the power that turned Paul round and changed him from a narrow-minded ecclesiastical fanatic into the great missionary of the Gentiles was the dynamic personality of Jesus Christ.

* * *

We are meeting here in the earliest month of the year and have hardly got used to writing 1960 instead of 1959, but has it ever occurred to you why the year is dated thus? Have you ever paused to consider what power it was that changed the

[1] 2 Corinthians 10¹⁰

centuries out of their course? It was the dynamic personality of Jesus Christ. After all, many attempts had been made to change the calender. It was suggested that the calendar should date from the building of Rome. It was decreed that after the name of the year should appear the magic letters A.U.C. (ab urbe condita)—from the building of the city. But it lasted so short a time that, if I may say so, you had never heard of it, had you? "Let us count time from the French Revolution," said men of great power in Europe's affairs. It lasted thirteen years. "Let us count time from an important conjunction of the planets," said La Place, the astronomer. It lasted three years. The most amusing illustration of all came my way recently when a distinguished Mohammedan wrote to me. At the top of his paper at one side was the number of the years as Moham-medans reckon them, viz. the Heggira, or flight of Mohammed from Mecca to Medina, but at the other side of his notepaper was the number 1960, as though in having to write both num-bers he confessed the small power of Mohammed compared with the might of Jesus Christ. "One name alone is stamped on the brow of the hurrying centuries," said Dr. Fitchett, "and it is the name of Jesus Christ." He adds, "Here is a peasant in the darkest age of the world; he lived in a subject province; he never wrote a sentence which has been preserved, He died when He had scarcely reached manhood and He died cast out by His own race and abandoned by His scanty handful of followers, and yet twenty centuries after He hung on the Cross, His birth is accepted, by believers and unbelievers alike, as the point whence all the centuries must be counted . . . He has lifted, with His pierced hands, empires off their hinges, turned the stream of the centuries out of its channel, and still governs the ages." The dynamic power of Jesus Christ!

Many a newspaper today will fill its columns with attacks on everything Jesus Christ stands for, but at the top of the page, in printing the date, it will pay tribute to His power.

*　　　*　　　*

Let us look at Him again tonight, for one of our dangers is

that we have become sentimental about Him. If you were away for Christmas and went to church, I expect some of you at least heard a sermon on the text, "There was no room for Him in the inn," and the preacher frequently (and legitimately, of course), pleads that Christ should be given a place in the human heart. Thousands of sermons have been preached on the picture of Christ gently knocking at the door. We have all seen Him depicted for us as the Friend of little children, the gentle Shepherd with the lambs, the lonely Man outcast by His fellows, the tragic Figure Who hangs on the Cross—and all this is true.

But wait a moment! Do you remember a word of His that begins, "Women of Jerusalem, weep not for Me!" We have seen pictures of Jesus in a beautiful pastoral landscape, with His men following behind, or Jesus teaching and preaching, with people lounging on the green grass in front of Him. We have seen pictures of Jesus in a spotless robe, healing a young girl, with lovely flowing hair, of some invisible disease. But sometimes I wish I could smash the stained-glass windows and tear up the sentimental pictures. If you could see the stinking Jerusalem bazaar even as it is today, and if you could imagine Jesus walking through that with its bug-infested beggars exhibiting their revolting sores and discharging ulcers; if you could have taken in the harshness of some of His sayings, it would correct your perspective. As Donald Miller said in his book, *The People of God*: "The sentimentalised Jesus of our time is not One before whom men would fall on their faces, and certainly He would frighten away no devils! He is One whom nobody would crucify, and for whom few, if any, would be willing to die. He could not have brought the Church into being, nor could He have sustained it through all the tortuous course of the long centuries." And I invite you to listen while I read some grim passages to you.

"I came not to bring peace, but a sword! For I came to set a man at variance against his father, and the daughter against her mother, and the daughter-in-law against her mother-in-law: and a man's foes shall be they of his own household. He that loveth father or mother more than Me is not worthy of Me; and he that loveth son or daughter more than Me is not worthy of Me. And he that doth not take his cross and follow after Me, is not worthy of Me." (Matthew 10, ³⁴⁻³⁸).

"Ye generation of vipers, how shall ye escape the damnation of hell? Woe unto you, scribes and Pharisees, hypocrites!" (Matthew 3⁷, 23¹³).

"His eyes were as a flame of fire; . . . His voice was as the sound of many waters. . . . Out of His mouth proceeded a sharp two-edged sword and His countenance was as the sun shining in its strength. And when I saw Him, I fell at His feet as one dead." (Revelation 1, ¹⁴⁻¹⁷).

Let us remember that although the idea of hell was caricatured by the vicious spiritual sadism of our grandfathers, the origin of the idea of hell lay in the words of Jesus. It was He Who spoke of a door that was shut and of an agelong flame, and of weeping and gnashing of teeth.

Let us remember that it was He who said, "If thine hand offend thee, cut it off, and if thine eye offend thee, pluck it out." (Matt. 5²⁹⁻³⁰). Certainly the words are not to be taken literally. But there is nothing sloppy or sentimental in the teaching of Jesus, for in these words He is really saying that if your job (that which your hand finds to do) imperils your soul, throw it up. He is saying that it is no good talking about "seeing life," if it imperils the soul to do so. It is better to live a one-eyed life and put up with your alleged frustration.

No one in the world ever spoke such tender, gentle, kindly words to sinners as Jesus did, but no one in the world ever said such dreadful things about sin. Even the tender parable of the Prodigal, you see, contains words like these: "This, my son, was dead and is alive again; he was lost and is found." *Dead! Lost!* So these are the words that describe what sin can do to you!

I have heard people in their prayers, and ministers in church, plead that they might have a vision of God: "Reveal to us Thy presence and show to us Thy face." I know that I have often

P   225

used similar words myself. But if you are a slum landlord; if you have just chalked a swastika on a Jew's front-door; if you have blackened by gossip somebody's name; if you have been cruel to a child; if you have encouraged some young person in sin, if you have, by your flirtation, broken up a home and smashed another's marriage, I don't think you will be very happy about seeing His face and you will not be able to sing sincerely:

> "Jesus, the very thought of Thee
> With sweetness fills the breast;
> But sweeter far Thy face to see,
> And in Thy presence rest."

Sweetness! I think you would be amongst those who cry to the hills, fall on us, and to the mountains, cover us, and as for resting quietly in His presence, I think you might feel like John on Patmos: "His eyes were as a flame of fire, and from His mouth proceeded a sharp two edged sword, and when I saw Him, I fell at His feet as one dead."

* * *

There are two types of men who make me more angry than most. I hope you will think my anger is righteous indignation and not just personal hostility!

1. The first is the conceited egotist who seems to have forgotten the best definition in the world of egotism, viz. that "it is the anaesthetic which God allows us to take in order to deaden the pain of feeling fools." I think of the egotist who frankly thinks of Jesus as an easy-going, weak personality. Gentle Jesus in fact! Such an egotist imagines that in that inevitable encounter which must come to us all when the soul is confronted by Christ, Jesus will pat him on the back and say, "Let's all be matey in heaven. I know you never lifted a finger to help another person, and I know you made your money in ways better forgotten; that you made your wife hate you, and your children dreaded the sound of your voice; I am aware that no one ever found out about this and that and the other. But never mind, it is all over. You didn't mean any harm. Come along

into heaven and be happy." Oh it won't be like that, you know, not when you see His face! You won't be able to say "Gentle Jesus" then. You will "fall at His feet as one dead."

Why, some of these self-important egotists actually patronise Jesus! I have heard them do so. They will say to me, "Yes, I have heard somewhere about the City Temple. I will come along one Sunday and hear you." Do they want me to say, "Oh, how very kind of you!" May I say, with throttled down anger, that I do not want them to hear *me*? I want them to get in touch with *Him*. Many do not realise that they are on the road to hell and that their stained-glass picture of gentle Jesus is just as misleading as it could possibly be. But nothing, nothing can break the shell of their complacent egotism. The eyes of the soul are so heavily bandaged that nothing will make it see, until at last the ruthless hand of Reality, in some dreadful day of judgment, tears the bandage from those eyes and men see themselves—which they may be able to bear—and see the *awful* face of Christ and feel the impact of His terrible purity, which will surely bring them flat on their faces. What other posture is possible for them, for even the *saint* said, "When I saw Him, I fell at His feet as one dead"?

2. The second class of person I find it hard to bear is the pimply young man who mutters that religion is all right for women: as much as to say, of course, that for he-men, like himself, it has really failed to appeal. It is effeminate and sentimental and credulous and feeble and a kind of crutch on which the weak may lean, but which strong men like himself do not need! Oh you little puppy! So now you can feel with your finger the faintest down on your upper lip and you can smoke half-way through a pipe without being sick, and you think of yourself as a he-man! Indeed, one such puppy, to whom I was introduced, told me that he was a scientist! I looked at him in amazement for he was about nineteen. I thought the word scientist was a word one applied to men like Einstein and Dr. Bronowski and Professor A. C. Lovell, but I find that if you have taken chemistry and physics in your G.C.E. you may now call yourself a "scientist"! And this little pathological specimen

talked as though the Christian religion was not a strong enough, manly enough thing for him!

Of course Christianity *is* all right for women. It has given to some of the finest women in the world the qualities we admire. When I look at the weedy youth before me I wonder how he would have reacted to the tests and trials and temptations of some of the great women in the world like Perpetua, St Teresa, the Maid of Orleans, Florence Nightingale, Nurse Cavell, Mary Slessor, Amy Wilson Carmichael and Ida Scudder.

But if he means that Christianity is not a manly enough religion, I can only deduce that he has never seen the real Jesus. I wonder how long our puppy would have stayed with Paul in his trials, tortures and imprisonment. I wonder if he regards Augustine as a real man, Augustine whose thought dominated the mind of Western Europe for centuries! I wonder if Livingstone would have tolerated our "scientist" in the forests and swamps of Africa. And I wonder where he would have been when Latimer said to Ridley, as they were both burned at the stake for Christ's sake, "Be of good cheer, Master Ridley, and play the man, for this day we shall, by God's grace, light such a candle in England as shall never be put out." No, I think our little puppy had better go back to Peckham in a nice warm train and creep into bed with a bag of peppermints and his hot-water bottle, and a copy of one of our modern, sloppy love-stories and keep his mouth shut about Christ's religion. He isn't big enough for it yet. God help us, who amongst us is?

Oh, men and women, let the wind of Reality—bleak and cold though it may be—blow away our silly egotism, our foolish pride, our futile excuses our cowardly hide-outs. Let us remember together that the day will come when no excuse will hide us any longer.

When I am introduced to a worldling, it is really amusing to me the way in which he will try to make contact with me. As soon as he knows I am a parson, he will rake up some uncle of his who once wanted to be a missionary, or he will tell me that he once had an aunt in Bloomsbury who was a big Baptist! Isn't it pathetic, and isn't it dreadful when you think that one day he will be face to face with Reality, and that all of us will have all our excuses and disguises and pretences, and silly, futile mannerisms stripped away from us? Yes, my friend, hold your head as high as you like! It will be bowed before Him at last, "for in the name of Jesus every knee shall bow and every tongue confess that Jesus Christ is Lord, to the glory of God the Father."

Do not imagine that you can hold any door closed against Him at the last. Your hidden motives, your business life, your secret sex life, your family life, your social life will all lie open before the eyes of Him with whom we have to do, and no Bluebeard hand of yours will be able to keep any door shut against Him.

What is your definition of a fanatic? I think my description of one would be a person who becomes very excited and emphatic about things which are really of no importance. Do you think Jesus was a fanatic? Do you think He used the language we have been quoting about things that really do not matter? If He were no more than a man, however loving and gentle and kind, Who walked across the stage of history two thousand years ago, saying beautiful things and doing lovely deeds, well, we may be able to escape His challenge. But if this Man is as much of God as can be poured into a human life without disrupting its humanity—and this is how I describe divinity; if He really had the values for us of God Himself, and if what He says is not a human opinion, but a divine revelation, then remember He is standing just as near to you as He was to the Scribes and Pharisees and the people of His day. Remember that what He said to them He says to us, and the God He revealed to them is the God with Whom we still have to do. The challenge He made to them He makes to us.

I enjoy talking to you about the love and forgiveness and gentleness of God, but do let us sometimes look at another side of His nature. There lies before each one of us, if we have not reached it already, the point at which there is an inescapable encounter with Reality, an inevitable meeting with God. I should like to think that tonight you are making up your mind not to pretend, or pose, or hide, or try to escape any more, but that you have looked at the real Christ tonight and decided to respond to His challenge.

"He hath sounded forth the trumpet that shall never call retreat;
He is sifting out the hearts of men before His judgment-seat;
O, be swift, my soul, to answer Him; be jubilant, my feet!
    For GOD is marching on."

Where Dwellest Thou?

John 1[38-9]: "They say unto Him, 'Where dwellest Thou?'
He saith unto them, 'Come and see,' and they came and
saw where He abode, and they abode with Him."

Psalm 91[1]: "He that dwellest in the secret place of the
Most High, that abideth under the shadow of the Almighty, shall say of the Lord, He is my fortress." (Revised Version margin).

Thomas à Kempis: "The proud and covetous can never
rest. The poor and humble in spirit dwell in a multitude
of peace."

"SHOW me your home and you show me your heart." There
is much truth in that saying. There are homes full of a
quiet peace and strength. They receive you and welcome you
and your mind is rested in them. There are homes full of unrest and disquietude, homes that chafe and irritate the spirit.
Wealth has nothing to do with it. I suppose the quality of the
emotional atmosphere is the determining factor, though this
often seems to find its expression in the furniture and decora-
tions, and especially the ornaments, carpets and pictures.

We *dwell* not only in material homes, but in homes made of
feeling, the latter often being translated into the former. "The
humble in spirit," says à Kempis, "dwell in a multitude of
peace."

* * *

Christ dwelt, we are told, in the bosom of the Father. That
was His home. He lived, we are taught, a pre-incarnate life in
unimaginable glory and in perfect harmony and closest unity

231

with God the Father. Then He became man and "dwelt" among us—the word means "put up His tent in our camp"—full of grace and truth, bringing the atmosphere of heaven to the unimportant dwellings of an unimportant town in an unimportant country at the unimportant end of the Mediterranean Sea. Sometimes He was homesick and cried out for the dwelling He had left for our sake. As He put it Himself in that great prayer to God, "Glorify Thou Me with the glory I had with Thee before the world was."[1] Yet on this earth He dwelt in what à Kempis called, "a multitude of peace".

That does not mean He was never ruffled. The New Testament has stories of His fierce outbursts of anger as when He overturned the tables of the moneychangers; of His overwhelming grief as when, seeing the city, He wept over it.[2] (The Greek word means He broke down and sobbed.) The New Testament speaks of His terrible agony in Gethsemane when He was "appalled and agitated".[3] Dr. David Smith translates, "He began to be sorrowful and *very homesick.*"[4]

It does mean that in the depths of His nature there was peace. We are so often the reverse. We maintain a calm exterior but, far below, there is a nagging worry, or a devouring fear, a seething jealousy, or a bitter resentment. Jesus was like the sea, often stormy on the surface, but in the depths there was an unbroken silence and inviolable peace. "Master, where dwellest Thou?" He dwelt "in a multitude of peace".

* * *

That is the kind of peace you and I want, the more so because we dwell in a world that is as hectic and frightened and unrestful as this world has ever been. If someone should ask us, "Where dwellest thou?" one answer would be, "We dwell in a world of fear and bewilderment and worry, of hectic rush and unceasing scramble; a world in which men carry on by means of phenobarbitone." Indeed we live in a country in which sixty-

[1] John 17[5]
[2] Luke 19[41]
[3] Matthew 26[37], Mark 14[33] (Moffatt).
[4] *Disciples' Commentary on the Gospels*, Vol. 1, pp. 419-20 (Hodder and Stoughton).

seven million sleeping tablets were prescribed in one year under the National Health Scheme—and remember that most people who use sleeping tablets are private patients, and in their case the figure is unknown.

Let us tonight see if we can get any help in the search for a dwelling place of peace. Can we live where Jesus did "in a multitude of peace"? Listen! "He that dwelleth in the secret place of the Most High; he that abides under the shadow of the Almighty, shall say of the Lord, He is my refuge and my fortress. He is the dwelling place where I have gathered that which will sustain me in the hour of fear and darkness and unrest." All that sounds very easy. "Turn to God, realise His presence, live under the shadow of His wings, and so on." And when we hear this advice we say, "Yes, quite, I really must do that." But in truth we do not know quite how to go about it. It is one of the greatest "religious difficulties" that we do not know how to *take* what our religion *offers*. Jesus says, "My peace I give unto you." What a gift! But the problem is how to take it, how to make it our own.

* * *

I have been reading recently the writings of Miss M. V. Dunlop of the Guild of Health, and she has been of great help to me. I should like to pass on something of her message.[1]

A difficulty of which I had for years been conscious is the old difficulty of the gap between intellectual acceptance and emotional realisation. I may be intellectually certain of God's forgiveness, but it is not at all easy to "feel forgiven". There is no hypocrisy here. A hypocrite is not a person who does not live up to his belief. None of us does. A hypocrite is a person who does not even *try* to live up to his beliefs. This is quite different. It is the difficulty of a person who does not know *how to lay hold on* the thing he intellectually believes to be true and worthwhile.

[1] See her *Introduction to Contemplative Meditation* and *Stillness and Strength and Contemplative Meditation*, obtainable from her at 3 Longdown, Guildford, 1s. 6d. and 2s. 3d. respectively.

I must try to make this clear by repeated illustration, and if I speak in the first person I shall offend no one. I ask myself. "Do I really trust God?" As President of The Methodist Church for one year, I have travelled around a great deal lately. On every recent Saturday night I have trusted my hostess to provide breakfast on Sunday morning. I have not found it necessary to say to her on arrival, "Have you laid in enough food for tomorrow's breakfast?" I have not said on retiring to bed, "You won't forget to get breakfast, will you?" I have not wakened in the night, stolen along the passage, knocked gently at her bedroom door and said, "Breakfast won't be forgotten, will it?" I TRUST her and therefore I dismiss the matter from my mind. Indeed, it usually does not even arise in the mind. Without it doing so, *I dwell in the atmosphere of trust*.

But, frankly, do we trust God like that? Do you know anyone who does? I trust doctors, psychiatrists, relatives, friends—I trust drugs and pills and potions before I trust God. If I really *trusted* Him, I should not worry. Having done all *I* could do in a situation—an important point—I should be able to put the matter from my mind. I don't *dwell* in an atmosphere of trust. *I still dwell far too often in the dwelling of fear*. Where *dwellest* thou?

Take another illustration! Let us suppose that I have suffered a grievous injury from someone and that I feel resentful about it. I *know* intellectually that resentment is wrong. I have read a great deal about resentment. I even know that if it is harboured in the deep mind over a long period it can cause physical illness. I confess it to God. I ask Him to take it away. But *I go on feeling resentful*. I haven't changed my dwelling place. I still live in the atmosphere of resentment. Knowing isn't enough. Willing isn't enough. How does one change one's feelings? How does one move into a better dwelling?

Many of us, ministers especially, if honest, would admit that we know intellectually some kind of answer to almost all the questions men can ask about God. And we are not such hypocrites as to preach what we do not believe. We exert our wills too and try hard. But any psychologist will tell you that

234

what you *feel* is the dynamic energy in personality. If in the street I see a bully twisting a child's arm, I do not pause and intellectually consider the situation. I do not coldly engage my will and decide to help. It is my *feeling* of anger and outrage that hurls me into the situation to deliver the child. It is *feeling* that releases power. How, in the field of religion, can I change my feelings?

*   *   *

Always, you see, there is an emotion in which at any given moment we can be said to "*dwell*". Often we do not attend to it at all. A child at a party dwells in an atmosphere of happiness. He does not even think how happy he is. Similarly a mother in the sick room of her child does not consciously think, "How worried I am!" She is dwelling in anxious care, and incidentally her anxiety affects her child by infection. I could tell you a true story of even a tiny baby in a children's ward, who fretted and lost weight until the matron replaced a nurse who was passing through a worrying time, with a nurse who "dwelt in a multitude of peace". Then the child, no longer infected by the nurse's unrest, began at once to recover.

How can we change our feelings? It is not that we do not know the truth or that we are feeble of will, but how little the feelings are in the control of the will!

Miss Dunlop calls her method Contemplative Meditation. It differs from what is usually called Meditation and which she calls Discursive Meditation, in which the mind broods, say, on a saying of Christ and *thinks* about it. This has value, but is not the soundest way of altering the feelings.

Contemplative Meditation depends for its efficacy on the principle of auto-suggestion, and that is no disparagement of it, for although prayer is not to be dismissed as "only auto-suggestion" yet some kinds of auto-suggestion are forms of prayer. But whereas auto-suggestion focuses the mind on "*I*" ("Every day in every way *I* am getting better and better"), this method allows a great truth about *God* to soak into the mind until it pervades the *feeling* part of the mind.

So we are urged to repeat a sentence like, "I will be still and rest in Thee, Spirit of Peace within me," and to repeat it over and over again as often as the mind tends to drift away. At first this means repeating it silently, almost continuously, for say five minutes, not thinking out its meaning and implications, but allowing its feeling to colour and stain our minds.

*   *   *

I have only been practising this method seriously for a short time, but already I find it helps me in a significant way. I never realised before how easy it is to dwell in the emotional atmosphere normal to an event. In other words, we allow our surroundings to determine what we feel, wrongly supposing that the feelings which outward conditions can impose are stronger than the feelings which we can lay hold of by this kind of meditation. For example, if some upsetting incident occurs, one tends immediately to be upset, and, to use our figure of speech, to "dwell" in that emotion. We accept the emotion that is born out of the occasion and dwell in irritation, or anger, or depression, or resentment, and so on and, of course, it is doubly bad to do this, bad for us—even bad for our health—and capable of infecting others. The truth is that one *can* alter one's reaction *if one refuses to give to those negative feelings like irritation, for instance, the attention that gives them their power over us*, and one can alter one's reaction the more quickly if one has practised, over a period, the art of inserting into the mind those positive ideas which are the opposite of the negative feelings which so easily flood the mind. We *can* draw on the store of feelings laid up for our use during our "dwelling in the secret place of the most high"; feelings borrowed, not from the incident which has upset us, but from God's presence within the soul. "He who dwelleth continually in the secret place of the Most High; he who abideth under the shadow of the Almighty, shall say of the Lord, He is my fortress," i.e. from God, he gets the weapons with which to react to this demanding situation without yielding to its negative and unhealthy effects. To change the figure he is like a sponge in water. Is the water in the sponge or is the sponge in the water? We can "abide in His words". We in them. They in us.

I can remember reading some years ago some words of Fay Inchfawn describing, I think, her own mother. Looking after little children and running a home, with its many monotonous duties, can be a very exhausting thing and must carry a constant temptation to be short-tempered and to become hectic and irritable. Miss Inchfawn said that as a tiny child she can remember her mother slipping away for perhaps not more than ten minutes, and coming back mistress of herself. Further, the hectic atmosphere disappeared. It was only when the child grew up and questioned her mother that the truth emerged, and it is the precious truth that I am trying to convey to you that if we can make time daily to dwell quietly, for even a few moments, in the presence of God, and assert those qualities in God which are the opposite of the emotions which destroy our peace, we can banish the latter and allow the former to take their place.

*   *   *

All this means hard work on ourselves at first. When we begin this method our minds dash away to other matters and results are so slow that we tend to give it all up. But I have become persuaded that this method of affirmation is the way in which we can take what God offers. The trouble is that we ask God in one sentence for serenity, but we do not know how to take it. No sooner is the petition for serenity off our lips than we *dwell* in an atmosphere of fear and anxiety again, and many of us feel helpless even as we make the petition. We are like men who ask the hotel manager for a hot bath, and then, though he consents, they find that they cannot turn on the taps. We tend to believe that only an outward change of circumstances can do for us what we want done. If I had more money. . . . If I were married. . . . If so and so didn't live with us. . . . If I could leave home. . . . If I had passed my examinations . . . If I could get away from this and that . . . and so on. But *has any soul ever come to possess spiritual qualities merely through altered external conditions?*

237

The altered external conditions may make the qualities less necessary and we may not feel our lack of them so desperately, but we are not changed within. We are like candidates who have evaded the examination, not candidates who have passed it, and unless our minds have been made to work differently and feel differently, we shall soon revert to the negative mental habits that destroy our peace. Are all the people who are married, rich, healthy or clever free from anxiety?

So let me reiterate. This method of praying is psychologically sound and it has New Testament sanction. One of the most significant things Jesus ever said is recorded in Mark 11²⁴: "All things whatsoever ye pray and ask for, believe that ye have received them and ye shall have them." So let us take some quality in God which is the opposite of the quality in our own lives that we want to lose, and let us include it in a positive sentence about Him. For example, if we are hectic and restless, short tempered and unquiet, we should use some such sentence as this: "I will be still and rest in Thee, Thou Spirit of Peace within me." Let us, with the body completely relaxed, repeat such a sentence over and over and over again, not actively thinking about it or about its implications, but letting the *feel* of it sink deeply into the mind. The point of repetition is that unless we constantly repeat the words, other thoughts and feelings will exclude those which we want to promote, and they are to be resolutely ignored. We are to attend to the sentence of affirmation.

It is not as though serenity and the other qualities we need had to be dumped into us. They are already there. We have been given them. ("Believe that ye *have received them.* . . .") All we need to do is to realise the fact, to believe that we have received them. This seems to me the real and practical way by which fret and fever can be banished; quietude and peace can supervene. The healing of the spirit follows, and in some cases this will mean the healing of the body also.

One thing is very certain: over the years our minds will take their quality from the emotional atmosphere in which they habitually *dwell*. What we *are*, depends on what we constantly think. "As a man thinketh in his heart, so is he." I have been thinking of some of the people who have consulted me recently. Some minds live always in fear. Some live in sex, and it dominates their entire life. Some think only of money and some of social status. Some live in ambition and some in pride, and some in overweening conceit. Some people live in an atmosphere of failure, of self-depreciation and defeat. Some live in an atmosphere of petty gossip or grumbling, some in negative thoughts and chronic unhappiness. Some live always in the atmosphere of grievance. Whatever happens something is sure to be wrong! How miserable they look, and are, and how miserable they can make others, banishing laughter even from the faces of otherwise happy children! Some, thank God, live in eternal serenity, radiant joy, unbreakable goodwill and inviolable peace. Where dwellest *thou*?

None of our difficulties is greater than the God Who dwells within us and whose nature contains the opposite of those feelings and qualities we want to lose.

*   *   *

I have read of a Valley of Roses in California, where roses bloom on both sides of a road for mile after mile. Travellers, it is said, who pass along the road, even in a motor car, find that the fragrance pervades their clothing, and those who meet them in the busy city do not need to say, "Where have you been?" for the fragrance that emanates from them tells its own tale. What of those who *dwell* in the valley? Always they remind others of roses. We read of those who "took knowledge of Peter and John that *they had been with Jesus*". How good it would be for us, and for all whose lives touch ours if we dwelt with Him and took from His hands the gifts He offers! How good it would be if we reminded others of Him, if there emanated from us the fragrance of His glorious life! How good, how very good it would be if men in their hearts, if not with their lips, said of you and me, "They have been with Jesus."

"'Master, where dwellest Thou?' He saith unto them, 'Come and see.' They came, therefore, and saw where He abode and *they abode with Him*." Most of the Gospel is there, isn't it? And to us all He says, "Come!" In the valley of His friendship there is plenty of room for all of us to make our dwellings.

Why I Believe in Life after Death[1]

I WANT to believe in life after death. Let me be quite honest about that. No man at death has exhausted all his possibilities and I want to go on. I want to realise all that as yet is embryonic, or only partly developed and imperfectly expressed in my personality. I want to meet my dear ones again. I want to know the answer to problems that baffle me, and men much wiser than me, this side of the grave. If there is a God at all—and of course I believe most sincerely that there is—I want to know Him and know more about Him and have deeper communion with Him. If there is no God, I want to know what the final reality is and what the universe is for, and what everything *means*. I've only just begun to live. I want to LIVE.

Of course, the critic and the cynic will say, "Ah, there you are! He has admitted it. Belief in a future life is just wishful thinking."

But what, in heaven's name, is wrong with wishful thinking? Because I *wish* that my dear one should recover from some terrible illness, does my wishing preclude the recovery? I read once of a lonely refugee child who wished desperately that he had a father and mother, brother and sisters. He thought they were all dead. Wishful thinking played a big part in his life. He wanted the relationships other boys had. But wishful thinking did not mean that his relatives did not exist and that he would never see them again. As it happened they were all alive. In fact, finally he was reunited with them. And the reality was far better than the dream. The

[1] This chapter, preached in substance in the City Temple, was printed in *The Sunday Express* and is here reproduced by permission of the Editor.

wishful thinking failed only at the point that it did not wish enough. The truth was better than the wish.

The fact that I *wish* to be reunited with my dead dear ones does not preclude the reality. If God is what I think He is, the reality of a further life will be far fairer than the dream. If I am hungry, I *wish* for bread. I want bread badly. If the universe makes sense, then the wanting is a pointer to the likelihood that bread exists. If, in the universe, there is a widespread craving which can *never* be satisfied; in which the material for satisfaction does not exist, then the universe itself is irrational. We live in a madhouse, and it is no good trying to think our way through any problems at all.

* * *

One lovely Spring morning I found a lark's nest in a field, and I held in my hand a lark's egg. Within that little, brown egg there was life. It was a very shut-in life. Yet what promise there was of a wider life that would begin when the little bird inside broke the shell and escaped. Within the egg were wings. Within the egg was the apparatus—not yet fully developed—which would be capable of producing the lovely song of the lark as, later, it flew up into the sunlight of a summer morning.

I feel that there we have an illustration of something that is true about man. No one can prove it mathematically, of course. But I cannot believe that the universe is purposeless and meaningless. The structure of the bird within the egg is meaningless unless there will come the chance to fly and to sing. What is the point of producing powers which can never be used? Wings mean air to fly in. Eyes mean something to see. A throat means a chance one day to sing.

Don't you feel sometimes as though this life is meaningless unless there is another? If man perishes at death, then the universe is as irrational as it would be if every bird died at the moment of hatching out. Some people never really *live* here at all. They never have a chance to express all their possibilities. They live a cramped life, full of frustration and pain, and as shut in as a bird inside the egg, but they *could* live if they had the chance. The apparatus is there. All of us have faculties we never fully use, longings we never fully realise—yes, and friendships that surely death cannot cut off for ever. Those friendships are made of love; the final "stuff" of the universe. If anything is strong enough to withstand the shock of death, love is. I have not the slightest doubt, in my own mind, that for those who love, reunion after death is certain. I feel that the very way in which our minds work suggests that the universe is rational, that it makes sense. And for a rational world, survival of death is essential. Without another life, this life is like a dirty trick played by a malignant, unjust fiend or imbecile.

*   *   *

The evidence of "Spiritualism" is impressive. I put the word in inverted commas partly because I do not like it, and partly because it means, in certain quarters, a quasi-religious inclusion of all kinds of weird phenomena which prove nothing more than the complexity of the human mind and of the existence of its many dark alleys in which at present we all grope, unable to find their significance or where they lead.

But serious psychic research provides evidence which convinces me that the living have communicated with the so-called dead. When one has cut out all the suspected material, all the intended deception and all the false conclusions of the self-deceived; when one has given due place to all the possible alternative theories to account for the phenomena, then, for myself, I am convinced that the dead live and that in some cases—relatively few—communication has been established with them. Frankly, it takes more credulity to accept some of the alternative hypotheses than it does to accept the theory that the living have made contact with the dead.

*   *   *

I want to slip in a warning here. What I have just written does not mean that I advise all bereaved people to seek out a medium and try to contact some loved one who is dead. Maybe such activity does a disservice to the dead. (I do not write that sentence without evidence.) Maybe it could lead to a greater sense of frustration and forlorn desolation than the bereaved person feels already. (Here again I could give illustrations.) In my view it is better for most bereaved persons to be content with wordless communion rather than seek communication by means of the services of a medium. Words may be received and puzzled over by the seeker when they are not messages from the dead at all. Their apparent triviality or even frivolity may hurt deeply. Silence at the seance may seem a snub. The difficulties and dangers are many. But the door is wide open and beckoning for an investigator with scientific training and an integrated and unemotional mind, who has not suffered the death of one dear to him, to make dispassionate enquiry in the field of psychical research. In this field I strongly believe we shall find, in the next fifty years, many discoveries that illumine our understanding of the universe and enrich our personal lives, especially if those who do the research are real scientists and use the same methods as are used in other sciences. The ideals of ruthless acceptance of facts, undeviating honesty in reporting, impartial examination of evidence and the exclusion of all emotion are required as much in this field as they are in physics.

It is thought by some that the dead have access to the living during sleep. Some of my own dreams point that way. More importantly I read a well-authenticated account of a man who dreamed that he must go to a certain house and tell the owner to look in a certain book—which he was able to name—for in it he would find a message that would comfort him and be of significance to him. With many misgivings and feeling an utter fool, the dreamer went to the house indicated and told his story. The householder found the book, and in it a loose sheet of paper with writing on it by his son who had been killed some weeks before. On the paper the dead man had written material which not only had a bearing on the lives of all in the house, but which provided amazing evidence of the son's survival and of his continued interest in family affairs. The dead man presumably could not "get through" to members of his family, but had found a stranger whose mental make-up made a communication possible. Perhaps a certain psychic "wave-length" was needed.

Single instances of this kind would not carry much weight, but the records of the Society for Psychical Research contain many similar stories carefully authenticated from reliable sources by reliable people, and to my mind it is mentally dishonest, and indeed impossible, to sweep them all away as imaginative nonsense, or to disregard their evidential value. One of the greatest mistakes which scientists are prone to make is to suppose that the universe necessarily ends at the point at which our physical senses fail to register its phenomena.

* * *

Life after death, if there is such a thing, is presumably very much a spiritual affair. We must, therefore, include the views of the great religious teachers. I cannot think of one who does not teach or imply a life that goes on after this one. The Buddha spoke of repeated existences. Hinduism and Mohammedanism and Confucianism have their heavens where life goes on in rebirths or with houris or ancestors. Christ, for me, stands above them all. And it is impressive that He does not argue. He does what is sometimes more convincing. He *assumes* a life after death. To a revolutionary dying on a cross next His own, He does not say, "My faith is that we shall meet again," or, "I hope we shall meet hereafter," or "There is a chance that we shall meet again." He says, "Today you will be with Me in Paradise." If He was not sure, it was a terribly dishonest thing to say. If Jesus Christ was sure about a matter so much within His sphere of authority, I feel it more than presumptuous to say, "You were wrong. There is no life after this." When the expert speaks on his own subject, I feel that if he does not know, no-one does, and to deny is rather like telling Einstein he has got his sums wrong, or telling Shakespeare he cannot write a play, or Beethoven that his sonatas are musically valueless. Surely we may say of Jesus in regard to spiritual things, "Others abide our question. Thou art free."

*   *   *

I would like to add another word. Most ministers have watched people die. If you had visited a sick person until he became so weak that he could not raise a hand, let alone his head from the pillow, and if you had then seen him sit up in bed, and watched his face shine suddenly with a radiance not of this world, and heard him call to—I should write *respond to*— a dear one who had died a score of years before; if then, with a look of calm triumph and unspeakable happiness on his face, the patient had fallen back dead, with the name of that dear one still echoing through the silent death-chamber, then, like me, in your heart you would want no further argument. You would say, "His beloved came to meet him and they are together once more." If that is a trick of the nervous system, or the delusion of a disordered brain, it is strangely convincing to the watcher, and if its unauthenticity were established, it would almost argue an obscene, deceptive trick; a beastliness at the heart of things.

I have seen this happen. I believe that men go on living after death. I believe that they then *begin* to realise what living is. I believe that spiritually they go on there from where they leave off here. I believe that by making the right reactions they go on to an incredible joy and blessedness; a fullness of life and of joyous communion with God beyond our present ability to imagine. I believe that that is the purpose of God for us all, and that at last, all His purposes will be fulfilled and all His dreams come true.

The Inns of Increasing Happiness

THOSE who enjoyed reading the life of Gladys Aylward, the servant-maid who became a missionary in China, will probably have seen the film based on her story. The film was called, "The Inn of the Sixth Happiness." I have rather borrowed from the title for our subject this morning and called the sermon, "The Inns of Increasing Happiness," for a reason which I hope will appear.

Among my letters last week was one from an old friend in Leeds, who was writing on behalf of a lady who lost her husband,—a man who was my friend also. The letter I received indicated that the lady was worried about the text in John 14²: "In My Father's house are many mansions." A mansion, as she pointed out, is a house in itself. What did the text mean? Did it mean the separation of our loved ones after death— each in his own mansion?

*   *   *

Let us look at the passage very closely. Take first the phrase, "My Father's house." Again and again in the Bible, the word "house" does not mean a building, but a community. "Bless the Lord, O house of Levi," we read (Psalm 135²⁰). Or again, "O house of Jacob let us walk in the light of the Lord" (Isaiah 2⁵). In Jeremiah (11¹⁰) we read, "The house of Israel have broken my covenant." And when we come to the New Testament, we read of the blessing the disciples were to give, "Peace be to this house!" (Luke 10⁵), meaning, of course, "the members of this household." In Acts 11¹⁴ we read of the angel sending Peter, "who," said the angel, "shall speak unto thee words whereby thou shalt be saved, thou and all thy house." Jesus Himself said He was sent unto "the lost sheep of the house of Israel" (Matthew 15²⁴).

So far, then, we may translate, "Among, or for, the members of My Father's household, there are many mansions."

Now the word for "mansions" has been the theme of much discussion. The word is "monai" and the commentators differ. Some think it means an abiding-place, a place where you remain, and that seems the sense of the relevant verb, "menein", "to remain". Professor C. Kingsley Barrett, of Durham University, in my opinion one of our greatest scholars, in his Commentary (p. 381) supports this view, and an earlier great scholar, R. H. Lightfoot, in his commentary (p. 275), seems to do so also.

But I am very attracted by the interpretation given by the late Archbishop Temple, who, as if there were no doubt about it at all, translates, "In My Father's house are many resting-places," and then adds, "The resting-places are wayside caravanserais—shelters at stages along the road where travellers may rest on their journey." He then explains that in the east it was the custom—and still is, where railways and motor cars have not yet penetrated—for travellers to send a dragoman (or interpreter) forward to make preparation for them in the next of the resting-places along the road, so that when they themselves arrive they find comfort as well as shelter.[1] The famous Dr. Westcott in his Commentary agrees here.[2] He says the word translated "mansions" means "resting-places or stations on a great road where travellers found refreshment." "This," he adds, "appears to be the true meaning of the Greek word here."

Well, when such scholars differ we can take our choice and we can translate our text anew. "For the members of My Father's household there are many inns at the side of the road." And then, referring perhaps to some earlier saying of His own

[1] *Readings in St. John's Gospel*, Vol. 2 p. 226 (Macmillan)
[2] *Commentary on St. John*, pp. 200-1

not recorded in the Gospels, Jesus adds, "If it were not so, should I have told you that I go to prepare a place for you . . .?"

*　　*　　*

I must say I find the thought infinitely appealing. What is it like to die? I think of it like this: when the long day is over, you will walk in the scented dusk down the last valley; and not alone, for He, the Companion of all men, has pledged His word to be with you. And at the end of that valley, all hushed and quiet, you will see, shining through the trees, the lights of an inn. One evening the lamps will be lighted for you in the inn of new beginnings. And when you draw near to the inn, you will hear the music and the dancing.

But then, after a rest, you will sally forth in the bright dawn of the eternal morning and find a great white road leading onward and upward toward the next "inn of happiness," the next stage of progress, and *if we keep to God's road* they will be inns of increasing happiness, of deeper and deeper communion with God, of clearer and clearer understanding of His mind and heart and will, until at last we become all that God can make us and are united with Him for ever.

This final dwelling place—to describe which there are no words—must be a union of the soul with God so marvellous that we cannot conceive it. It is called by the saints and mystics "the beatific vision." Beyond that final bliss no further journeying is conceivable. The soul has reached its goal. Human nature has achieved its climax. Then, in very truth, it could be said of the soul,

"Here he lies where he longed to be;
　Home is the sailor, home from the sea,
　And the hunter, home from the hill."

*　　*　　*

It is good to have that vision in mind, but that is a long way ahead. And before that the road "winds uphill all the way," and there is much for the soul to learn which it can only learn by activity and struggle.

I think that would not only be the desire, but the expectation of most of us, and there is one very common heresy which we must avoid. It is the heresy of supposing that the soul continues for ever in the state in which it crosses the threshold called death; that its destiny is decided by the act of dying. It was this heresy that spurred men on to "save" their fellows quickly, for it was believed, that if death overtook them when they were unsaved, they would land in hell for ever. It is the reason why men asked for time to prepare for death and prayed to be delivered from "battle, murder and sudden death," without time to repent. Missionary enterprise at one period was immensely stimulated by the belief that the "heathen" by their thousands were daily falling into hell. But is the Good Shepherd hindered by the accident of death from continuing His work? Does He stop caring for the sheep?

Surely the truth must be that, in the vast perspective of the soul's history, death is a very minor incident and does nothing to determine the soul's destiny. Agadir would be intolerable if, believing in the importance of every human life to God, one did not at the same time believe in the unimportance of death.

In parenthesis, since the tragedy is so much in our minds, let us realise that the size of the tragedy does not increase the size of the problem.[1] The *problem* set us by the tragedy is the same as that of one child swept away by the tide. Man has to learn how to control, master, or evade the effect of the huge energies which are inherent in this planet as God made it, and the learning is often long and sometimes tragic. How much we have learned through the pain of others!

With immense sympathy with sufferers we note several points about the recent earthquake:

[1] At Agadir, in North Africa, just before this sermon was preached (March 1960), 12,000 people perished in an earthquake.

(1) Those whose houses were built on rock and were "earthquake-proof" found that their houses remained unharmed and the occupants safe. In earlier earthquakes, notably that in Quetta in 1935, earthquake-proof buildings remained intact. Not even their chimneys fell. We are told in the Press that the new Agadir will be built of earthquake-proof dwellings founded on rock. A great lesson has been learnt.

(2) If, knowing that earthquakes do occur in this area, men build huge blocks of stone buildings, where does the blame lie for the disaster? When Dr. T. Nakamura, Professor of Architecture at Tokyo University, was sent out by the Japanese Government for the purpose of examining the facts of the San Francisco earthquake, in his report he used this remarkable sentence: "Dishonest mortar was responsible for nearly all the earthquake damage in San Francisco." I am not hinting that this was so at Agadir but I am suggesting that man could have built more wisely. Indeed, he now plans to do so.

(3) It is always precarious theology to link a natural calamity with a divine judgment. Matthew Arnold said long ago:

> "Earthquakes do not scorn
> The just man to entomb,
> Nor lightning stand aside
> To find his virtues room."

(4) Professor J. W. Judd, in his book, "Volcanoes," writes: "The first impression produced upon the mind when the phenomena of volcanic action are studied, is that we have here exhibitions of destructive violence, the effects of which must be entirely mischievous and disastrous to the living beings on the earth's surface. A little consideration, however, will convince us that the grand and terrible displays of volcanic energy have given rise to exaggerated assertions concerning their destructive effects. Internal forces continually at work

within the earth's crust, perform a series of most important functions in connection with the economy of the globe; and were the actions of the forces to die out, our planet would soon cease to be fit for the habitation of living beings. By the admirable balancing of external and internal forces on our own globe, the conditions necessary to animal and vegetable existence are almost constantly maintained, and thus interruptions of such conditions which are produced by hurricanes and floods, or by volcanic outbursts and earthquakes, may safely be regarded as the insignificant accidents of what is on the whole a very perfectly working piece of machinery."

Though we rightly sympathise with all who suffered in mind and body as a result of the earthquake, not forgetting the relatives of the dead, the dead themselves go on where they left off. I ministered for a time in Manchester. Then I ministered in Leeds. It seemed a great change, and through it I left some friends and made others. Now, as I look back after thirty-five years, the change seems relatively unimportant, and I think we must try to accept the view that, in the perspective of the soul's adventure, it really is of minor importance whether we function on this side of death or the other. Surely one goes on where one left off. Where there is life, there is always the prospect of growth and development. Surely death is finally as unimportant to the soul as going to sleep at night, awaking the next morning and going on with one's life with scarcely a break in the stream of consciousness.

The soul longs to go on being active; serving, learning, climbing.

> "She desires no isles of the blest, no quiet seats of the just,
>   To rest in a golden grove, or to bask in a summer sky.
>   Give her the wages of going on, and not to die."[1]

Says the Master, "You will not die. The tomb is only a milestone. You will go on where you left off. And there are inns at the side of the road. You will rest a little and have fellow-

[1] Tennyson, "Wages"

ship with your friends and with Me. I go ahead to prepare for you. And then, with new-found strength and cleared vision, you will take up the journey once more."

*　　*　　*

Some may think, "Your thought disturbs me. I lost my wife a score of years ago. She was a saint. She will have gone far ahead of me on the great white road. She may be resting in an inn miles ahead of any I can reach when I die."

Well, we must not carry figures of speech too far! In the country of mathematics you are far ahead of your little son doing his arithmetic homework at the same table where you, a chartered accountant, let us say, are working out a tricky balance sheet. But you have rich fellowship and much fun together. There is a great gulf fixed at the moment between you and your little boy in the world of mathematics, but love can bridge the gulf and make fellowship possible.

Christ is miles ahead of us. He has arrived. He has reached the goal. He is one with the Father. But He promised fellowship with a dying thief. He knew—after His death—a bereaved woman in a garden and greeted her by name. He came back to her garden. And while our dear ones may make progress, it will not hinder fellowship. If we cannot race forward to them, they will be free to come back to our modest inn at the side of the road.

*　　*　　*

With this thought of progress after death along a great white road, with inns of rest and happiness at the side of it, let us think a little about luggage.

I spent a holiday years ago with a party of friends in another land. We planned, one day, to leave our hotel and carry enough luggage for one night and stay at an inn up in the mountains, and go on from there the next day and return by a roundabout route. We had to get across a glacier and the walk was to be very rough and exacting, so we were advised to take as little luggage as possible. Most of us men just had pyjamas and toothbrush, a razor and a comb, and the inevitable "mac" in case it rained. But one man had a small tin trunk strapped to his back. How we teased him about it! He was a great sport and did not mind the teasing. Further, since he carried it himself, no one could grumble. But, believe it or not, he brought hair cream—for one night—and a hot-water bottle, and, since the doctor had ordered daily glucose, he had brought a whole packet of it and a bottle of lime juice in which to take it! He had a change of this and that and a spare pair of boots which he wore round his neck by the laces. I forget the other things he had, but they would have done most men for a week!

Are we a bit like this about the next life? Do you remember how in the war the Emigration Officer made restrictions on what one could carry. No jewellery, very little currency, limited luggage. . . . Sometimes I think it will be rather like that when we set off for the country on the other side of death. Will the angel say, "You can't take that. That's no use to you. You won't want that!" Is there a voice saying, "In the Father's spirit kingdom there are many inns at the side of the road, but you won't want wealth or sex. The power you had over others you won't be able to use there. The status you've acquired doesn't count in that country. Your pomposity and self-importance and pride and 'getting your own way' have no relevance there. That dominating disposition won't influence the innkeepers there, and I should keep quiet about your university degrees and the fact that your great grandfather was a missionary"? So many things that seem so very important here have no importance there. They turn out to be "junk" that we leave behind.

He Who told His disciples on earth not to travel with too much equipment—you remember, "no gold or silver, nor brass in your purse, no wallet, neither two coats, nor shoes nor staff," —may be saying to us, "Take love and willingness to serve, and humility by which men learn; take goodwill, and take the power to laugh, especially at yourself. Take these for your journey, but you won't want much. You'll only spend a night or two at each of the inns, and you won't want much luggage, and most of the things you are collecting now, you'll have to leave behind before you reach the first inn."

*　　*　　*

Indeed, has it struck you that perhaps we build our own inns of happiness there as we do here? He may prepare them, but do we have to supply Him with the materials?

I heard of a dream a rich man had about heaven. In the dream he was being shown round. A lovely mansion was shown him. "Whose is this?" he asked. "That," said the guide, "is your gardener's." They came to a hovel. "Whose is this?" he asked. "That," said the guide, "is yours. You see, *you didn't give us enough material to prepare anything better!*"

Does Christ say, "For the members of My Father's house there are, on the other side, many inns at the side of the road. I go to prepare yours"? Yes, but what material have we provided?

*　　*　　*

Men and women, sometimes it is a good thing to look ahead, even far ahead. God's will for all of us is ultimately union with Himself, so that finally we have not a wish left that is out of harmony with Himself, and no desire save His glory. Finally, for us *all*—for God will not be satisfied with less—is a glory too wonderful, too august for any language. But first the striving, here and hereafter, possibly even through other lives on earth, for we may have to come back and take some of earth's examinations again if we fail too badly.[1] But the glory will be worth everything it costs, and in the light of it everything, except sin, will have been worthwhile, everything!

[1] I do not find the idea of Reincarnation incompatible with Christian Teaching. Indeed it was for a long time an accepted part of Christian belief. I have examined the matter in "*The Case for Reincarnation*", obtainable 1/6 post free from The City Temple, Holborn Viaduct, London, EC1.

"Strive man, to win that glory;
  Toil, man, to gain that light;
  Send hope before to grasp it,
  Till hope be lost in sight.
  Exult, O dust and ashes;
  The Lord shall be thy part:
  His only, His for ever
  Thou shalt be, and thou art."

Date Due